FUNCTIONAL ANALYSIS AND OPTIMIZATION

FUNCTIONAL ANALYSIS AND OPTIMIZATION

Edited by

E. R. CAIANIELLO

Istituto di Fisica Teorica

Università di Napoli, Naples, Italy

1966

New York   **ACADEMIC PRESS**   *London*

ACADEMIC PRESS INC.
111 Fifth Avenue, New York, New York 10003

United Kingdom Edition published by
ACADEMIC PRESS INC. (LONDON) LTD.
Berkeley Square House, London W.1

LIBRARY OF CONGRESS CATALOG CARD NUMBER: 66-26272

PRINTED IN THE UNITED STATES OF AMERICA

List of Contributors

Numbers in parentheses indicate the pages on which the authors' contributions begin.

H. A. ANTOSIEWICZ, *Department of Mathematics, University of Southern California, Los Angeles, California* (1)

JEAN PIERRE AUBIN, *Electricité de France, Dirèction des Etudes et Recherches, Service E.R.C.A., Paris, France* (7)

A. V. BALAKRISHNAN, *Department of Engineering, University of California, Los Angeles, California* (15)

E. R. CAIANIELLO, *Istituto di Fisica Teorica, Università di Napoli, Naples, Italy* (37)

C. CASTAING, *Laboratoire d'Automatique Théorique, Faculté des Sciences, Université de Caen, Caen, Calvados, France* (47)

ROBERTO CONTI, *Instituto Matematico, Università di Firenze, Florence, Italy* (51)

W. DE BACKER,* *CETIS, Scientific Data Processing Center, EURATOM C.C.R., Ispra, Italy* (55)

JIM DOUGLAS, JR., *Rice University, Houston, Texas* (65)

WENDELL H. FLEMING, *Brown University, Providence, Rhode Island* (67)

HUBERT HALKIN,† *Bell Telephone Laboratories, Whippany, New Jersey* (85)

ROBERT LATTÉS, *Groupe Metra-International (SEMA—Société d'Informatique Appliquée) Paris, France* (99)

J. H. LIONS, *Department of Mathematics, Institut Henri Poincaré, Paris, France* (115)

LAWRENCE MARKUS, *University of Minnesota, Institute of Technology, Center for Control Science, Minneapolis, Minnesota* (133)

J. J. MOREAU, *Faculté des Sciences, University of Montpellier, Montpellier, France* (145)

C. MUSES, *Centre de Recherches en Mathématiques et Morphologie, Pully-Lausanne, Switzerland* (171)

A. STRASZAK, *Polish Academy of Sciences, Institute for Automation, Warsaw, Poland* (213)

*Present address: University of Louvain, Louvain, Belgium.
†Present address: Department of Mathematics, University of California, San Diego, La Jolla, California.

v

Preface

The contents of this volume, better than any comments by the Editor, will show how great and fruitful is the contribution that a skillful use of modern methods of functional analysis can bring to the study and solution of challenging problems posed by recent developments in science and technology.

Linear mathematics is of little or no avail in a realistic study of stability conditions, optimal performance of systems with feedback, organizational principles in assemblies of communicating elements, etc. Thus, a whole new branch of mathematics has come into existence for the study of this vast class of phenomena, in short, optimization.

As is always the case with all beginnings, many results were at first derived with too narrow a scope, or with methods of only heuristic value. The intervention of functional analysis permits the recognition of the underlying unity of many seemingly different problems, opens new, powerful ways of attack, as well as enlarging the horizon of the pure mathematicians, who always find stimulation and incentive in an effective interaction with colleagues from other fields of natural science.

The purpose of this 7th International School of Ravello (June 1965), which the generous support of NATO made possible, was twofold: to hear eminent specialists speak on the general state of the art and of their own work; to bring together active researchers of the interested areas and have them pose problems to the mathematicians and find with them and among themselves a common language and understanding.

The scientific organization and direction of the School are due to Professor J. L. Lions, to whom belongs the credit for the gratifying success of this initiative, with our warmest personal thanks. Thanks are also due to Academic Press for their ever-efficient and understanding cooperation.

Naples, Italy   E. R. CAIANIELLO
December, 1966

vii

Contents

On a Generalization of the Bang-Bang Principle
C. CASTAING

On Linear Controllability
ROBERTO CONTI

Some Computational Aspects of the Theory of Optimal Control
W. DE BACKER

The Approximate Solution of an Unstable Physical Problem Subject to Constraints
JIM DOUGLAS, Jr.

Optimal Control of Diffusion Processes
WENDELL H. FLEMING

Convexity and Control Theory
Hubert Halkin

Non-Well-Set Problems and the Method of Quasi Reversibility
Robert Lattés

On Some Optimization Problems for Linear Parabolic Equations
J. L. Lions

Controllability and Observability
LAWRENCE MARKUS

Convexity and Duality
J. J. MOREAU

The First Nondistributive Algebra, with Relations to Optimization and Control Theory
C. MUSES

Suboptimal Supervisory Control
A. STRASZAK

Linear Control Systems—Controllability

H. A. ANTOSIEWICZ

Department of Mathematics
University of Southern California
Los Angeles, California

1. This is a brief outline of some geometric aspects of the theory of linear control systems,

$$\dot{x} = A(t)x + B(t)u(t) + c(t) \tag{1}$$

in an n-dimensional real normed space X. For all details we refer to the bibliography, especially ($1,4$).

We suppose throughout that the set of admissible controls is the closed unit ball U in a Lebesgue space $L_Y{}^r(K)$, where K is an interval $[0,T]$ in $\mathbf{R}$, Y an m-dimensional real normed space, and $1 < r \leqslant \infty$. The coefficients on the right of (1) are assumed to be (at least) integrable in K; in particular, the elements of $B(t)$ are the values of functions belonging to $L_{\mathbf{R}}{}^s(K)$ with $s = r/(r-1)$.

The solution of the homogeneous matrix equation associated with (1), whose value at $t = 0$ is the identity, will be denoted by $t \to R(t)$.

2. Recall that (1) is said to be ϵ-approximately controllable in U relative to two given points x_0 and x_1 in X if x_0 can be transferred in time T via a solution of (1) with $u \in U$ into a closed ball with center x_1 and radius $\epsilon > 0$ (1). If x_0 can be transferred to x_1, i.e., if we may take $\epsilon = 0$, (1) is called (strictly) controllable in U.

The classical variation-of-parameters formula shows that (1) is ϵ-approximately controllable in U if and only if the closed ball in X with center

$$z(T) = x_1 - R(T)\left[x_0 + \int_0^T R^{-1}(t)c(t)\,dt\right]$$

1

and radius $\epsilon \geqslant 0$ meets the image of U by the mapping

$$\Lambda_T: u \to \int_0^T V(T, t) u(t) \, dt$$

of $L_Y^r(K)$ into X, where $V(T, t) = R(T) R^{-1}(t) B(t)$ for every $t \in K$.

Clearly, Λ_T is a continuous linear mapping, and so $\Lambda_T(U)$ is a bounded convex subset of X (symmetric with respect to the origin). In fact, $\Lambda_T(U)$ is closed, hence compact. If $1 < r < \infty$, this follows directly from the weak compactness of U in $L_Y^r(K)$ $(1, 12)$; if $r = \infty$, it is a consequence of a theorem of Lyapunov (13).

Thus necessary and sufficient conditions for the ϵ-approximate controllability of (1) can be given on the basis of the classical separation theorem for compact convex sets (1) [see also $(5, 6, 9, 12, 17)$].

Equation (1) *is* ϵ-*approximately controllable in* U *if and only if*

$$|\langle z(T), x' \rangle| - \epsilon \|x'\| \leqslant \left(\int_0^T \|V'(T, t) x'\|^s \, ds \right)^{1/s}, \qquad s = r/(r-1), \qquad (2)$$

for every x' *in* X'. (3)

These conditions are testable in the sense that they involve only the given data and the fundamental system of solutions of the homogeneous equation associated with (1). Their explicit form depends on the given norms in X and Y.

3. Observe that, for each x' in X', both sides of (2) are continuous functions of T. This implies, as a corollary of (3), the following existence theorem for time-optimal controls (1):

If (1) *is* ϵ-*approximately controllable in* $U \subset L_Y^r(K), 1 < r \leqslant \infty$, *there exists a least interval* $K_0 = [0, T_0] \subset K$ *such that* (1) *is* ϵ-*approximately controllable in* $U \subset L_Y^r(K_0)$. (4)

It follows that there is at least one $x_0' \in X'$ for which (2) holds as equality when T is replaced by T_0. Hence, in particular, if (1) is (strictly) controllable in $U \subset L_Y^r(K)$, there is at least one $x_0' \in X'$ and at least one time-optimal control $u_0 \in U \subset L_Y^r(K_0)$ for which

$$\int_0^{T_0} \langle V(T_0, t) u_0(t), x_0' \rangle \, dt = \left(\int_0^{T_0} \|V'(T_0, t) x_0'\|^s \, dt \right)^{1/s}$$

or, equivalently,

$$\int_0^{T_0} \langle B(t)u_0(t), \psi_0(t)\rangle \, dt = \left(\int_0^{T_0} \|B'(t)\psi_0(t)\|^s \, dt\right)^{1/s} \tag{5}$$

where $\psi_0 : t \to R^{-1\prime}(t) R'(T_0) x_0'$ is the solution of the adjoint equation

$$x' = -A'(t)x' \tag{6}$$

in X' such that $\psi_0(T_0) = x_0'$. Therefore, the form of each time-optimal control can be deduced by use of Hölder's inequality (6, 10).

If $r = \infty$, hence $s = 1$, (5) shows that to each time-optimal control $u_0 \in U \subset L_Y^\infty(K_0)$ there corresponds a solution ψ_0 of (6) in K_0 for which

$$\langle B(t)u_0(t), \psi_0(t)\rangle = \|B'(t)\psi_0(t)\|$$

a.e. in K_0 (2). This is a particular case of Pontryagin's maximum principle (11), since the Hamiltonian function for (1) attains its maximum in the closed unit ball in Y wherever $\langle B(t)y, x'\rangle$ assumes its maximum value $\|B'(t)x'\|$.

4. If (1) is controllable in U, i.e., if $z(T) \in \Lambda_T(U)$, there exist in general more than one $u \in U$ such that $z(T) = \Lambda_T(u)$. Moreover, if Λ_T is onto [or, equivalently, the origin in X is in the interior of $\Lambda_T(U)$], there is always a $u \in U$ with $\|u\| = 1$ for which $z(T) = \Lambda_T(u)$ (6).

Suppose (1) is controllable in $U \subset L_Y^r(K)$ and $z(T) \in \mathrm{bd}\,\Lambda_T (U)$. There exists a unique $u \in U$ with $\|u\| = 1$ for which $z(T) = \Lambda_T(u)$ if either $1 < r < \infty$, $Y = l_m^p$ with $1 < p < \infty$ and Λ_T is onto or $1 < r \leqslant \infty$, $Y = l_m^\infty$ and Λ_T is normal. (7)

As a consequence, the time-optimal controls are, *a fortiori*, unique in these cases (4, 6, 13).

(3) shows, when $X = l_n^2$, $Y = l_m^2$, that (1) is controllable in $U \subset L_Y^2(K)$ if and only if the matrix

$$C(T) = \int_0^T V(T,t) V'(T,t)\, dt - z(T) z'(T)$$

is positive semidefinite (1, 8). This allows us to determine explicitly the time-optimal controls $u \in U$ with $\|u\| = 1$ in terms of the component of $z(T)$ in the nullspace of $C(T)$ and to give simple algebraic conditions for their uniqueness (1).

5. For approximate controllability, a different optimization problem often arises, that of the existence of a "least" control (*1*).

Suppose (1) *is ϵ-approximately controllable in U and let U_0 be the set of controls for which $\|\Lambda_T(u) - z(T)\| \leqslant \epsilon$. There exists a $u_0 \in U_0$ such that $\|u_0\| = \inf\{\|u\| : u \in U_0\}$. Moreover, if $0 \in' U_0$, then*

$$\inf\{\|u\| : u \in U_0\} = \sup\left\{|\langle z(T), x'\rangle| - \epsilon\|x'\| : \int_0^T \|V'(T,t)x'\|^s \, dt = 1\right\},$$

where $s = r/(r-1)$. (8)

Here the right-hand side is computable from the given data.

Another optimization concerns the distance of the set of reachable points from the desired terminal point (*1, 6*).

Suppose (1) *is ϵ-approximately controllable in U; let U_0 be the set of controls for which $\|\Lambda_T(u) - z(T)\| \leqslant \epsilon$, and define*

$$\sigma = \sup\left\{|\langle z(T), x'\rangle| - \left(\int_0^T \|V'(T,t)x'\|^s \, dt\right)^{1/s} : \|x'\| = 1\right\},$$

where $s = r/(r-1)$. Then $\max\{0, \sigma\} = \inf\{\|\Lambda_T(u) - z(T)\| : u \in U_0\}$. (9)

6. The synthesis problem for (1) has been extensively studied (*2, 11, 14*) [see also (*3, 6*)]. The most promising techniques appear to be those in (*2, 3, 14*), which are based on the method of steepest descent.

The case, here excluded, when the admissible controls belong to a subset of $L_Y^1(K)$ has been treated, for example, in (*10, 12, 15*).

The present approach applies equally well to problems in which a point from a given compact convex set is to be transferred via a solution of (1) with $u \in U \subset L_Y^r(K)$ into another given compact convex set (*7*). For a discussion of various other extensions we refer to (*4*).

REFERENCES

1. H. A. Antosiewicz, Linear Control Systems, *Arch. Rat. Mech. Anal.* **12**, 313–324 (1963).
2. T. G. Babunashvili, The Synthesis of Linear Optimal Systems, *Dokl. Akad. Nauk SSSR* **155**, 295–298 (1964).

3. A. V. Balakrishnan, An Operator Theoretic Formulation of a Class of Control Problems and a Steepest Descent Method of Solution, *J. SIAM Control* **A1**, 109–127 (1963).
4. R. Conti, Notes on Optimal Control Theory, Univ. Maryland Lecture Ser. No. 43, College Park and Baltimore, Maryland, 1964.
5. R. Conti, Sul problema della controllabilità di un sistema lineare, *Atti. Acad. Naz. Lincei Rend. Classe Sci. Fis. Mat. Nat.* **37**, 146–149 (1964).
6. R. Conti, Contributions to Linear Control Theory, *J. Differential Eqs.* **1**, 427–445 (1965).
7. R. Gabasov and F. M. Kirillova, The Solution of Certain Problems in the Theory of Optimal Processes, *Avtomat. i Telemeh.* **25**, 1058–1066 (1964).
8. R. E. Kalman, Y. C. Ho, and K. S. Narenda, Controllability of Linear Dynamical Systems, *Contrib. Differential Eqs.* **1**, 189–213 (1963).
9. N. N. Krasovskii, On the Theory of Optimum Regulation, *Avtomat. i Telemeh.* **18**, 960–970 (1957).
10. N. N. Krasovskii, On the Theory of Optimum Control, *Prikl. Mat. Meh.* **23**, 625–639 (1959).
11. N. N. Krasovskii, On a Method of Constructing Optimal Trajectories, *Mat. Sb.* **53**(95), 195–206 (1961).
12. E. Kreindler, Contributions to the Theory of Time-Optimal Control, *J. Franklin Inst.* **275**, 314–344 (1963).
13. J. P. LaSalle, Time Optimal Control Systems, *Proc. Natl. Acad. Sci. U.S.* **45**, 573–577 (1959).
14. L. W. Neustadt, Synthesizing Time Optimal Control Systems, *J. Math. Anal. Appl.* **1**, 484–493 (1960).
15. L. W. Neustadt, Minimum Effort Control Systems, *J. SIAM Control* **A1**, 16–31 (1962).
16. L. S. Pontryagin, V. G. Boltyanskii, R. V. Gamkrelidze, and E. F. Mishchenko, "The Mathematical Theory of Optimal Processes." Wiley (Interscience), New York, 1962.
17. W. T. Reid, Ordinary Linear Differential Operators of Minimum Norm, *Duke Math. J.* **29**, 591–606 (1962).

Approximation of Variational Inequations

JEAN PIERRE AUBIN

*Electricité de France, Direction des Etudes et Recherches
Service E.R.C.A., Paris, France*

I. Introduction

Let V be a real Hilbert space, K be a closed convex subset of V, $a(u, v)$ be a continuous coercive bilinear form on $V \times V$; i.e.,

$$a(v, v) \geqslant c\|v\|^2, \qquad c > 0, \quad v \in V. \tag{1.1}$$

We recall the following:

Theorem A (*3*). If $f \in V'$, there exists a unique element u in K which satisfies the following inequation:

$$a(u, u-v) \leqslant (f, u-v) \qquad \text{for all } v \text{ of } K. \tag{1.2}$$

Remark 1.1. We do not assume here that the bilinear form $a(u, v)$ is symmetric. If $a(u, v)$ is symmetric, Theorem A is well known, and the solution u minimizes on K the functional $I(v) = a(v, v) - 2(f, v)$ (compare the lectures of J. Moreau).

We shall replace the inequation (1.2) by another inequation defined on a space V_h. With suitable assumptions we shall prove (Theorems 2.1 and 3.1) that the solutions u_h "converge" to the solution u of (1.2) when h goes to 0. Before that, we shall give two examples of such inequations:

Example 1.1. Let Ω be a bounded open subset of R^n, E be a subset of Ω. The space V will be the space $H_0^1(\Omega)$ of functions u of $L^2(\Omega)$ with derivatives $D_i u$ in $L^2(\Omega)$, for which the restriction to the boundary Γ of Ω vanishes (in a generalized way).

The convex closed subset will be the space of functions u greater than 1 in E. We take $f = 0$.

7

We consider the following bilinear form on $V \times V$,

$$a(u, v) = \sum_{i,j=1}^{n} \int_{\Omega} a_{ij}(x) \, D_i u \cdot D_j v \, dx, \tag{1.3}$$

where

(a) $a_{ij}(x) \in L^{\infty}(\Omega)$,

(b) $\sum_{i,j=1}^{n} a_{ij}(x) \phi_i \phi_j \geq c|\phi|^2$, $c > 0$, almost everywhere on Ω. $\tag{1.4}$

We can prove (3) that the solution u of (1.2) is equal to 1 on Ω, and that the distribution

$$v \rightarrow a(u, v) = L(u) \tag{1.5}$$

is positive. Then $L(u)$ is a positive measure on Ω, which is the capacity of E relatively to Ω and to the form $a(u, v)$ defined by (1.4).

Example 1.2. In this example V is the Sobolev space $H^1(\Omega)$, K the closed convex subset of functions for which the restriction to Γ is nonnegative, and $a(u, v)$ the following bilinear form:

$$a(u, v) = \sum_{i,j=1}^{n} \int_{\Omega} a_{ij}(x) \, D_i u \cdot D_j v \, dx + \int_{\Omega} a_0(x) \, u \cdot v \, dx, \tag{1.6}$$

where

(a) $a_{ij}(x)$, $a_0(x) \in L^{\infty}(\Omega)$,

(b) $a_0(x) \geq c$, $\sum_{i,j=1}^{n} a_{ij}(x) \phi_i \phi_j \geq c|\phi|^2$ almost everywhere on Ω. $\tag{1.7}$

Then, the solution u of inequation (1.2) is the solution of this boundary-value problem:

(a) $Au = -\sum_{i,j=1}^{n} D_j(a_{ij}(x) \, D_i u) = f$ on Ω,

(b) $u|\Gamma \geq 0$, $\dfrac{\partial u}{\partial v_A} \geq 0$, $\tag{1.8}$

(c) $u \dfrac{\partial u}{\partial v_A} = 0$.

[cf. (2)].

II. Approximation

We associate to a parameter $h = (h_1, h_2, \ldots, h_n) \in]0, 1[^n$ a Hilbert space V_h, an operator $r_h \in \mathscr{L}(V, V_h)$, and an operator $p_h \in \mathscr{L}(V_h, V)$.
We assume that

$$\begin{array}{ll}
\text{(a)} & p_h \text{ is an isomorphism of } V_h \text{ into } V, \\
\text{(b)} & \|v_h\|_h = \|p_h v_h\|.
\end{array} \tag{2.1}$$

Let K_h be a closed convex subset of V_h such that

$$\begin{array}{ll}
\text{(a)} & r_h K \subset K_h, \\
\text{(b)} & p_h K_h \subset K.
\end{array} \tag{2.2}$$

We consider the following bilinear form:

$$a_h(u_h, v_h) = a(p_h u_h, p_h v_h). \tag{2.3}$$

This form is evidently continuous and coercive. Then it follows from Theorem A that there exists a unique solution $u_h \in K_h$ of the inequation

$$a_h(u_h, u_h - v_h) \leqslant (f, p_h u_h - p_h v_h) \qquad \text{for all } v_h \in K_h. \tag{2.4}$$

We shall prove, as a corollary of Theorem 3.1:

Theorem 2.1. We assume (2.1)–(2.3) and that

$$p_h r_h v \text{ converges to } v \text{ in } V \text{ for all } v \in V \text{ when } h \text{ goes to } 0. \tag{2.5}$$

Then, if u is the solution of (1.2) and u_h the solution of (2.4), we have

$$p_h u_h \in K \qquad \text{and} \qquad \|u - p_h u_h\| \text{ goes to } 0 \text{ with } h. \tag{2.6}$$

Remark 2.1. We have in fact the following inequality:

$$c\|u - p_h u_h\|^2 \leqslant \|f - A p_h u_h\|_* \|u - p_h r_h u\|. \tag{2.7}$$

This implies that the norm (in V) of error $u - p_h u_h$ decreases as the square root of the norm of truncation error $u - p_h r_h u$. When $K = V$, we have more precise results (1, Chap. IV, §2). More generally, if we assume that $a_h(u_h, v_h)$ is a continuous bilinear form on $V_h \times V_h$, which satisfies

$$\begin{array}{ll}
\text{(a)} & a_h(u_h, u_h) \geqslant c\|u_h\|_h^2, \qquad c \text{ independent of } h, \\
\text{(b)} & \lim_{h=0} [a_h(r_h u, v_h) - a(u, p_h v_h)] = 0 \qquad \text{if } \|p_h v_h\| \leqslant \text{cst},
\end{array} \tag{2.8}$$

Theorem 2.1 is again true. We shall give a construction of bilinear forms $a_h(u_h, v_h)$ such that the solutions u_h converge to u.

III. Partial Approximations

We assume that there exist Hilbert spaces V_i $(i=1,\ldots,n)$ (included in a same separate locally convex space) such that

$$V \text{ is a closed linear subset of } \bigcap_{i=1}^{n} V_i, \tag{3.1}$$

with the canonical topology defined by

$$\|v\|^2 = \sum_{i=1}^{n} \|v\|^2_{V_i}. \tag{3.2}$$

Let $a_{ij}(u_i, v_j)$ be continuous bilinear forms on $V_i \times V_j$ such that

$$
\begin{aligned}
\text{(a)} \quad & |a_{ij}(u_i, v_j)| \leqslant M_{ij} \|u_i\|_{V_i} \|v_j\|_{V_j}, \\
\text{(b)} \quad & \sum_{i,j=1}^{n} a_{ij}(u_i, u_j) \geqslant c \sum_{i=1}^{n} \|u_i\|^2_{V_i}.
\end{aligned}
\tag{3.3}
$$

Using (3.2) it is seen that

$$a(u, v) = \sum_{i,j=1}^{n} a_{ij}(u, v) \tag{3.4}$$

is continuous and coercive on $V \times V$.

We consider now a family of spaces V_h, of operators $r_h \in \mathscr{L}(V_i, V_h)$ and of operators $p_h{}^i \in \mathscr{L}(V_h, V_i)$ which satisfies

(a) $\|u_h\|_h^2 = \sum_{i=1}^{n} \|p_h{}^i u_h\|^2_{V_i}$ is a norm on V_h,

(b) $p_h{}^i r_h u_i$ converges to u_i in V_i (for all $u_i \in V_i$), $\qquad$ (3.5)

(c)   if $p_h{}^i u_h$ converges in each space V_i, there exists $u \in V$ such that $u = \lim_{h=0} p_h{}^i u_h$ for every $i=1, \ldots, n$ (for a weak convergence).

We introduce the following bilinear form on $V_h \times V_h$:

$$a_h(u_h, v_h) = \sum_{i,j=1}^{n} a_{ij}(p_h{}^i u_h, p_h{}^j v_h). \tag{3.6}$$

From our assumption (3.5) it follows that $a_h(u_h, v_h)$ is continuous and coercive.

We suppose now that there exists $p_h \in \mathscr{L}(V_h, V)$ such that

(a) $p_h^i u_h$ converges to u in each V_i implies that $p_h u_h$ goes to u in V,

(b)   there exists a closed convex subset K_h such that
$$r_h K \subset K_h, \quad p_h K_h \subset K.$$

(3.7)

Let f be an element of V'. Then, if $(\cdot, \cdot)_i$ denotes the scalar product which defines the duality of V_i and V_i', there exists $f_i \in V_i'$ such that

$$(f, v) = \sum_{i=1}^{n} (f_i, v)_i. \tag{3.8}$$

Theorem A implies that there exists a unique solution of the inequation

$$a_h(u_h, u_h - v_h) \leqslant \sum_{i=1}^{n} (f_i, p_h^i u_h - p_h^j v_h) \qquad \text{for all } v_h \in K_h. \tag{3.9}$$

Theorem 3.1. The assumptions (3.1) and (3.3)–(3.7) imply that the solutions u_h of (3.9) converge to the solution u of (1.2) in the following way:

(a) $u = \lim_{h=0} p_h^i u_h$ in each space V_i $(i=1,\ldots,n)$,

(b) $u = \lim_{h=0} p_h u_h$ in K.

(3.10)

Proof. (1) *Stability and weak convergence.* We choose an arbitrary $v \in K$ and we replace v_h in (3.9) by $r_h v$ (which belongs to K_h). Hence, using (3.3), we have

$$c \sum_i \|p_h^i u_h\|^2_{V_i} \leqslant \sum_{i,j} M_{ij} \|p_h^i u_h\|_{V_i} \|p_h^j r_h v\|_{V_j} + \sum_i \|f_i\|_{V_i'} \|p_h^i u_h\|_{V_i}$$
$$+ \sum_i \|f_i\|_{V_i'} \|p_h^i r_h v\|_{V_i} \leqslant \frac{c}{2} \sum_i \|p_h^i u_h\|^2_{V_i} + k_1. \tag{3.11}$$

It follows from (3.11) that

$$\|p_h^i u_h\|_i \leqslant k_2 \qquad \text{for every } i = 1, \ldots, n, \tag{3.12}$$

and then we can extract a sequence h_n such that, using (3.5c) and (3.7),

$$p_{h_n}^i u_{h_n} \text{ converges weakly to } u_* \text{ in each } V_i, \qquad u_* \in K. \tag{3.13}$$

(2) *Strong convergence.* To simplify the notation we denote $h_n = h$ and $\epsilon_h{}^i = u_* - p_h{}^i u_h$. Then we remark that, using (3.9),

$$c \sum_i \|\epsilon_h{}^i\|_{V_i}^2 \leqslant \sum_{i,j} a_{ij}(u_*, \epsilon_h{}^j) + \sum_{i,j} a_{ij}(p_h{}^i u_h, p_h{}^j r_h u_* - u_*)$$
$$+ \sum_i (f_i, p_h{}^i u_h - p_h{}^i r_h u_*)_i. \tag{3.14}$$

Using (3.13) and (3.5b), we see that

$$\sum \|\epsilon_h{}^i\|_{V_i}^2 \qquad \text{converges to 0.} \tag{3.15}$$

(3) It remains to be shown that u_* is the solution of (1.2). But, if we replace v_h in (3.3) by $r_h v$, for arbitrary v of K, we have

$$\sum_{i,j} a_{ij}(p_h{}^i u_h, p_h{}^j u_h - p_h{}^j r_h v) \leqslant \sum_i (f_i, p_h{}^i u_h - p_h{}^i r_h v)_i. \tag{3.16}$$

Since $p_h{}^i u_h$ converges strongly to u_* in V_i and $p_h{}^i r_h v$ converges strongly to v in V_i, the limit in (3.16) exists and we obtain

$$a(u_*, u_* - v) \leqslant \sum (f_i, u_* - v)_i = (f_i, u_* - v) \qquad \text{for every } v \in K. \tag{3.17}$$

Then u_* is the unique solution of (1.2) and $p_h u_h$ converges to u_* in K.

IV. Example

We shall now give an example of approximation of Example 1.1. If V_i is the space of functions $u \in L^2(\Omega)$ for which the derivative $D_i u$ belongs to $L^2(\Omega)$, assumption (3.1) is satisfied. We take

$$a_{ij}(u_i, v_j) = \int_\Omega a_{ij}(x) D_i u_i \cdot D_j v_j \, dx, \tag{4.1}$$

and (3.3) follows from (1.4).

We have to define the spaces V_h, where $h = (h_1, \ldots, h_n)$. We denote $\alpha = (\alpha_1, \ldots, \alpha_n)$ a multi-integer of $\mathbf{Z}_n$, and

$$\varpi_h(\alpha) = \prod_{i=1}^n [(\alpha_i - 1)h_i, \alpha_i h_i] \tag{4.2}$$

$X_h(\alpha)$ the characteristic function of $\varpi_h(\alpha)$.

$$X_h{}^2(\alpha) = h^{-1} X_h * X_h(\alpha), \qquad X_h = X_h(0) \tag{4.3}$$

(* denotes the convolution product).

The support of $X_h{}^2(\alpha)$ is the cube $\varpi_h{}^1(\alpha) = \prod_{i=1}^{n} [(\alpha_i - 2)h_i, \alpha_i h_i]$. Then we define

$$\mathscr{R}_h(\Omega) = \{\alpha \in \mathbf{Z}^n \text{ such that } \varpi_h{}^1(\alpha) \text{ is included in } \Omega\}. \qquad (4.4)$$

The space V_h is the space of finite sequences $u_h = (u_h(\alpha))$ defined on $\mathscr{R}_h(\Omega)$ [with $u_h(\alpha) = 0$ if $\alpha \notin \mathscr{R}_h(\Omega)$].

We construct the operators $p_h{}^i$ in the following way. First, we consider

$$p_h{}^0 u_h = \sum_a u_h(\alpha) X_h(\alpha) \in L^2(\Omega). \qquad (4.5)$$

Then, we define

$$p_h{}^i u_h = h_i^{-1} X_{h_i} * \sum_a u_h(\alpha) X_h(\alpha) \in V \qquad (4.6)$$

and

$$p_h u_h = h^{-1} X_h * \sum_a u_h(\alpha) X_h(\alpha) \in V = H_0^1(\Omega). \qquad (4.7)$$

We suppose now that the subset E is smooth. Then, if $\phi \in H_0^1(\Omega)$, we can construct an operator γ_h such that

(a) if $\phi \in K$, $\gamma_h \phi \geqslant 1$, on the union of $\varpi_h{}^1(\alpha)$ which intersects E, with support in the union of $\varpi_h{}^1(\alpha)$ when $\alpha \in \mathscr{R}_h(\Omega)$;

(b) $\gamma_h \phi$ converges to ϕ in $H_0^1(\Omega)$ when h goes to 0.

$$(4.8)$$

We thus define the operator r_h by

$$r_h(\phi) = \left(\int \gamma_h(\phi) \cdot X_h{}^2(\alpha) \, dx \right)_{\alpha \in \mathbf{Z}_n}. \qquad (4.9)$$

We can prove (1, Chap. II) that assumptions (3.5) are satisfied.

The closed convex subset K_h of V_h is the set of sequences $u_h = (u_h(\alpha))$ such that

$$u_h(\alpha) \geqslant 1 \qquad \text{if } \varpi_h{}^1(\alpha) \text{ intersects } E. \qquad (4.10)$$

We can easily see that [using the fact that $\sum_a X_h{}^2(\alpha) = 1$]

$$K_h = r_h K, \qquad p_h K_h \subset K. \qquad (4.11)$$

Finally, we have to compute the bilinear form (3.6).

We note that

$$D_i p_h{}^i u_h = \nabla_{hi} p_h{}^0 u_h = p_h{}^0 \nabla_{hi} u_h, \qquad \nabla_{hi} = h_i^{-1}(\tau_{hi} - 1), \qquad (4.12)$$

and we deduce that

$$a_h(u_h, v_h) = \sum_{i,j=1}^{n} \sum_{\alpha} \nabla_{hi} u_h(\alpha) \nabla_{hj} v_h(\alpha) \left(\int_{\Omega} a_{ij}(x) \, X_h(\alpha) \, dx \right). \qquad (4.13)$$

This scheme of approximation is classical. If we compute

$$a_h(u_h, v_h) = a(p_h u_h, p_h v_h),$$

we obtain another scheme (1, Chap. IV).

We now have to resolve the following inequation:

$$a_h(u_h, u_h - v_h) \leqslant 0. \qquad (4.14)$$

Thus this is a problem of "quadratic programmation." Theorem 3.1 implies that the solution u_h of (4.14) satisfies (3.10); $p_h u_h$ converges to u in K.

REFERENCES

1. J. P. Aubin, Approximation des espaces de distributions, to appear in memoirs of SMF.
2. J. L. Lions and G. Stampacchia, to appear in memoirs of SMF.
3. G. Stampacchia, Equations elliptiques du second ordre à coefficients discontinus. Seminaire J. Leray, College de France, Paris, May 1964.
4. G. Stampacchia, Formes bilineaires coercitives sur les ensembles convexes, *Compt. Rend.* **258**, 4413 (1964).

On the State-Space Theory of Nonlinear Systems[1]

A. V. Balakrishnan

Department of Engineering, University of California
Los Angeles, California

I. Introduction

In recent years there has been an increasing need for a general theoretical framework for dealing with the kind of "systems-optimization" problems arising in the broad area of information and control (including computer) systems. The first step towards this end is to develop a general descriptive theory of systems based on their external behavior, whether they are deterministic or random, whether they are sequential machines (or automata), or whether they are "continuous" systems (such as the lumped or distributed parameter systems in more classical engineering terminology). The work of Zadeh (*1*), in which he uses the concept of state as the basic unifying element, is perhaps the first systematic effort in this direction. In particular he develops a state-space theory for linear systems with finite-dimensional state spaces. In (*2, 3*) the present author has extended this theory to linear systems without the restriction of finite dimensionality, thus embracing nondynamic systems, random systems, and systems described by partial differential equations. The main purpose of this paper is to extend the theory to nonlinear systems, or, rather, to present the first results in the extension to nonlinear systems. As a preliminary to this extension, we study linear systems under more general conditions than in (*2, 3*), thus preparing the way for the nonlinear theory. In particular we derive state-input relations for nonlinear systems by appropriately topologizing the reduced state space. For a treatment of optimization problems in this framework, see (*4–6*) for linear systems and (*7*) for nonlinear systems.

[1] The research reported in this paper is supported in part by the Air Force Office of Scientific Research, Applied Mathematics Division, U.S. Air Force, under Grant AFOSR 700-65.

We begin in Section II with a brief description of the main concepts and necessary definitions. Some of the special notation used is explained in Section III. Section IV is devoted to linear systems. The main body of results for nonlinear systems is given in Section V.

II. Basic Concepts and Definitions

We collect here the basic concepts and definitions of state-space theory. For more elaboration, as well as more background and motivation, reference may be made to Zadeh's work (1) and also to Kalman's (8). A "system" for our purposes here is characterized by an input, an output, and state, all functions of time t, $-\infty < t < \infty$. The input functions denoted $u(t)$ have their range in a Banach space X_1, the output functions denoted $v(t)$ in another and possibly different Banach space X_2. The state function denoted $x(t)$ has its range in an abstract set denoted Σ. A minimal assumption on the functions $u(t)$ and $v(t)$ will be that they are strongly measurable. By a *state-space description* we mean the following relations connecting input, state, and output:

$$v(t) = Z(t, a; x(a); u(s), a < s < t) \qquad t > a, \qquad (2.1)$$

$$v(t) = Z(t, b; x(b); u(s), - < s < t) \qquad t > b > a, \qquad (2.2)$$

where (2.1) is defined for every $x(a)$ and (2.2) implies that we can find a state $x(b)$ (independent of the input in $t > b$) such that (2.2) holds. In this paper we shall deal only with "time-invariant" systems, in which the system behavior commutes with the operation of translation in time [see (2) if further elaboration is required]. Hence we shall henceforth rewrite (2.1) as

$$v(t) = Z(t - a; x(a); u(s + a), 0 < s < t - a) \qquad t > a,$$

and since a is arbitrary, we shall set it equal to zero, following common practice. Hence the basic definitions (2.1) and (2.2) will finally be written

$$v(t) = \dot{B}(t; x(0); u(s), 0 < s < t) \qquad t > 0, \qquad (2.3)$$

$$v(t) = Z(t - \tau; x(\tau); u(s), \tau < s < t) \qquad t > \tau > 0. \qquad (2.4)$$

It is understood that in all these definitions, all the functions are defined only almost everywhere in t in $[0, \infty)$. We note that (2.3) is a mapping defined on the product space $\Sigma \times U$, U denoting the class of admissible input functions, into the space V of another class of functions, with range in X_2. Although we may take the admissible input class in quite arbitrary fashion, we shall, for the purposes of this paper, take it as a linear space, in fact, a complete locally convex space, to be defined more precisely (and more restrictively) later; and similarly for the class V. It would appear that there would be ground for considerable generalization here.

By definition, a "system" in our terminology is "linear" if Σ is a linear vector space, U is a linear vector space, and the mapping (2.3) is linear on the product space $\Sigma \times U$. In the case of a linear system, therefore, we may rewrite (2.3) as

$$v(t) = Z_i(t; x(0)) + Z_s(t; u(s), 0 < s < t),$$

where $Z_i(t; \cdot)$ denotes the output corresponding to the zero input ("the zero-input response") and $Z_s(t, \cdot)$ denotes the output corresponding to the zero state at time zero ("zero-state response"). $Z_i(t; \cdot)$ is a linear functional on Σ and $Z_s(., .)$ is a linear transformation defined on U.

Before studying the general nonlinear case, it is convenient to briefly examine linear systems to set the pattern so to speak, and perhaps bring the essential differences to focus. Our treatment of linear systems is also more general than our previous work in (2, 3) in that, besides allowing the input and output to be Banach-space-valued, the topology used on the state space is also different, and in particular, the system weight functions need not be continuous.

III. Notation

Since the notation for some of the function spaces we shall need is not sufficiently standardized, we shall find it convenient to indicate separately what these spaces are and how we shall denote them. Let X be a Banach space. We shall denote by $B_p(X;n)$ the class of all strongly (Lebesgue) measurable functions $x(t)$, $0 < t < n$, with range in X, such that

$$\int_0^n \|x(t)\|^p \, dt < \infty.$$

This becomes a Banach space under the norm

$$\|x(\cdot)\| = \left[\int_0^n \|x(t)\|^p \, dt\right]^{1/p} \tag{3.1}$$

for each p in $1 \leqslant p \leqslant \infty$. By convention $p = \infty$ denotes the Banach space of essentially bounded functions. We shall let

$$B_p(X) = \bigcup_n B_p(X;n)$$

denote the strict inductive limit of the spaces $B_p(X;n)$. Then $B_p(X)$ is a complete locally convex space, with the right side of (3.1) defining a pseudo norm for each n. We shall denote by $E[X;Y]$ the space of linear bounded transformations mapping X into Y, the topology being the "uniform operator topology," so that it is a Banach space.

IV. Linear Time-Invariant Systems

As part of the definition of linearity, the state space Σ is assumed to be a linear vector space. Because of time invariance, we may, as we have seen, take zero as the arbitrary reference time and all functions of time may be taken as defined for $t \geqslant 0$. The input functions denoted $u(\cdot)$ will be taken to be in $B_p(X_1)$, and the output functions $v(\cdot)$ to be in $B_p(X_2)$, where X_1 and X_2 are arbitrary Banach spaces. The input and output functions are now such that they need not be defined on sets of measure zero. Of course, p and $\tilde{p}$ need not be the same. The basic definitions for a linear time-invariant system connecting input and output and state are

$$v(t) = Z_i[t; x(0)] + Z_s[t; u(s), 0 < s < t] \qquad\qquad t > 0, \tag{4.1}$$

$$v(t) = Z_i[t-\tau; x(\tau)] + Z_s[t-\tau; u(s+\tau), 0 < s < t-\tau] \qquad \text{a.e. } t-\tau > 0. \tag{4.2}$$

Here both (4.1) and (4.2) are only defined almost everywhere.

Let us begin by studying the zero-input response. For each x in Σ, we define a mapping into $B_p(X_2)$ by

$$v(\cdot) = Lx,$$

where

$$v(t) = Z_i(t; x).$$

Because of the linearity, it is readily verified that L is a linear transformation of Σ. Let Σ_0 be the subspace in Σ defined by

$$\Sigma_0 = x \in \Sigma / Lx = 0$$

and let

$$\Sigma_R = F(\Sigma / \Sigma_0), \text{ factor space modulo } \Sigma_0.$$

Then it is clear that L defines a one-to-one mapping defined on all of Σ_R into $B_p(X_2)$. We now introduce a topology on Σ_R by that induced by L—that is to say, a set E in Σ_R is defined to be open if and only if LE is open relative to $L\Sigma_R$, or

$$LE = \mathcal{O} \cap L\Sigma_R, \qquad \text{where } \mathcal{O} \text{ is open in } B_p(X_2).$$

Thus topologized, Σ_R is a locally convex (linear topological) space. Let us denote the "shift" operator on $B_p(X_2)$ by $S(t)$:

$$S(t)\,v(\sigma) = v(t+\sigma), \qquad \sigma \geqslant 0; t > 0.$$

It is easily seen that $S(t)$ is a linear continuous transformation for each t and that $S(t)$ is a semigroup in $0 \leqslant t \leqslant \infty$, defining $S(0)$ to be the identity. Now from (4.1) and (4.2) we have that

$$Z_i(t+\sigma; x) = Z_i(\sigma; x(t)), \qquad \sigma > 0, t > 0,$$

which implies that

$$S(t)L\Sigma_R \subset L\Sigma_R$$

We now define the transformation $T(t)$ for each positive t on Σ_R by

$$T(t)x = L^{-1}S(t)Lx. \tag{4.3}$$

It is readily seen that $T(t)$ is a linear continuous transformation on and that it is also a semigroup in t in $0 \leqslant t < \infty$. Let D denote the domain of elements in $B_p(X_2)$ for which

$$\lim_{\Delta \to 0} \frac{1}{\Delta} \int_0^\Delta v(s)\,ds$$

exists. For $v(\cdot)$ in D we define a function (transformation) $f_0(\cdot)$ by

$$f_0(v) = \lim_{\Delta \to 0} \frac{1}{\Delta} \int_0^\Delta v(s)\,dx.$$

We note that for any x in Σ_R, $S(t)Lx \in D$ for almost all t and

$$Z_i(t;x) = f_0(S(t)Lx) \qquad \text{a.e. in } t \geqslant 0, \tag{4.4}$$

or

$$(Lx)(t) = f_0(LT(t)x) \qquad \text{a.e. in } t \geqslant 0.$$

Next let us examine the relation between the zero-input response and the zero-state response. From the linearity and time invariance and imposing suitable continuity conditions it would follow that

$$Z_s(t;u(s), 0 < s < t) = \int_0^t W(t-s)u(s)ds,$$

where $W(\cdot)$ is a generalized function with values in $E[X_2;X_2]$. Here we shall make the assumption (H) that $W(\cdot)$ is a member of $B_\infty(E(X_1;X_2))$. This is certainly a restrictive assumption but one from which generalizations are readily made. For any element b of X_1, let

$$u_n(s) = \begin{cases} nb & 0 < s < 1/n, \\ 0 & \text{otherwise.} \end{cases}$$

Then for any $\sigma > 1/n$ we have, by definition, a state $x(\sigma)$ such that

$$y(t) = n \int_0^{1/n} W(t-s)b\,ds = Z_i(t-\sigma;x(\sigma)), \qquad \text{a.e. } t > \sigma.$$

We shall show first that $\{x(\sigma)\}$ as σ goes to $1/n$ is a directed Cauchy sequence in Σ_R. For this it is enough to show that $\{Lx(\sigma)\}$ is a directed Cauchy sequence in $B_p(X_2)$. Now, denoting the pseudo norm given by the right side of (3.1) by p_n, we have

$$p_n(L(x(\sigma_1) - x(\sigma_2))) = \left[\int_0^n \|v(s+\sigma_1) - v(s+\sigma_2)\|^p\,ds \right]^{1/p}$$

and using the fact that

$$v(s+\sigma) = n \int_0^{1/n} W(s+\sigma-t)b\,dt$$

where $W(\cdot)$ is essentially bounded in each finite interval, it follows that $\{Lx(\sigma)\}$ is a directed Cauchy sequence, having the function $v(s+1/n)$ for its limit. We shall now complete Σ_R in its topology and denote the completed space by $\overline{\Sigma}_R$. We may then denote the limit of $x(\sigma)$ by $x(1/n)$ and we then have

$$v(t+1/n) = Z_i(t; x(1/n)) = f_0(S(t)Lx(1/n)) \qquad \text{a.e. } t \geqslant 0/n.$$

It also follows that the sequence $\{Lx(1/n)\}$ has for its limit [in the topology of $B_{\bar{p}}(X_2)$] the function

$$W(t)b \qquad 0 \leqslant t.$$

Hence there is also an element x in $\overline{\Sigma}_R$ such that

$$W(\cdot)b = Lx; \qquad W(t)b = f_0(S(t)Lx) \qquad \text{a.e.}$$

Clearly, x itself depends linearly on b; in fact,

$$x = Bb,$$

where B is a linear continuous transformation mapping X_1 into $\overline{\Sigma}_R$. Hence we finally have that

$$W(\cdot)b = LBb,$$
$$W(t)b = f_0(S(t)LBb) \qquad \text{a.e.}$$

Next we observe that the integral

$$\int_0^t S(t-s)LBu(s)\,ds = v \tag{4.5}$$

exists as a Pettis integral, where the element v is the function

$$v(s) = \int_0^t W(t+s-\sigma)u(\sigma)\,d\sigma.$$

Moreover, we observe that v belongs to the domain D and

$$f_0(v) = \int_0^t W(t-\sigma)u(\sigma)\,d\sigma.$$

Hence it follows that we can write

$$\int_0^t W(t-\sigma)u(\sigma)\,d\sigma = f_0\left(\int_0^t S(t-\sigma)LBu(\sigma)\,d\sigma\right).$$

Since $\overline{\Sigma}_R$ is complete, it follows that the integral

$$\int_0^t T(t-\sigma)\,Bu(\sigma)\,d\sigma$$

also exists as a Pettis integral and is equal to $L^{-1}v$, where v is defined in (4.5). If we define a transformation $g_0(\cdot)$ on

$$L^{-1}(D \cap L\overline{\Sigma}_R)$$

by

$$g_0(x) = f_0(Lx),$$

we finally have that

$$\int_0^t W(t-\sigma)u(\sigma)\,d\sigma = g_0\left(\int_0^t T(t-\sigma)\,Bu(\sigma)\,d\sigma\right).$$

If we now define the state function $x(t)$ by

$$x(t) = T(t)x(0) + \int_0^t T(t-s)\,Bu(s)\,ds, \qquad (4.6)$$

the output in (2.1) is given by

$$v(t) = g_0(x(t)) \qquad \text{a.e. } t \geqslant 0. \qquad (4.7)$$

Equation (4.6) provides the state-input relation sought, and (4.6) together with (4.7) yields the complete description. A dynamic equation corresponding to (4.6) can be written

$$\dot{x}(t) = A_s x(t) + Bu(t) \qquad \text{a.e.} \qquad (4.8)$$

under certain additional conditions as shown in (2). In (4.8) A_s is the infinitesimal generator of the semigroup $T(t)$. If the infinitesimal generator of $S(t)$ is denoted A, we have that

$$A_s = L^{-1}AL.$$

Simplifications arise if the state space can be specialized. The case where it is finite-dimensional has been treated in (2). In this case

$$T(t) = \exp(A_s t),$$

and A_s is, of course, a linear bounded transformation on $\overline{\Sigma}_R$; thus (4.8) holds without any restrictions. It is readily seen that

$$D \cap L\overline{\Sigma}_R = L\overline{\Sigma}_R$$

and that the zero-input response is actually infinitely differentiable. The transformation B is also linear bounded. In fact if $\{e_i\}$ is a basis for $\overline{\Sigma}_R$ we have that

$$Bb = a_i(b)\,e_i,$$

where the a_i are linear (continuous) functionals on X_1. It readily follows also that $v(t)$ also satisfies a differential equation of the form

$$\sum_0^m \alpha_k v^k(t) = \sum_i \sum_{k=0}^{m-1} a_i(u^k(t))\,c_{k,i}, \tag{4.9}$$

where the $\{\alpha_k\}$ are scalars and $\{c_{k,i}\}$ are elements in $g(\overline{\Sigma}_R)$, m being the degree of the minimal polynomial of A_s, and, of course, the necessary differentiability of $u(t)$ is assumed. It is clear from (4.9) that the range of $v(t)$ is finite-dimensional, or, in other words, X_2 may be taken as finite-dimensional without loss of generality. Similarly, the input $u(t)$ only appears thru the linear functionals $a_i(u(t))$, so that the effective input space is also finite-dimensional. In other words, if the state space is finite-dimensional, we may as well assume that X_1 and X_2 are also finite-dimensional. On the other hand, the state space can be infinite-dimensional, even though X_1 and X_2 are finite-dimensional, as shown in (2).

The next level is to consider the state space to be a Banach space. The semigroup $T(t)$ may be taken uniformly continuous or merely strongly continuous. We can produce stochastic systems as examples of this; as an example of the former we may take

$$\sum_0^m \alpha_k v^k(t) = u(t),$$

where the α_k are real variables and $u(t)$ is a random process with finite second moments. As an example of the latter we may consider

$$\dot{v}(t) = \mathcal{T}v(t) + u(t),$$

where $\mathcal{T}$ is a random variable which is negative with probability 1 and $u(t)$ and $v(t)$ are one-dimensional random processes with finite second moments.

In this case we have that $X_1 = X_2 = \overline{\Sigma}_R =$ an L_2 space over a probability measure space. Other examples may be found in distributed parameter systems governed by partial differential equations (3). Examples where the state space has perforce to be merely locally convex are (deterministic) nondynamic systems, as shown in (2), where the input-output relation has the form

$$v(t) = \int_{-\infty}^{t} w(t-\sigma)u(\sigma)\,d\sigma,$$

where

$$w(t) \text{ is in } L_p[0,T] \text{ for each } T > 0.$$

We note that as a result of assumption (H) the system is such that the state function is continuous from the right; also the response is well defined for a delta-function input, the corresponding state function also being continuous from the right.

V. Nonlinear Systems

We shall now examine the state-space description of time-invariant systems without restricting them to be linear. The attendant generality is gained to some extent at the expense of the kind of representation theory we were able to obtain in the linear case. In fact, we shall have to replace some restrictions before any useful theory can be evolved.

The state space Σ is now merely an abstract set. As before, since we are only going to consider time-invariant systems, we may take the arbitrary initial time to be zero. The input $u(\cdot)$ will again be in $B_p(X_1)$ and the output $v(\cdot)$ in $B_{\bar{p}}(X_2)$. The basic definition connecting input, state, and response is again embodied in

$$v(t) = Z(t; x(0); u(s), 0 < s < t) \qquad\qquad t > 0, \tag{5.1}$$

$$v(t) = Z(t-\tau; x(\ ); u(\tau+s), 0 < s < t-\tau) \qquad \text{a.e. } t > \tau > 0, \tag{5.2}$$

in the sense there is a state $x(\tau)$ for which (5.2) holds. We shall now restate (5.1) as a mapping on $\Sigma \times B_{\bar{p}}(X_1)$ into $B_p(X_2)$ denoted by

$$Z(x; u) = v. \tag{5.3}$$

As shown by (5.1), the main feature of this mapping or function is that it is a "physically realizable" or "causal" function of $u(\cdot)$. Thus for each $t > 0$ and any function $u(\cdot)$ in $B_{\bar{p}}(X_2)$ let us define the transformation $A(t;u)$:

$$A(t;u) = u,$$

where

$$u'(s) = \begin{cases} u(s) & 0 < s < t, \\ 0 & \text{otherwise}, \end{cases}$$

with a similar definition for any function $v(.)$ in $B_{\bar{p}}(X_2)$. Then physical realizability is characterized by

$$A(t;v) = Z(x;A(t;u)), \qquad 0 < t. \tag{5.4}$$

Let us denote the shift semigroup on $B_p(X_1)$ by $S_1(t)$ and the shift semigroup on $B_{\bar{p}}(X_2)$ similarly by $S_2(t)$. Then (5.2) can be rephrased more precisely as

$$S_2(t)Z(x;u) = Z(x(t);S_1(t)u) \tag{5.5}$$

in the sense that for each $t > 0$ there is a state $x(t)$ in Σ (there may be more than one such state) such that (5.5) holds. As before, Eq. (5.5) can be used to define a transformation on the state space. The first step in this is to introduce the notion of the reduced state space. In the linear case this could be done without considering the total response, but this is no longer possible here. We now define states x_1 and x_2 to be equivalent if

$$Z(x_1;u) = Z(x_2;u) \qquad \text{for every } u \text{ in } B_p(X_1). \tag{5.6}$$

Similarly, we may define two inputs u_1 and u_2 to be equivalent if

$$Z(x;u_1) = Z(x;u_2) \qquad \text{for every } x \text{ in } \Sigma. \tag{5.7}$$

It may be noted that the zero input is such that the shift semigroup $S_1(t)$ leaves it invariant. Let θ be any input which is such that $S(t)\theta$ is equivalent to θ for every $t > 0$. Then we define two states to be θ-equivalent if

$$Z(x_1;\theta) = Z(x_2;\theta). \tag{5.8}$$

It may be noted that in the linear case θ-equivalence for any θ implies equivalence in the sense of (5.6). In particular, we have been using zero-input equivalence in the linear case. Let the state space be now reduced modulo the equivalence relation (5.6) and let us denote the reduced state by Σ_R. Then clearly we may define (5.3) in the obvious manner on $\Sigma_R \times B_p(X_1)$. We next introduce a topology on Σ_R by defining open sets in the following way:

Any set of the form

$$E = \{xZ(x;u) \in O \cap Z(\Sigma_R;u)\},$$

where O is any open set in $B_{\bar{p}}(X_2)$ and u is a fixed element of $B_p(X_1)$, is open; and as u ranges over all of $B_p(X_1)$, we thus obtain a fundamental class of open sets. In other words, the topology is so defined that $Z(x;u)$ for each u is a continuous mapping of Σ_R into $B_{\bar{p}}(X_2)$. Since $B_{\bar{p}}(X_2)$ is complete, we may proceed to Σ_R in this topology and denote the completed space by $\overline{\Sigma}_R$. Then (5.3) may be extended to be defined on $\overline{\Sigma}_R \times B_p(X_1)$ in the usual way, so that the mapping $Z(\cdot;u)$ is continuous on $\overline{\Sigma}_R$ for fixed u.

Next let us consider (5.5), and let t be such that $x(t)$ therein is defined. There is only one $x(t)$ in Σ_R for which (5.5) is defined. For suppose x_1 and x_2 in Σ are such that

$$S_2(t)Z(x;u) = Z(x_1;S(t)u) = Z(x_2;S(t)u). \tag{5.9}$$

Let u' be any element of $B_p(X_1)$. Define $u(s)$ by

$$\tilde{u}(s) = \begin{cases} u(s) & 0 < s < t, \\ u'(s-t) & t < s, \end{cases}$$

so that $S(t)\tilde{u}=u'$. Next it is implicit in the definition (5.2) that $x(\tau)$ "depends" only on x and $u(s)$, $0 < s < \tau$. Thus we have

$$V(t+\sigma) = \begin{cases} Z[t+\sigma;x;\tilde{u}(s),0 < s < t+\sigma] & \sigma > 0, \\ Z[\sigma;x(t);u'(s),0 < s < \sigma] & \sigma > 0, \end{cases}$$

from which it follows that

$$Z(x_1;u') = Z(x_2;u'),$$

and u' being arbitrary, x_1 and x_2 are equivalent. Hence we may define a mapping on $\Sigma_R \times B_p(X_1)$ into Σ_R by

$$S_2(t)Z(x;u) = Z(x(t);S(t)u) \qquad t > 0, \tag{5.10}$$

$$x(t) = X(t;x;u), \tag{5.11}$$

which, as we have noted, is a casual function of u. Here (5.11) is defined for almost every $t > 0$. By taking appropriate limits, (5.11) can clearly be extended to the completed space $\overline{\Sigma}_R$. Next, rewriting (5.11) as

$$x(t) = X(t; x(0); u)$$

we see that more generally for any t, $\Delta > 0$,

$$x(t+\Delta) = X(\Delta; x(t); S(t)u), \tag{5.12}$$

$$x = X(0; x; u).$$

If θ is an element such that $S(t)\theta$ is equivalent to θ for every t, then if we define for each t

$$T(t)x = X(t; x; \theta), \tag{5.13}$$

it is readily verified that $T(t)$ is a semigroup of transformations, nonlinear in general. It should be noted that (5.13) is defined on the space $\overline{\Sigma}_R$ and not on the equivalence classes of zero-input equivalent states. It can clearly be redefined on the latter space, preserving the semigroup property. We also note that (5.13) is of significance for those systems in which zero-input equivalence implies equivalence.

Next let us use the transformation $f_0(\cdot)$ as defined in Section IV. Then we have that if

$$v = Z(x; u),$$

excepting a set of measure zero:

$$v(t)) = \begin{cases} f_0(S_2(t)Z(x; u)), \\ f_0(Z(x(t); S_1(t)u)). \end{cases} \tag{5.14}$$

We now make the smoothness assumption (H_1) that for every x in $\overline{\Sigma}_R$,

$$f_0(Z(x; S_1(t)u)) = \begin{cases} \lim\limits_{\Delta \to 0} \Delta^{-1} \int\limits_0^\Delta Z(\sigma; x; u(t+s), 0 < s < \sigma)\, d\sigma, \\ g(x; u(t)) \qquad \text{a.e. in } t, \end{cases}$$

where $g(.;.)$ is a transformation mapping $\overline{\Sigma}_R \times X_1$ into X_2. We observe that for the linear systems of Section IV, the function $g(.;.)$ depends only on x, and, as we shall see in the examples below, this is also true for a large class of nonlinear systems as well. Using H_1, (5.14) can be written

$$v(t) = g(x(t); u(t)). \tag{5.15}$$

In (5.12) and (5.15) we have the first stage of generalization to nonlinear systems of (4.6) and (4.7), respectively. It is true that (5.12) is not as concrete as (4.7), but this is the price one has to pay for generality. It should be noted in this connection that the state space Σ_R may not even be a linear space. Examples will be given below where under additional assumptions it is possible to express (5.12) more concretely.

A dynamic equation corresponding to (5.12) and generalizing (4.8) can be obtained in the following way: Since it makes no sense in general to "differentiate" $x(t)$ we consider rather

$$Z(x(t); u'),$$

where u' is any element of $B_p(X_1)$. Now, using (5.10),

$$\Delta^{-1}[Z(x(t+); u') - Z(x(t); u'] = \Delta^{-1} S_2(\Delta)[Z(x(t); \tilde{u}) - Z(x(t); u')]$$
$$+ \Delta^{-1}(S_2(\Delta) - I) Z(x(t); u'),$$

where

$$u(s) = \begin{cases} u(t+s) & 0 < s < \Delta, \\ u'(s-\Delta) & s > \Delta. \end{cases}$$

As Δ goes to zero, assuming the existence of the limits, we obtain

$$d/dt \, Z(x(t); u') = AZ(x(t); u') + B(x(t); u(t); u'), \qquad (5.16)$$

where A is the infinitesimal generator of the semigroup $S_2(t)$.

Equation (5.16) would appear to be not too useful. If we assume (H$_2$) that $\overline{\Sigma}_R$ is a linear space (or, Σ_R is a linear space and linear topological space in the induced topology, so that the completion $\overline{\Sigma}_R$ is then also a linear space), then of course we can obtain a dynamic equation by considering

$$\lim_{\Delta \to 0} \Delta^{-1}(x(t+\Delta) - x(t)).$$

Let us also assume (H$_3$) that the input $u(\cdot)$ is such that (in the topology of $\overline{\Sigma}_R$)

$$\lim_{\Delta \to 0} \Delta^{-1}[X(\Delta; x; S_1(t)u) - X(0; x; S(t)u)] = F(x; u(t)) \qquad \text{a.e. in } t$$

for x in some subset of $\overline{\Sigma}_R$, where $F(\cdot; \cdot)$ maps a suitable subset of $_R \times \overline{\Sigma}X_1$ into $\overline{\Sigma}_R$. If we assume that $x(t)$ is in this subset for each t, we have

$$\Delta^{-1}[x(t+\Delta) - x(t)] = \Delta^{-1}[X(\Delta; x(t); S(t)u) - X(0; x(t); S(t)u)],$$

which as Δ tends to zero has the limit

$$F(x(t); u(t)).$$

Or, we have the dynamic equation

$$\dot{x}(t) = F(x(t); u(t)) \qquad \text{a.e.}, \tag{5.17}$$

which is then the general result corresponding to (4.8). It is to be noted however, that we have had to make assumptions H_1, H_2, and H_3 in the process. Conversely, to establish existence and uniqueness of solutions of (5.17) we have to make additional assumptions, as a rule. For some recent results (for the case where Σ_R can be assumed to be a Hilbert space) for this latter problem, see (7).

We have mentioned briefly the class of systems for which zero-input equivalence implies equivalence. This would appear to be a useful constraint, and many classes of nonlinear systems (including some examples we shall study below) fall into this category. It is convenient to topologize the reduced state space in this case using the zero-input response, and we shall call the resulting topology the "zero-input" topology. (This topology is, of course, coarser than the more general topology.) We note that (5.13) defines a semigroup of continuous (albeit nonlinear) transformations on $\overline{\Sigma}_R$. Also, using (5.10), we have

$$S_2(t) Z(x; 0) = Z(T(t) x; 0),$$

and from (5.16), where u' can now be replaced by the zero element, we have

$$d/dt\, Z(x(t); 0) = AZ(x(t); 0) + B(x(t); u(t)), \tag{5.18}$$

which is clearly potentially more useful than (5.16) when Σ_R is not a linear space.

Examples

We shall now proceed to illustrate the theory with some examples. Let us first consider the system defined in terms of the input-output relation

$$v(t) = \int\limits_{-\infty}^{t} \int\limits_{-\infty}^{t} W(t-s_1, t-s_2) u(s_1) u(s_2)\, ds_1\, ds_2, \tag{5.19}$$

where $X_1 = X_2 =$ the complex-number field, and the weight function $W(\cdot,\cdot)$ is continuous on compact subsets of the positive quadrant of the plane. For the state space Σ here we take the class of set functions countably additive on the Borel field with compact support. This is obviously a linear space, and using the well-known correspondence between these set functions and functions of bounded variation, we shall denote the point functions by $U(\cdot)$ and introduce the shift semigroup $T(t)$:

$$T(t)x = y; \qquad\qquad x \sim U, \quad y \sim U',$$

$$U'(s) = \begin{cases} U(t+s) & s \leqslant -t, \\ U(0) & 0 > s > -t. \end{cases}$$

The zero-input response using (5.19) can then be expressed as

$$Z(t;x;0) = \begin{cases} Z(0;T(t)x;0), \\ \displaystyle\int_{-\infty}^{0}\int_{-\infty}^{0} W(-s_1,-s_2)\,dU(t+s_1)\,dU(t+s_2). \end{cases}$$

Let us denote the delta function in the usual definition by δ. The class of functions continuous on $[0,\infty)$ provides a determining set of functionals for Σ, and with reference to this set we can define the integral

$$\int_{0}^{t} T(t-s)\,u(s)\,ds,$$

and the corresponding element in Σ is a set function absolutely continuous with respect to Lebesgue measure, with density function given by

$$u(t+s) \qquad -t < s < 0,$$

$$0 \qquad\qquad -t > s.$$

If we now define the transformation on Σ by

$$x(t) = T(t)x(0) + \int_{0}^{t} T(t-s)\,\delta u(s)\,ds \qquad\qquad (5.20)$$

and a function on Σ by

$$g(x) = \int_{-\infty}^{0}\int_{-\infty}^{0} W(-s_1,-s_2)\,dU(s_1)\,dU(s_2),$$

we have that

$$v(t) = g(x(t)), \tag{5.21}$$

as can be readily verified by an appropriate change of variable in (5.19). Also $g(\cdot)$ is a homogeneous polynomial of second degree on Σ. We thus have a state-space representation for (5.19), but, of course, the state space is not necessarily reduced, and (5.20) is not a relation in the reduced state space, necessarily, unless the mapping $g[T(t)x]$ of Σ into $B_{\bar{p}}(X_2)$ is one-to-one. If the latter is true, then zero-input equivalence obviously implies equivalence, and the operator $T(t)$ is clearly continuous in the zero-input topology for each t, and we have the state relations, etc., as indicated in the general theory.

It is therefore of interest to consider the case where the mapping $g[T(t)x]$ is not one-to-one. For this we shall consider the example where

$$W(s_1, s_2) = \sum_{i=1}^{n} \sum_{j=1}^{n} a_{ij} \exp(\lambda_i s_1) \exp(\lambda_j s_2). \tag{5.22}$$

Then suppose

$$g(T(t)x_1) = g(T(t)x_2) \qquad t > 0. \tag{5.23}$$

By a direct calculation from (5.22) it can then be verified that

$$g(T(t)(x_1 - x_2)) = 0 \qquad t > 0.$$

Moreover the set of elements x for which

$$g(T(t)x) = 0 \qquad t > 0 \tag{5.24}$$

is also readily verified to be a linear subspace of Σ. Again zero-input equivalence can be readily shown to imply equivalence. Hence Σ_R is simply the linear space modulo the subspace defined by (5.24). On the other hand, this space is seen to be finite-dimensional, and the Euclidean topology is equivalent to the zero-input topology. If we denote the mapping of Σ onto Σ_R by P, then of course P is linear, and if for x_1, x_2 in Σ,

$$Px_1 = Px_2,$$

then also

$$PT(t)x_1 = PT(t)x_2.$$

Hence we can define a transformation on Σ_R by

$$\tilde{T}(t) Px = PT(t) x \qquad (5.25)$$

and $\tilde{T}(t)$ is again a semigroup, and from (5.20) we have

$$Px(t) = \tilde{T}(t) Px(0) + \int_0^t \tilde{T}(t-s) Bu(s) \, ds, \qquad (5.26)$$

where

$$P\delta = B. \qquad (5.27)$$

The semigroup $\tilde{T}(t)$ has the form

$$\tilde{T}(t) = \exp(At),$$

where A is a linear transformation on the finite-dimensional space Σ_R, and the element B in (5.27) is defined by the relations

$$\int_{-\infty}^{0} \exp(-\lambda_i s) b(s) \, ds = 1 \qquad i = 1, \ldots, n,$$

and we also have

$$\int_{-\infty}^{0} \int_{-\infty}^{0} W(t-s_1, t-s_2) b(s_1) b(s_2) \, ds_1 \, ds_2 = W(t,t) \qquad t > 0. \quad (5.28)$$

Also we can define the function (functional) $\tilde{g}(\cdot)$ on Σ_R by

$$\tilde{g}(Px) = g(x).$$

This is well defined, since if for x_1, x_2 in Σ,

$$Px_1 = Px_2,$$

then the equality

$$g(T(t) x_1) = g(T(t) x_2) \qquad t > 0$$

is seen to hold for t equal to zero as well. Now $g(\cdot)$ is readily seen to be a second-degree homogeneous polynomial on the space Σ_R, and the final (reduced) state relations for this example are thus given by

$$x(t) = \exp(At) x(0) + \int_0^t \exp[(t-s) A] Bu(s) \, ds, \qquad (5.29)$$

$$v(t) = \tilde{g}(x(t)), \qquad (5.30)$$

with the corresponding "dynamic" equation,

$$\dot{x}(t) = Ax(t) + Bu(t) \qquad \text{a.e.}$$

However, there is no "differential equation" connecting $v(t)$ and $u(t)$, unlike the linear case in general. It should be noted in this example that the zero-input topology is equivalent to the Euclidean topology. We can also state a sort of a converse to this example; if the system is defined by (5.19) and if the mapping p onto the reduced (with respect to zero-input) state space is linear, and Σ_R is finite-dimensional, then the weight function $W(.,.)$ must have the form

$$W(s_1, s_2) = \sum \sum a_{ij} P_i(s_1) P_j(s_2) \exp(\lambda_i s_1) \exp(\lambda_j s_2), \qquad (5.31)$$

where the $P_i(\cdot)$ are polynomials. This is immediate from (5.29). It is likely that this is true under the weaker hypothesis that Σ_R is a normed linear space [as in the linear case (2)], but we shall not pursue this point further here.

We can generalize this example in several directions. First we can generalize (5.19) to

$$v(t) = \sum_1^N \int_{-\infty}^t \cdots \int_{-\infty}^t W_k(t - s_1, \ldots, t - s_k) u(s_1) \cdots u(s_k) \, ds_1 \cdots ds_k \qquad (5.32)$$

and (5.20) again provides a state-input relation, and we have only to define the function $g(\cdot)$ by

$$g(x) = \sum_1^N \int_{-\infty}^0 \cdots \int_{-\infty}^0 W_k(-s_1, -s_2, \ldots, -s_k) \, dU(s_1) \cdots dU(s_k), \qquad (5.33)$$

and it is to be noted that $g(\cdot)$ is a polynomial of degree N on the linear space Σ. As before, if the mapping $g[T(t)x]$, mapping Σ into $B_{\bar{p}}(X_2)$, is one-to-one, then (5.20) is the desired state-input relation, with

$$v(t) = g(x(t)).$$

We can also clearly generalize (5.31), by taking in (5.31),

$$W_k(s_1, \ldots, s_k) = \sum_{i_1=1}^m \cdots \sum_{i_k=1}^m a_{i_1, \ldots, i_k} P_{i_1}(s_1) \cdots P_{i_k}(s_k) \exp \sum_{j=1}^k \lambda_{i_j} s_j,$$

leading to finite-dimensional reduced state space, with the state equation given by (5.29).

As a final generalization of (5.19) we may consider

$$v(t) = \int_{-\infty}^{t} \phi(t-s; u(s)) \, ds, \tag{5.34}$$

where $\phi(.,.)$ is defined and Lesbesgue-measurable on $[0, \infty] \times [-\infty, \infty]$ and (5.34) is a summable integral for each input function $u(\cdot)$ that is p-summable and vanishes outside compact intervals, and the corresponding output $v(\cdot)$ is p-summable, also on finite intervals. For our initial state space Σ we may take the class (linear space) of all p-summable functions vanishing outside compact intervals of $(-\infty, 0]$. We may add set functions with atomic parts to this class, by requiring that suitable limits exist. In particular, then, the δ-function will be in Σ, and it is readily verified that (5.20) defines an acceptable state-input relation. Let

$$g(x) = \int_{-\infty}^{0} \phi(t-s; u(s)) \, ds.$$

Then

$$v(t) = g(x(t)).$$

As before, the mapping $g(T(t)x)$ is one-to-one, then (5.20) is also the desired reduced state-input relation. We can, of course, generalize (5.34) to the form

$$v(t) = \sum_{k=1}^{N} \int_{-\infty}^{t} \cdots \int_{-\infty}^{t} \phi_k(t-s_1, \ldots, t-s_k; u(s_1), \ldots, u(s_k)) \, ds_1 \cdots ds_k. \tag{5.35}$$

We can extend these considerations to examples where X_1 and X_2 are Banach spaces to some extent. Thus (5.35) can be extended to functions $\phi_k(\cdot)$ defined on the product of product spaces $(0, \infty]^k \times (X_1^k)$ with range in X_2, the integral taken as a Bochner integral. To obtain the analogue of (5.32) we have only to replace the integrand therein by

$$L_k(t-s_1, \ldots, t-s_k; u(s_1), \ldots, u(s_k)),$$

where for each fixed s_i, $L_k(.,.)$ is a k-linear form defined on the product space $[X_1]^k$, with range in X_2, and the integral is again taken as a Bochner integral. The analogue of (5.31) for arbitrary Banach spaces does not lead to anything interesting, since if the state space is finite-dimensional, (5.29) must hold, so that the input would enter only as linear functionals on X_1; unlike the linear case, however, the output space X_2 can of course be infinite-dimensional.

We can also clearly extend considerations under suitable limiting conditions to infinite-series versions of (5.32) and (5.35).

As a contrast to these examples, we may consider examples where the state-input relation is nonlinear and the output-state relation is linear. More specifically, let X be a Banach space, and let us consider the system described by the equations

$$\dot{x}(t) = F(x(t), u(t)) \qquad x(t) \in X, \quad u(t) \in X_1, \tag{5.36}$$

$$v(t) = L(x(t)), \tag{5.37}$$

where L is a linear transformation mapping X into X_2, and sufficient conditions are placed on the function $F(.,.)$ so that existence and uniqueness of solutions for the initial-value problem for (5.36) are guaranteed. [Such conditions are well known for the finite-dimensional case (9), and for recent results for the infinite-dimensional case see (7).] We note that X can be taken as the state space for the system. If the solution is continuous in the appropriate sense with respect to the initial value for the case of zero input, then zero-input equivalence implies equivalence, so that X is also the reduced state space.

REFERENCES

1. L. Zadeh and C. A. Desoer, "Linear System Theory, the State Space Approach," McGraw-Hill, New York, 1963.
2. A. V. Balakrishnan, Linear Systems with Infinite Dimensional State Spaces, *Proc. Symp. System Theory*, Brooklyn Polytechnic Institute, Brooklyn, New York, 1965.
3. A. V. Balakrishnan, On the State Space Theory of Linear Systems, *J. Math. Anal. Appl.* **14** (3) (1965).
4. J. L. Lions, On Some Optimization Problems for Linear Parabolic Equations, this volume.
5. A. V. Balakrishnan, Optimal Control Problems in Banach Spaces, *J. SIAM Control* **3** (10) (1965).

6. A. V. Balakrishnan, Semigroup Theory and Control Theory, *Proc. IFIP*, Spartan Books, Washington, D.C., 1965.
7. J. L. Lions, Optimisation pour certaines classes d'equations d'evolution non-lineaire, to be published.
8. R. E. Kalman, Mathematical Description of Linear Dynamical Systems, *J. SIAM Control* (1963).
9. G. Sansone, Equazioni Differenziali nel Campo Reale, vol. 2, 2nd ed., Zanichelli, Bologna, 1949.

Nonlinear Problems Posed by Decision Equations

E. R. Caianiello

Istituto di Fisica Teorica, Università di Napoli, Naples, Italy

I. Introduction

First, let me state clearly that I do not claim to be a mathematician: as a theoretical physicist, my task is not to compete with mathematicians, but rather to ask questions of them, such as can be gathered from Nature itself, with pains and luck.

The study of the brain offers enormous difficulties, because of the very large number of elements in mutual interactions; the most important thing is to understand at which level it is useful to begin a study of the brain. For instance, it would not be useful to look at the brain as a collection of atoms and molecules and to study their interactions by means of the wave mechanics. In 1961 I gave a mathematical model of neuronal behavior (*1*), to which it may be useful to refer here, to start with. The model is essentially based on the three following abstractions;

(1) Neurons are binary elements, and their behavior is described by means of highly nonlinear equations. We shall call them *neuronic or decision equations*; their detailed form, at least for a qualitative study, is not very important.

(2) Memory is accounted for by means of *mnemonic equations*; more precisely, if we indicate with a_{hk} the coupling coefficient between a neuron h and a neuron k, the mnemonic equations describe the variability of such a coefficient as a function of the activity of the neurons h and k.

(3) *Adiabatic learning hypothesis*: Since the processes described by mnemonic equations are very slow with respect to those described by neuronic equations, we are allowed, in a first approximation, to consider the coupling coefficients as constant.

This last approximation is quite often used in physics; for example in the

37

Born-Oppenheimer model of molecular motion, nuclei are supposed to be at rest, and only the motion of electrons is taken into account.

I propose in this lecture to sketch briefly some of the mathematical problems with which the study of brain or brainlike machines confronts us. Details may be found in the cited references or in forthcoming papers.

II. Decision Equations and Reverberations

Let us introduce the Heaviside function,

$$1(x) = \begin{cases} 1, & x > 0, \\ 0, & x \leqslant 0. \end{cases}$$

We represent the response at a time t of a neuron h to the stimuli which come to it from all other neurons in the following way:

$$u_h(t+\tau) = 1\left[\sum_{k=1}^{n} \sum_{r=0}^{n(h)} a_{hk}^{(r)} u_k(t-r\tau) - S_h\right], \tag{1}$$

where τ is a delay in the response of the neuron h and S_h its threshold (note that in a realistic model of the brain the summation symbol should be substituted by Stieltjes integrals). We are interested in finding out which are the periodic solutions of (1), or *reverberations* of assigned period R. To this end let us first make a simplification consisting of the quantization of the time variable t; from now on we write

$$t = m\tau. \tag{2}$$

By means of (2), Eq. (1) becomes

$$u_{h,m+1} = 1\left(\sum_{k,r} a_{hk}^{(r)} u_{k,m-r} - S_h\right). \tag{3}$$

Indicating by $u_h(t)$ the argument of the 1-function, (1) can be written

$$v_h(t+\tau) = \sum_{kr} a_{hk}^{(r)} 1[v_k(t-r\tau)] - S_h, \tag{4}$$

and therefore (3) becomes

$$v_{h,m+1} = \sum_{kr} a_{hk}^{(r)} 1[v_{k,m-r}] - S_h. \tag{5}$$

Now introducing the vectors

$$\mathbf{v}_j \equiv \begin{pmatrix} v_{1,j} \\ \vdots \\ v_{N,j} \end{pmatrix}, \qquad \mathbf{S} \equiv \begin{pmatrix} S_1 \\ \vdots \\ S_N \end{pmatrix}$$

and indicating by $A^{(r)}$ the matrix

$$\|a_{hk}^{(r)}\|,$$

Eq. (5) can be written

$$\mathbf{v}_{m+1} = \sum_r A^{(r)} 1[\mathbf{v}_{m-r}] - \mathbf{S}, \tag{6}$$

from which it clearly appears that a reverberation of period R exists if, and only if, the following equality holds:

$$\mathbf{v}_{m+R} \equiv \mathbf{v}_m. \tag{7}$$

We can therefore conclude that the search for reverberations of period R is equivalent to finding the solutions of (6) with the condition (7).

III. A Transformation of the Neuronic Equations: An Algebraic Problem

The high nonlinearity of neuronic equations presents some advantages, as we are going to show. More precisely, the choice of the $1(x)$ function preserves here for the product operation a property close to that which holds for the sum operation with linear systems. Let us first introduce the $\theta(x)$ function defined as

$$\theta(x) = \begin{cases} 1 & x > 0, \\ \tfrac{1}{2} & x = 0, \\ 0 & x < 0, \end{cases}$$

then note that the following equality holds:

$$\theta(x) = \tfrac{1}{2}(1 + \operatorname{sgn} x),$$

where

$$\operatorname{sgn} x \equiv \sigma(x) = \begin{cases} 1 & x > 0, \\ 0 & x = 0, \\ -1 & x < 0. \end{cases}$$

Of course it is

$$\sigma(xy) = \sigma(x)\,\sigma(y).$$

If we then consider the equations

$$X_\alpha = \sum_\beta A_{\alpha\beta} 1[x_\beta] - S_\alpha \qquad (\alpha = 1, 2, \ldots, N),$$

they can also be written[1]

$$\mathbf{X} = A[\tfrac{1}{2}\mathbf{1} + \tfrac{1}{2}\sigma(\mathbf{x})] - \mathbf{S},$$

or, in the more convenient form,

$$\mathbf{X} = \tfrac{1}{2}A\sigma(\mathbf{x}) + (\tfrac{1}{2}A\mathbf{1} - \mathbf{S}). \tag{8}$$

Let us now consider only the equations of a form which we shall call *normal*, i.e., equations for which the following condition is fulfilled:

$$\tfrac{1}{2}A\mathbf{1} - \mathbf{S} = 0.$$

This is a necessary condition, in the language of automata theory, for the self-duality of our system, which is necessary for every state [i.e., value of $u_n(t)$, all h, at a given time t] to belong to a reverberation, transients being thus forbidden (2). We restrict our attention here to this special case. Then (8) becomes

$$\mathbf{X} = \tfrac{1}{2}A\sigma(\mathbf{x}).$$

After that if we are given two normal systems,

$$X_\alpha = \sum_\beta B_{\alpha\beta}\,\sigma(x_\beta), \tag{9a}$$

$$Y_{\alpha'} = \sum_{\beta'} B'_{\alpha'\beta'}\,\sigma(y_{\beta'}), \tag{9b}$$

their Cartesian product can be written

$$X_\alpha Y_{\alpha'} = \sum_{\beta,\beta'} B'_{\alpha\beta} B_{\alpha'\beta'}\,\sigma(x_\beta y_{\beta'}).$$

So, if we have the equation

$$\mathbf{Z} = C\sigma(\mathbf{z}), \tag{10}$$

where

$$C = B \times B', \tag{11}$$

---

[1] Note that the use of the signum function $\sigma(x)$ instead of $1(x)$ is justified provided that the zero value of x is somehow excluded.

and if we know two solutions **X** and **Y**, respectively, for (9a) and (9b), we are able to construct a solution **Z** of (10), provided condition (11) is satisfied.

If we now have a normal system,

$$X_\alpha \equiv \rho_\alpha \sigma(x_\alpha) = \sum_\beta B_{\alpha\beta} \sigma(x_\beta),$$

where ρ_α is the absolute value of X_α, we may write this as

$$\sum_\beta (B_{\alpha\beta} - \rho_\beta \delta_{\alpha\beta}) \sigma(x_\beta) = 0.$$

These equations are equivalent to the conditions

(a) $$\Delta \equiv \det (B_{\alpha\beta} - \rho_\beta \delta_{\alpha\beta}) = 0,$$

(b) $$\sigma(x_h) = K\Delta_{1,h} = \pm 1,$$

(c) $$\Delta_{11}^2 = \Delta_{12}^2 = \ldots = \Delta_{1N}^2,$$

and the posed problem is thus seen to be equivalent to the familiar (although not easier) one of searching for all positive solutions ρ_β of (a), (b), and (c).

IV. An Analytical Problem

The equations we have been dealing with have, if referred to a realistic system of neurons, essentially the form

$$\phi_h(x, y, z; t+\tau)$$

$$= \sum_k \int_{-\infty}^{+\infty} dx' \int_{-\infty}^{+\infty} dy' \int_{-\infty}^{+\infty} dz' \int_{-\infty}^{t} dt' \, K_{hk}(x, x'; y, y'; z, z'; t, t')$$

$$\times 1[\phi_k(x', y', z', t')] - S_h(x, y, z, t),$$

where $\phi_h(x, y, z; t)$ represents the *effective excitation*, i.e., excitation minus threshold, reaching a neuron of species h located at point x, y, z at time t. The threshold of that neuron has been indicated by $S_h(x, y, z; t)$. The kernels K_{hk} contain all information related to the neurons' density distribution, connectivity, and time decay for each neuronic species. Kernels K_{hk} should be obtained experimentally, by observing the neuron fields (3).

Equations of this type are being studied by de Luca and the author; in several particular cases complete solutions are available. Let us consider, as an example, the equation

$$u(x, t+\tau) = 1\left[-\int_0^t u(x, t')\,dt' + \int_0^x u(x', t)\,dx'\right].$$ (12)

To this equation we have added an initial condition consisting of the requirement that at times $t \leqslant 0$, all neurons of the positive x axis are kept excited. In such a case the solution of equation (12) has been found to be

$$u(x, t) = 1\left[x - mt + \binom{m}{2}\tau\right] \qquad m\tau \leqslant t \leqslant (m+1)\tau.$$

The equation

$$x - mt + \binom{m}{2}\tau = 0$$

represents a straight line, for each fixed value of m, and the intersections of each pair of consecutive straight lines belong to a parabola, the equation of which is

$$x = \frac{t-\tau}{2\tau}\,t.$$

V. Equation of a Single Neuron (4)

The equation describing the behavior of a single neuron is basically a *decision equation*, whose form can be assumed, in general, to be

$$u(t+\tau) = 1\left[A(t) - \int_{-\infty}^t K(t-t')\,u(t')\,dt' - S\right].$$ (13a)

The most interesting problems connected with (13a) are the following:

(1) $K(t)$ and S are known—to determine the output $U(t)$ of the neuron as a function of the applied stimulus $A(t)$. This may take conveniently the form of determining the frequency response $n(t)$ for the given stimulus.

(2) $K(t)$ and S are unknown, totally or because the general form of $K(t)$ is known, but not the parameters which specify it in detail—to determine $K(t)$ and S by measuring the frequency response of the system caused by the application of a suitable known stimulus $A(t)$, e.g., a constant one.

(3) $K(t)$ and S are known—to determine the unknown applied stimulus $A(t)$ from measurements of the frequency response caused by it. $A(t)$ will be found, in general, to belong to a class of functions, all giving the same response within a fixed error; this class must be specified.

(4) Another important question arises when studying an actual experimental situation; the *external* stimulus one is able to apply to the system may affect it in a way unknown to us *a priori*, so that it may be necessary to devise computational techniques which also yield the actual dependence of $A(t)$ in (13a) on the applied external stimulus. This question is particularly important in the study of neuronal responses.

We have developed techniques which allow us to find the solution of such an equation for a generic kernel; a case of marked biological interest arises when the kernel has the form

$$K(t) = \lambda e^{-\alpha t},$$

λ and α being two positive constants, characteristic of the neuron. For this case we have solved completely questions (1)–(4), with results that are in good agreement with the experimental data, consisting of the frequency response of motoneurons, stimulated by means of currents. In the case of a kernel of the previous form, (13a) can be written

$$u(t+\tau) = 1\left[E(t) - \int_{-\infty}^{t} \exp\left[-\alpha(t-t')\right]u(t')\,dt'\right], \tag{13b}$$

where we have set

$$E(t) = (A(t) - S)/\lambda.$$

In many special cases the problem can be solved in closed form. We have studied the following:

(a)
$$E = \text{const.,}$$

(b)
$$E \begin{cases} \leqslant 0 & t < 0, \\ = \text{const.} & t > 0, \end{cases}$$

(c)
$$E = a + be^{-\gamma t} \qquad a, b, \gamma, \text{ are constants.}$$

All these cases have a biological interest; the last one, particularly, is met when studying *adaptation* problems. To handle (13a) it has been useful to define the following quantities:

$$\Delta_{2k} = t_{2k+1} - t_{2k} \qquad \text{time interval during which the neuron is active,}$$

$$\Delta_{2k+1} = t_{2k+2} - t_{2k+1} \qquad \text{time interval during which the neuron is inactive.}$$

Assuming that all intervals Δ are $> \tau$, we have obtained the following results for a generic excitation $E(t)$:

$$\exp(\alpha\Delta_{2k}) \ [\alpha E(t_{2k} + \Delta_{2k}) - 1] = \alpha E(t_{2k}) - \beta,$$

$$\exp(\alpha\Delta_{2k+1}) E(t_{2k+1} + \Delta_{2k+1}) - E(t_{2k+1}) = (\beta - 1)/\alpha.$$

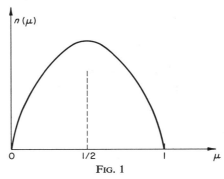

Fig. 1

These are recursion equations in Δ_{2k} and Δ_{2k+1} if $E(t)$ is an assigned function, which enables us to determine the sequence of activity and inactivity intervals for the studied neuron.

In the case of *constant* excitation, we have found for the frequency the following expression:

$$n(\mu) = \alpha/\ln\{1 + [\beta(\beta - 1)/\mu(1 - \mu)]\} \tag{14}$$

where we have set

$$\mu = \alpha E.$$

Moreover, μ is constrained to vary in the interval $(0, 1)$. Note that, apart from a transient term, (14) represents the frequency in steady conditions for variable excitations going to a constant value.

The plot of n as function of μ has the behavior illustrated in Fig. 1. It is a symmetrical function with respect to the axis $\mu = \frac{1}{2}$, which increases in the interval $(0, \frac{1}{2})$.

Experimental results provided by Granit (5) give a frequency-response curve as a function of excitation whose behavior is very close to that shown in Fig. 1, devoid of the last decreasing part, corresponding to quite high values of the excitation. The curve shown in Fig. 1 can be approximated by a parabola in suitable intervals around $\mu = 1/2$, of the equation

$$n(\mu) = \{\alpha/\beta(\beta - 1)\}\,\mu(1 - \mu).$$

VI. Concluding Remarks

The study of (13b) in the case of the excitation

$$\mu(t) = \rho + ve^{-ht} \tag{15}$$

has shown the existence of *adaptation* phenomena, provided the parameters contained in the excitation satisfy suitable conditions. Adaptation essentially consists of finding a frequency response in some neurons at the onset of the stimulus that is greater than the one found in stationary conditions. Such a phenomenon finds an immediate interpretation in the framework of our model. Suppose, in fact, that a constant external current I_0 is suddenly applied; one expects, on physical and biological grounds, that the current acting on the system will be of the type

$$I = I_0(1 - e^{-ht}) \qquad (I_0 > 0);$$

if this generates in the system itself an *effective stimulus* of the type

$$\mu(t) = \xi I + \eta\,dI/dt + \zeta, \tag{16}$$

where ξ, η, and ζ are parameters characteristic of the system, equation (16) coincides with (15) if it is

$$\rho = \xi I_0 + \zeta, \qquad v = I_0(\eta h - \xi),$$

which gives reason of the adaptation phenomenon.

E. R. CAIANIELLO

We shall conclude by observing that an excitation of type (16) is produced if we suppose that a neuron receives (as is true in some cases) a facilitation given by $aI(t)$ $(a > 0)$ from the central zone of the receptory field and an inhibition from the peripheral zone of it given by $-bI(t-\theta)$ $(b > 0)$ (θ is the delay caused by the greater traveling distance of the signal); the effective stimulus is

$$\mu(t) = aI(t) - bI(t-\theta) \simeq (a-b)I(t) + b\theta \, dI/dt,$$

so that

$$\rho = (a-b)I_0, \qquad v = I_0[hb\theta - (a-b)].$$

This is, of course, only one of the mechanisms which we can invoke to explain adaptation from the standpoint of our model, possibly the simplest one.

REFERENCES

1. E. R. Caianiello, Outline of a Theory of Thought Processes and Thinking Machines, *J. Theoret. Biol.* **1**, 204–235 (1961).
2. C. Crocchiolo and A. Drago, Linear Separability and State Reverberations, in press, 1966.
3. F. Lauria, Mathematical Approach to the Study of a Cerebral Cortex. Histological Methods of Calculating the Coupling Coefficients in the Neuronic Equations, *J. Theoret. Biol.* **8**, 5, 54–70 (1965).
4. E. R. Caianiello and A. de Luca, Decision Equation for Binary Systems. Application to Neuronal Behavior, 1965.
5. R. Granit, D. Kernell, and G. K. Shortess, Quantitative Aspects of Repetitive Firing of Mammalian Motoneurons Caused by Injected Currents, *J. Physiol.* (*London*) **168**, 911–931 (1963).

On a Generalization of the Bang-Bang Principle

C. CASTAING ·

Laboratoire d'Automatique Théorique, Faculté des Sciences
Université de Caen, Caen, Calvados, France

This paper is an attempt to extend the bang-bang principle to Banach infinite-dimensional spaces. We begin to give some definitions and notations. $C_E(T)$ is the vector space of continuous mappings of a compact space T into a Banach space E. A linear mapping m from $C_E(T)$ into a Banach space F is called *linear majorable mapping* if there is a positive measure μ on T such that the following condition is satisfied:

$$\|m(f)\|_F \leqslant \int |f| \, d\mu,$$

where $|f|:t \to \|f(t)\|_E$, $t \in T$ for every $f \in C_E(T)$. The preceding condition implies that m is a linear continuous mapping of $C_E(T)$ [equipped with the strong topology of $L_E^1(T,\mu)$] into F. Consequently, there is a unique linear continuous extension m of $L_E^1(T,\mu)$ into F. For every $f \in L_E^1(T,\mu)$ we shall note $\int f \, dm$ instead of $m(f)$. We shall suppose that E is a separable and reflexive Banach space and μ is nonatomic. Let S be a bounded closed and convex set in E and denote by $\check{S}$ the set of all extreme points of $\check{S}$. Let B (resp. $\dot{B}$) be the set of all functions $f \in L_E^\infty(T,\mu)$ such that $f(t) \in S$ (resp. $f(t) \in \check{S}$) (a.e. $t \in T$). We shall note

$$[\dot{B}] = \left\{ \int f \, dm / f \in \dot{B} \right\}, \qquad [B] = \left\{ \int f \, dm / f \in B \right\}.$$

Lemma. B is $\sigma(L^1, L^\infty)$ convex and compact in $L_E^1(T,\mu)$.

Theorem 1. $\dot{B}$ is $\sigma(L^1, L^\infty)$ dense in B.

Theorem 2. (a) $[B]$ is convex and $\sigma(F, F')$ compact in F. (b) The (weak) $\sigma(F, F')$ closure of $[\dot{B}]$ is $[B]$.

Corollary 1. If $f \to \int f \, dm$ is weakly compact, we have the following properties:

(a) $[B]$ is convex and strongly compact in F.

(b) The closure of $[\dot{B}]$ is convex and strongly compact in F.

Corollary 2. Let m be a majorable vector measure defined on a compact space T. Suppose that $|m|$ is nonatomic. Then the weak closure of the set of all elements $m(A)$, where A describes the set $\mathscr{X}$ of all $|m|$-measurable sets in T, is convex and $\sigma(F, F')$ compact in F.

Study of the Finite-Dimensional Case

Let μ a positive nonatomic measure on a compact space T. Let K be a compact set in $\mathbf{R}^n$. Denote by S the convex hull of K, $\ddot{S}$ the set of all extreme points of S, and $\bar{\ddot{S}}$ the closure of $\ddot{S}$. We shall note

$$B_0 = \{f \in L^\infty_{\mathbf{R}^n}(T, \mu) / f(t) \in \ddot{S} \quad \text{a.e.}\},$$

$$B_1 = \{f \in L^\infty_{\mathbf{R}^n}(T, \mu) / f(t) \in \bar{\ddot{S}} \quad \text{a.e.}\},$$

$$B_2 = \{f \in L^\infty_{\mathbf{R}^n}(T, \mu) / f(t) \in K \quad \text{a.e.}\},$$

$$B_3 = \{f \in L^\infty_{\mathbf{R}^n}(T, \mu) / f(t) \in S \quad \text{a.e.}\}.$$

Let

$$[B_i] = \left\{ \int f \, d\mu / f \in B_i \right\} \quad \text{for } i = 0, 1, 2, 3.$$

Theorem 3. (a) B_3 is convex and compact in $\mathbf{R}^n$.

(b) $\overline{[B_0]} = [B_1] = [B_2] = [B_3]$.

(c) If T is metrizable, we have $[B_0] = [B_1] = [B_2] = [B_3]$.

To prove Theorem 3 we shall need the following two theorems, which generalize Filippov lemma.

Theorem 4. Let T be a locally compact space, U a metrizable compact space, and V a Hausdorff topological space. Let h be a continuous mapping of $T \times U$ into V. Let μ be a positive measure (Radon) on T and v a μ-measurable mapping of T into V such that $v(t) \in h(t, U)$ a.e. $t \in T$. Then there is a μ-measurable mapping u of T into U such that

$$v(t) = h(t, u(t)) \quad \text{a.e. } t \in T.$$

Theorem 5. Let T be a locally compact Polish space, U a Polish space, and V a metrizable space. Let h be a continuous mapping of $T \times U$ into V. Let μ be a positive measure (Radon) on T and v a μ-measurable mapping of T into V such that $v(t) \in h(t, U)$ a.e. $t \in T$. Then there is a μ-measurable mapping u of T into U such that

$$v(t) = h(t, u(t)) \qquad \text{a.e. } t \in T.$$

The details of proofs of the preceding theorems can be found in two sources: (1) Sur une extension du théorème de Lyapounov, *Compt. Rend.* **260**, 3838–3841 (1965); (2) Relèvement des applications mesurables, Séminaire d'Automatique Théorique, Faculté des Sciences, Université de Caen, Caen, France.

On Linear Controllability

ROBERTO CONTI

Istituto Matematico, Università di Firenze
Florence, Italy

1. The basic problem of linear controllability can be described as follows.

Problem A. With the following data

$\mathscr{X}, \mathscr{U}, \mathscr{V}, \mathscr{W}$ (real) linear spaces,

$L: \mathscr{X} \to \mathscr{U}$; $M: \mathscr{X} \to \mathscr{V}$; $N: \mathscr{X} \to \mathscr{W}$, linear mappings,

$\tilde{\mathscr{U}}, \tilde{\mathscr{V}}, \tilde{\mathscr{W}}$ given subsets,

determine the solutions $(x, u, v, w) \in \mathscr{X} \times \tilde{\mathscr{U}} \times \tilde{\mathscr{V}} \times \tilde{\mathscr{W}}$ of

$$Lx = u, \qquad Mx = v, \qquad Nx = w. \tag{1.1}$$

Then *controllability* (with respect to $\tilde{\mathscr{U}} \times \tilde{\mathscr{V}} \times \tilde{\mathscr{W}}$) will just mean solvability of (1.1) if we call *controls* the triplets (u, v, w) and *admissible controls* those belonging to the subset $\tilde{\mathscr{U}} \times \tilde{\mathscr{V}} \times \tilde{\mathscr{W}}$ (the elements x of $\mathscr{X}$ are called *trajectories*).

We shall make the following assumptions:

(H_1) L has a right inverse $L^+: \mathscr{U} \to \mathscr{X}$, $LL^+ = I_{\mathscr{U}}$.

(H_2) M_0, the restriction of M to $\mathscr{N}(L) = \{x : Lx = 0\}$, the null space of L, has the inverse $M_0^{-1}: \mathscr{V} \to \mathscr{N}(L)$, $M_0 M_0^{-1} = I_{\mathscr{V}}$, $M_0^{-1} M_0 = I_{\mathscr{N}(L)}$.

Then

$$x = M_0^{-1} v + (I_{\mathscr{X}} - M_0^{-1} M) L^+ u \tag{1.2}$$

is equivalent to

$$Lx = u, \qquad Mx = v. \tag{1.3}$$

Therefore, under (H_1) and (H_2), (1.1) is equivalent to

$$x = M_0^{-1} v + (I_{\mathscr{X}} - M_0^{-1} M) L^+ u, \qquad Nx = w. \tag{1.4}$$

51

Denoting by N_0 the restriction of N to $\mathcal{N}(L)$ and by Λ_1 and Λ_2 the two linear mappings

$$\Lambda_1 = N(I_{\mathscr{X}} - M_0^{-1} M) L^+ : \mathscr{U} \to \mathscr{W}, \tag{1.5}$$

$$\Lambda_2 = N_0 M_0^{-1} : \mathscr{V} \to \mathscr{W}. \tag{1.6}$$

Problem A will be equivalent, under (H_1) and (H_2), to

Problem B. Determine the solutions $(u, v, w) \in \tilde{\mathscr{U}} \times \tilde{\mathscr{V}} \times \tilde{\mathscr{W}}$ of

$$\Lambda_1 u + \Lambda_2 v = w \tag{1.7}$$

or else to

Problem C. Find the intersection of the two sets

$$\hat{\mathscr{W}} = \Lambda_1 \tilde{\mathscr{U}} + \Lambda_2 \tilde{\mathscr{V}}, \tilde{\mathscr{W}}.$$

Remark. Obviously our problem is a particular case of

Problem D. Given $\mathscr{U}, \mathscr{V}, \mathscr{W}, \tilde{\mathscr{U}}, \tilde{\mathscr{V}}, \tilde{\mathscr{W}}$ as before, and two linear mappings

$$\Lambda_1 : \mathscr{U} \to \mathscr{W}, \qquad \Lambda_2 : \mathscr{V} \to \mathscr{W}$$

[*not* necessarily defined by (1.5) and (1.6)], find the intersection set $\hat{\mathscr{W}} \cap \tilde{\mathscr{W}}$.

2. The assumption $\tilde{\mathscr{U}}, \tilde{\mathscr{V}}, \tilde{\mathscr{W}}$ are convex sets implies that $\hat{\mathscr{W}}$, hence $\hat{\mathscr{W}} \cap \tilde{\mathscr{W}}$, are convex sets.

The case

$$\dim \hat{\mathscr{W}} = \dim \tilde{\mathscr{W}} = 0 \tag{2.1}$$

has no interest, since the problems reduces to verify whether, given the three *points* $\tilde{u}, \tilde{v}, \tilde{w}$, the relation $\Lambda_1 \tilde{u} + \Lambda_2 \tilde{v} = \tilde{w}$ holds or not.

Also the case

$$\tilde{\mathscr{W}} = \mathscr{W} \tag{2.2}$$

has no interest, since $\Lambda_1 \tilde{\mathscr{U}} + \Lambda_2 \tilde{\mathscr{V}} \subseteq \mathscr{W}$ for *any* $\tilde{\mathscr{U}}, \tilde{\mathscr{V}}$.

On the contrary, if

$$\hat{\mathscr{W}} = \mathscr{W}, \tag{2.3}$$

the problem will have solutions for any $\tilde{\mathscr{W}}$, but this depends, not only on $\tilde{\mathscr{U}}, \tilde{\mathscr{V}}$ but also on Λ_1, Λ_2, which imply more than a mere verification.

In particular, we have (2.3), if

$$\Lambda_1 \widetilde{\mathscr{U}} = \mathscr{W},\tag{2.3'}$$

i.e., if $\widetilde{\mathscr{U}}$ is a subspace of $\mathscr{U}$ and the restriction of Λ_1 to $\widetilde{\mathscr{U}}$ is onto, or if

$$\Lambda_2 \widetilde{\mathscr{V}} = \mathscr{W},\tag{2.3''}$$

i.e., if $\widetilde{\mathscr{V}}$ is a subspace of $\mathscr{V}$ and the restriction of Λ_2 to $\widetilde{\mathscr{V}}$ is onto.

In the remaining cases the problem is that of determining the intersection of two proper, convex subsets of $\mathscr{W}$, one of which, at least, has dimension greater than zero. One of these two sets, $\widehat{\mathscr{W}}$, is a datum, whereas the other, $\widecheck{\mathscr{W}}$, is given indirectly by means of $\widetilde{\mathscr{U}}$, $\widetilde{\mathscr{V}}$, Λ_1, Λ_2.

3. When $\mathscr{W}$ is a linear *topological* space it is of interest to know whether $\widehat{\mathscr{W}}$, $\widecheck{\mathscr{W}}$ are closed or not.

In general $\widehat{\mathscr{W}}$ is a (given) closed set, but $\widecheck{\mathscr{W}}$ may turn out *not* to be closed and the following cases are possible:

$$\widecheck{\mathscr{W}} \subset \overline{\widecheck{\mathscr{W}}} = \mathscr{W},\tag{3.1}$$

$$\widecheck{\mathscr{W}} \subset \overline{\widecheck{\mathscr{W}}} \subset \mathscr{W},\tag{3.2}$$

$$\widecheck{\mathscr{W}} = \overline{\widecheck{\mathscr{W}}} \subset \mathscr{W}\tag{3.3}$$

[in addition to (2.3), already considered].

It should be noted that (3.3), i.e.,

$$\Lambda_1 \widetilde{\mathscr{U}} + \Lambda_2 \widetilde{\mathscr{V}} = \overline{\Lambda_1 \widetilde{\mathscr{U}} + \Lambda_2 \widetilde{\mathscr{V}}}\tag{3.3'}$$

does *not* follow, in general, from

$$\Lambda_1 \widetilde{\mathscr{U}} = \overline{\Lambda_1 \widetilde{\mathscr{U}}}, \qquad \Lambda_2 \widetilde{\mathscr{V}} = \overline{\Lambda_2 \widetilde{\mathscr{V}}}.\tag{3.3''}$$

4. Several examples of the different situations listed in the preceding paragraphs may be found in the literature on linear control. They refer, in general, to the case of an operator L of the type

$$Lx = x_t - A(t)x,$$

where t is a real variable ("time") on a compact interval $[0, T]$, x_t denotes a derivative, and $A(t)$ is an operator-valued function of t such that a "representation formula" of the type (1.2) can be written for the corresponding problem (1.3).

REFERENCES

Finite-Dimensional Case:

H. A. Antosiewicz, *Arch. Rat. Mech. Anal.* **12**, 313 (1963).

E. A. Barbashin, *Avtomat. i Telemeh.* **21**, 941, 1341 (1960).

R. Conti, *J. Differential Eqs.* **1**, 120 (1965).

R. Gabasov and L. S. Kirillova, *Dokl. Akad. Nauk SSSR* **156**, 1007 (1964).

L. S. Pontryagin, V. G. Boltyanskii, R. V. Gamkrelidze, and E. F. Mishchenko, "The Mathematical Theory of Optimal Processes." Wiley (Interscience), New York, 1962.

W. T. Reid, *Duke Math. J.* **29**, 591 (1962).

Infinite-Dimensional Case:

Yu. V. Egorov, *Dokl. Akad. Nauk SSSR* **145**, 720 (1962).

Yu. V. Egorov, *Mat. Sb.* **64** (106), 79 (1964).

H. O. Fattorini, *J. SIAM Control* **2**, 54 (1964).

W. L. Miranker, *Proc. Am. Math. Soc.* **12**, 243 (1961).

W. L. Miranker, *J. Math. Anal. Appl.* **10**, 378 (1965).

A. Pistoia, *Rend. Ist. Lombardo Sci. Lettere* **86**, 760 (1953).

P. K. C. Wang, *Advan. Control Systems* **1**, 75 (1964).

Some Computational Aspects of the Theory of Optimal Control

W. De Backer [1]

CETIS, Scientific Data Processing Center, EURATOM C.C.R.
Ispra, Italy

I. Introduction

In developing some remarks on the implementation on computers of the necessary conditions for optimality, as given by the maximum principle of Pontryagin, we intend to achieve two ultimate goals.

A. Taking into account the by now well-known sensitivity of the optimal solutions with respect to computation errors, it seems necessary to bring these into the focus of interest and not treat them merely as details of secondary importance.

B. To obtain some practical advantages in computation [for analog as well as for digital computers; for a discussion of these aspects see ref. (12)] we shall try to imply the necessary conditions of Pontryagin by a set of differential equations to be added to the original equations of the plant. Of course, this can only be done by some approximation, the influence of which should be evaluated together with the computation errors, especially those involved with the analog or numerical integration.

The remarks collected in this paper give no complete answer to the problems implied by these goals. On the contrary, the partial results we obtained convinced us that some difficulties should be solved on a more fundamental level. Especially, we should decide what we mean by the solution of a problem if errors are involved. This kind of question is connected with a mathematical definition of the concepts "simulation" and "approximation" and are discussed in (11) and (12).

[1]*Present address:* University of Louvain, Louvain, Belgium.

55

In what follows we shall refer frequently to the following equations, the basic definitions and underlying theorems of which can be found in (*1*).

$$\frac{dx}{dt} = f(x, u), \qquad x \in E^n, \quad u \in E^r,$$

$$x(t_0) = x_0, \tag{1}$$

$$J = \int_{t_0}^{t_1} f^\circ(x, u)\, dt, \tag{2}$$

$$H(\psi, x, u) = \sum_{i=0}^{n} \psi^i f^i(x, u), \tag{3}$$

$$\frac{d\psi^i}{dt} = -\frac{\partial H}{\partial x^i} \quad (i = 1, n), \qquad \psi^\circ(t) = -1, \tag{4}$$

$$u^* = \arg\max_{u \in U} H(\psi, x, u),$$
$$M(\psi, x) = H(\psi, x, u^*), \tag{5}$$

$$u \in U: \text{ control constraints of the type } q(u) \leqslant 0, \tag{6}$$

$$x \in G: \text{ state constraints of the type } g(x) \leqslant 0, \tag{7}$$

$$p(x, u) = \sum_{i=1}^{n} \frac{\partial g}{\partial x^i} f^i(x, u) = \frac{dg}{dt}. \tag{8}$$

II. Normalized Adjoint Variables

Optimal trajectories do not depend on the length of the adjoint vector $\psi = (\psi^\circ, \psi^1, \ldots, \psi^n)$ but only on its direction. Therefore, all transformations applied to (4) which only affect the length of $\psi(t)$ give rise to new equations which are all mathematically equivalent with respect to the optimal solution. However, they are not equivalent with respect to the impact of computation errors, and a qualitative study of these immediately leads to the use of normalized equations. Moreover, the length of ψ has no physical meaning, and *a priori* nothing can be said about its evolution. ψ may very well be unbounded even at finite times, which is, indeed, very undesirable behavior for computation.

The normalized adjoint equation we propose preserves unit length of ψ for all t:

$$\frac{d\psi^i}{dt} = -\frac{\partial H}{\partial x^i} + \left(\sum_{\alpha=0}^{n} \frac{\partial H}{\partial x^\alpha} \psi^\alpha\right)\psi^i \quad (i = 0, 1, \ldots, n), \tag{9}$$

$$\langle \psi_0, \psi_0 \rangle = 1, \qquad \psi_0 = \psi(t_0). \tag{10}$$

Note that it is not allowed to set $\psi^\circ(t) = -1$. The initial conditions (10) and $M(\psi_0, x_0) = 0$ can be implemented by a gradient technique, as explained in (8).

Also the optimization criterion is subject to normalization in the sense that the optimal solution does not depend on the value of coefficients a multiplying the function $f^0(x, u)$. It has been established by computational experience that values of a can be found which make the optimal solution less dependent upon errors.

In general, normalizing ordinary differential equations is a well-established technique in analog computation. For digital computers note that the floating-point representation only guarantees a normalization with respect to roundoff errors, but not with respect to truncation errors in numerical integration, a fact often overlooked.

III. The Maximization of $H(\psi, x, u)$

According to our computational concepts (see Section I.B), condition (5) is implied by the vector differential equation (11), which is to be solved simultaneously with Eqs. (1) and (9).

$$\frac{du}{dt} = k_H \frac{\partial}{\partial u} [H(\psi, x, u) - \tfrac{1}{2} l q^2(u)]. \tag{11}$$

k_H is a large positive parameter, whereas l is a large positive constant if $q(u) > 0$ and zero if $q(u) \leqslant 0$.

The justification of this implementation is based on following mathematical considerations.

A. For fixed values of x and ψ Eq. (11) performs the maximization of the function $(H - \tfrac{1}{2} l q^2)$ by the gradient technique. The second member $(\tfrac{1}{2} l q^2)$ of the object function is called the *penalty function* corresponding to the constraint $q(u) \leqslant 0$.

The control variable $u(t)$ tends asymptotically to an equilibrium value u^* which satisfies the necessary conditions for a maximum:

$$\frac{\partial H}{\partial u} = l q(u) \frac{\partial q}{\partial u}. \tag{12}$$

Considering now a series of values $l \to \infty$ we expect $lq(u) \to \nu$, where ν is the Lagrange multiplier for the constraint $q(u)$. Consequently, Eq. (12) contains the ordinary conditions for a maximum subject to constraints as a limit case. General considerations concerning this method can be found in (2) and theorems discussing the convergence of solutions are developed in (3).

In practice it is impossible and unnecessary to achieve the limit case. Indeed, since other computation errors already effect u, it is reasonable to accept a correspondingly important constraint violation $q(u) \leqslant \epsilon$. Therefore, it is sufficient to take $l > |\nu_{est}/\epsilon|$, where ν_{est} is an *a priori* estimate of ν.

Note also that whatever the value of $u(t)$ at a given instant t, we must wait only for a finite time η before $u(t+\eta)$ and u^* satisfy the tolerance relation induced by the other computation errors. This finite time $\eta(k_H) \to 0$ for $k_H \to \infty$. For the same reason the initial conditions of (11) are inessential.

B. The results obtained under A can be transposed to the general case where (1), (9), and (11) are solved simultaneously (x and ψ are no longer fixed) on the condition that k_H be a "nonessential" large parameter [or that $1/k_H$ is a nonessential small parameter; see (4) and the bibliography there]. That parameter k_H is nonessential means that the solution of system (1), (9), (11) converges to the solution of system (1), (9), (12) for $k_H \to \infty$. System (1), (9), (12) is "inert" in the sense of Andronov [see (4)] and the derivatives du/dt of the "fast" equation (12) are qualitatively negligible.

Necessary conditions for k_H to be nonessential are (1) that the fast equation (11) be asymptotically stable for fixed values of x and ψ (which is true by definition; see A), and (2) that the slow equations (1) and (9) do not produce too rapid changes of $u^*(\psi, x)$. Consequently, important errors are to be expected for the control variables at the switching points, if present. At these points $u(t)$, as given by (11), necessarily remains continuous. However, these errors are limited to some small interval $\eta(k_H)$ (see A) and there are good theoretical reasons, confirmed by computational experiences, to expect that their influence upon the optimal trajectory is not too important. Apart from these considerations, a drastic remedy would be to "freeze" (1) and (9) for an interval $\eta(k_H)$ at every switching joint.

In order that the errors due to the approximation of (1), (9), (12) by (1), (9), (11) be quantitatively small, it is necessary to find a lower bound for

k_H, which inevitably depends on the behavior of all other computation errors.

C. The fact that we are giving so much importance to a simultaneous integration of (1), (9), and (11) finds its roots in computational advantages which are evident for analog computers [implicit computation by high-gain amplifiers; see (8)], but for digital-computation techniques they merit some explanation.

By an implementation of (11) on a digital computer we clearly do not mean that we program a stepwise version of the gradient equation with constant time increments. This would add not only a new kind of error, but plunge us again into convergence difficulties (putting upper bounds on k_H), convergence acceleration problems, and all well-known troubles proper to these techniques. But we do mean that (11) is solved simultaneously with the other equations and by the same numerical integration method. This numerical integration is supposed to work with variable time increments which depend on a truncation error estimate for each step. This dependence must be such that the qualitative properties of the differential equations are preserved. We agree on the fact that in this way all difficulties are transferred to this variable step-error control (with the corresponding risk of sticking to small increments for large values of l and k_H, especially if interference with roundoff errors occurs). However, a unified approach to the influence of the truncation error is now possible for the whole set of equations [see (12)]. Although we are lacking computational experience on this particular point, our first trials have not deceived our expectations for practical situations.

IV. Jump Conditions for Adjoint Variables

Jump conditions have to be satisfied if the trajectory reaches or leaves a state constraint $g(x)=0$ [see (1, §36)] or passes a hypersurface $g(x)=0$ dividing the state space into two parts for which different $f(x,u)$ are valid [$\partial f^\alpha/\partial x^i$ discontinuous; see (1, §37, Ex. 1)]:

$$\psi^+(\tau) = \gamma[\psi^-(\tau) + \mu \operatorname{grad} g[x(\tau)]], \tag{13}$$

$$\langle \psi^+(\tau), \psi^+(\tau) \rangle = \langle \psi^-(\tau), \psi^-(\tau) \rangle = 1, \tag{14}$$

$$M[\psi^+(\tau), x(\tau)] = M[\psi^-(\tau), x(\tau)] = 0. \tag{15}$$

At the junction point $x(\tau)$, the integration of (1) and (9) has to be stopped (e.g., hold mode for analog computers) while the final $\psi^-(\tau)$ values are memorized. The $\psi^+(\tau)$ values to be imposed as new initial conditions for (9) are calculated by (13), γ and μ and $u^+(\tau)$ corresponding to the asymptotic solutions of the following set of differential equations:

$$\frac{du}{d\vartheta} = k_H \frac{\partial}{\partial u} [H(\psi^+(\tau), x(\tau), u) - \tfrac{1}{2}lq^2(u)], \tag{16}$$

$$\frac{d\gamma}{d\vartheta} = -k_\gamma [\langle \psi^+(\tau), \psi^+(\tau) \rangle - 1], \tag{17}$$

$$\frac{d\mu}{d\vartheta} = -k_\mu H(\psi^+(\tau), x(\tau), u) p(x(\tau), u). \tag{18}$$

Equations (16)–(18) are asymptotically stable on their own, such that their simultaneous behavior depends again on whether the parameter k_γ is large and nonessential with respect to k_μ and whether k_H is large and non-essential with respect to k_γ and k_μ,

$$k_H \gg k_\gamma \gg k_\mu. \tag{19}$$

Consequently, all comments developed in Section 3 can be repeated here.

V. State Constraints and Penalty Functions

The basic idea of approximating an optimization problem with constraints by a problem without constraints, but with a penalty function, can be applied also for the case of constraints in state space. Formally, the development is as follows. Take

$$f^{\circ *}(x, u) = f^\circ(x, u) + \tfrac{1}{2}k_p[p(x, u)]^2 \tag{20}$$

with

$$k_p \gg 0 \qquad \text{for } g(x) > 0,$$

$$k_p = 0 \qquad \text{for } g(x) \leqslant 0.$$

We now have for (11),

$$\frac{du}{dt} = k_H \left[\frac{\partial H}{\partial u} - lq(u) \frac{\partial q}{\partial u} - k_p p(x, u) \frac{\partial p}{\partial u} \right], \tag{21}$$

and for (4) (case of not normalized adjoint system),

$$\frac{d\psi}{dt} = -\frac{\partial H}{\partial x} + k_p p(x, u)\frac{\partial p}{\partial x}. \tag{22}$$

If for $l \to \infty$, $k_p \to \infty$, and $k_H \to \infty$ we obtain convergence of the optimal trajectories, then (21) and (22) coincide in the limit with the Gamkrelidze conditions [see (1, Chap. VI)] for $lq(u) \to \nu$ and $k_p p(x, u) \to \lambda$, and this implies automatically the condition $u \in \omega(x)$ on the constraint $g(x) = 0$. Remember that $\omega(x) = \Omega(x) \cap U$, with

$$\Omega(x) = \{u : p(x, u) = 0; \quad g(x) = 0; \quad x \text{ regular}\}.$$

Consequently, we can expect convergence of the controls as well as the trajectories.

Note also that the jump conditions for the adjoint variables at each constraint violation ($\partial f^{\circ *}/\partial x$ is discontinuous in x) remain valid in the limit.

Of course, other types of penalty functions can be proposed for the same state constraint. The following one has been studied, particularly in (6):

$$f^{\circ *}(x, u) = f^{\circ}(x, u) + \tfrac{1}{2}k_g[g(x)]^2. \tag{23}$$

This type of penalty has the advantage that no jump conditions have to be satisfied at $g(x) = 0$ ($\partial f^{\circ *}/\partial x$ continuous). Note that the maximum condition (5) is not affected by the penalty, and in these circumstances one can hardly imagine how to make the optimal controls converge to the Gamkrelidze condition $u \in \omega(x)$. In any case, computational tests failed in that respect.

Moreover, the optimal trajectories constructed with both types of penalty functions [(22) and (23)] proved to be extremely sensitive with respect to computation errors. For this reason it was numerically impossible to take values of k_p and k_g greater than their lower bound imposed by the accuracy.

VI. The Two-Point Boundary Problem

The most difficult point in the synthesis of optimal control remains the problem of the transversality conditions. Assume that the initial conditions for the adjoint vector ψ_0 have to be set such that the end point $x_1 = x(t_1)$ of the optimal trajectory coincides with a given point c. A logical extension of the techniques discussed in preceding sections would be as follows.

Define a distance function $\rho(x_1, c)$ to be minimized by the gradient equation

$$\frac{d\psi_0}{d\sigma} = -\left\langle \frac{\partial \rho}{\partial x_1}, \frac{\partial x_1}{\partial \psi_0} \right\rangle. \tag{24}$$

The implementation of this equation leads to the following remarks.

The values of $\partial x_1/\partial \psi_0$, which are called *initial-condition influence coefficients* or, shorter, *sensitivity coefficients*, can be calculated by the variational equations for the system $(x, \psi, u^*(\psi, u))$. However, at the switching points of the control variable, these variational equations are not defined, and jump conditions must be satisfied for the sensitivity coefficients [see (9)]. These jump conditions give no particular computational difficulties.

In any case (also for analog-hybrid computers) only a stepwise version of (24) can be implemented and practice shows that because of the behavior of $\partial x_1/\partial \psi_0$ this leads to unsurmountable difficulties (regions of high criticality and regions of slow convergence). Also, many authors have preferred to look for more specialized techniques, generally applicable for linear systems only [see bibliography in (8)]. We feel that all hope is not lost for (24), if we integrate the differential equation by a method referred to in Section III.C. It depends on the properties of a good control of the truncation error, but this more general problem goes beyond the scope of our subject.

VII. Conclusions

The proposed techniques, based on normalization, penalty functions, and nonessential large parameters, have been applied with variable success [see (8, 10, 13)] for low-order nonlinear optimization problems subject to state constraints.

The equations discussed in Sections II–IV gave results which were quantitatively satisfactory. The implementation of the methods of Section 5 could only give some qualitative information on the optimal trajectories we were looking for, and this was due to the high sensitivity of the initial conditions of ψ. For the same reason the suggestions of Section 6 failed until now. However, we feel that the shortcomings are on a more fundamental level.

(1) We were not able to give reasonable criteria for the lower bounds of the large parameters l, k_H, k_y, k_μ, k_p, and k_g. What we did in practice was to compare the trajectories for growing values of these parameters until their effect became negligible.

(2) We cannot give criteria for large parameters until we have clearly defined what we mean by the relative importance of errors of different kinds and how we allow them to contribute to the calculated optimal trajectories and controls.

(3) All approximations have been considered relative to the "other" errors, which are mainly those involved with analog and numerical integration and the numerical representation of variables and parameters. Consequently, the whole study falls back on an analysis of these last.

Questions 1–3 refer to general problems in computation. Yet we think that the sensitivity troubles of optimal trajectories should be attacked on this level. The implementation of the maximum principle is very attractive, especially for on-line computers, and it certainly merits the efforts of the error analysis we referred to.

REFERENCES

1. L. S. Pontryagin, V. G. Boltyanskii, R. V. Gamkrelidze, and E. F. Mishchenko, "The Mathematical Theory of Optimal Processes," Wiley, New York, 1962.
2. H. J. Kelley, Method of Gradients, *in* "Optimization Techniques" (G. Leitmann, ed.). Academic Press, New York, 1962, Chap. 6.
3. H. Rubin and P. Ungar, Motion under a Strong Constraining Force, *Commun. Pure Appl. Math.* **10**, 65–87 (1957).
4. L. Gumowski, Sensitivity Analysis and Lyapunov Stability, *in* "Sensitivity Methods in Control Theory" (L. Radanovič, ed.). Pergamon Press, New York, 1966.
5. G. A. Korn, Enforcing Pontryagin's Maximum Principle by Continuous Steepest Descent, *IEEE Trans. Electron. Computers* **13**(4), 475 (1964).
6. S. S. L. Chang, A Modified Maximum Principle for Optimal Control of a System with Bounded Phase Space Coordinates, *Proc. IFAC, Basel*, September 1963.
7. W. De Backer, The Maximum Principle, Its Computational Aspects and Its Relations to Other Optimization Techniques, *EURATOM Rep. EUR-590e*, 1963.
8. W. De Backer, Synthesis of Optimal Control and Hybrid Computation, *Proc. 4th AICA Conference*, p. 265, Presses Academiques Européennes, Brussels, 1966; *EURATOM Rep. EUR-2202e*.

64 W. DE BACKER

9. W. De Backer, Jump Conditions for Sensitivity Coefficients, "Sensitivity Methods in Control Theory" (L. Radanovič, ed.). Pergamon Press, New York, 1966.
10. W. De Backer, Nuclear Reactor Power Reduction in Minimum Time Including Restriction of Xenon Poisoning, *Actes du Congrès d'Automatique Théorique à Saclay, 1965*, p. 134, Dunod, Paris, 1966; *EURATOM Rep. EUR-2506e.*
11. W. De Backer and L. Verbeek, Study of Analog, Digital and Hybrid Computers Using Automata Theory, *Bulletin I.C.C. (Rome)* (4), 1966.
12. W. De Backer, Simulation of Differential Systems (to appear).
13. G. P. Caligiuri, Sull'utilizzazione con calcolatore analogico del principio del massimo per l'ottimizzazione di un sistema idro-termo-elettrico, Revue Calcolo, Roma.

The Approximate Solution of an Unstable Physical Problem Subject to Constraints

Jim Douglas, Jr.

Rice University, Houston, Texas

Consider the problem of finding an approximate determination of a function harmonic in a half-plane from approximate data given on a compact segment in the half-plane; i.e.,

$$\Delta u = u_{xx} + u_{yy} = 0, \qquad -\infty < x < \infty, \quad y > 0,$$

$$|u(x, Y) - g(x)| < \epsilon, \qquad -\infty < -X \leqslant x \leqslant X < \infty, \tag{1}$$

where Y is a positive constant. This problem is well known to be unstable, and it is necessary to specify some global information about the function u to make the question meaningful. What follows is a summary of a forth-coming paper of J. R. Cannon and the author giving a constraint on u that provides stability to u and a computing procedure for approximating u.

Nonnegative harmonic functions on the half-plane can be represented by a Poisson integral with a kernel,

$$P(x, y) = \frac{1}{\pi} \frac{y}{x^2 + y^2}, \tag{2}$$

being integrated against a nonnegative measure. Obviously, a harmonic function that is the difference of two nonnegative harmonic functions can be represented similarly by employing a signed measure. Impose the global constraint on u that it be representable in the form

$$u(x, y) = \int_{-\infty}^{\infty} P(x - \xi, y) \, d\mu(\xi), \qquad y > 0, \tag{3}$$

where μ is a signed measure with Jordan decomposition $\mu = \mu^+ - \mu^-$ such that

$$\mu^+([n, n+1)) + \mu^-([n, n+1)) \leqslant 1, \qquad n = 0, \pm 1, \pm 2, \ldots. \tag{4}$$

65

If $x_i = i\Delta x$ and $\xi_j = j\Delta x$, it can be shown easily that

$$\left| u(x_i, Y) - \sum_{x_i - Z \leqslant \xi_j \leqslant x_i + Z} P(x_i - \xi_{j+\frac{1}{2}}, Y)\, \mu([\xi_j, \xi_{j+1}]) \right| \leqslant C(Z^{-1} + \Delta x), \quad (5)$$

where C is a constant depending on Y.

Let U be defined by

$$U(x, y; \{a_j, b_j\}) = \sum_{|\xi_j - x| \leqslant Z} P(x - \xi_{j+\frac{1}{2}}, y)(a_j - b_j), \quad (6)$$

where

$$a_j, b_j \geqslant 0, \qquad j = 0, \pm 1, \pm 2, \ldots,$$

$$a_j = b_j = 0, \qquad |\xi_j| > X + Z, \quad (7)$$

$$\sum_{n \leqslant \xi_j < n+1} (a_j + b_j) \leqslant 1, \qquad n = 0, \pm 1, \pm 2, \ldots.$$

Note that $\{a_j\}$ corresponds to μ^+ and $\{b_j\}$ to μ^- in the discretization of μ. Determine the constants $\{a_j, b_j\}$ so that U gives the best minimax fit to the data $g(x)$ at points x_i:

$$\min_{\{a_j, b_j\}} \max_{|x_i| \leqslant X} |U(x_i, Y; \{a_j, b_j\}) - g(x_i)| = \eta. \quad (8)$$

The evaluation of a solution $\{a_j', b_j'\}$ of the minimax problem is a standard linear programming problem. It is clear that

$$\eta \leqslant \epsilon + C(Z^{-1} + \Delta x) \quad (9)$$

and that the function U resulting from using $\{a_j', b_j'\}$ in (6) differs from the harmonic function U^* resulting from summing on all j in (6) by no more than a multiple of Z^{-1} on any half-plane $\{y \geqslant y_0 > 0\}$. If $v = U^* - u$, then an analysis based primarily on a theorem of Carleman can be made to show that

$$\max_R |v(x, y)| \leqslant C(R)\eta^{\alpha(R)}, \quad (10)$$

where $\alpha(R) > 0$, for any compact subset R of the half-plane $\{y > 0\}$. The constant $C(R)$ can be estimated explicitly in terms of the specified data X, Y, Z, and R.

Optimal Control of Diffusion Processes

WENDELL H. FLEMING

Brown University, Providence, Rhode Island

In this article we are going to summarize, in most instances without detailed proof, some results about stochastic optimization problems. We shall usually be concerned with a class of continuous-parameter optimization problems which I shall call *Markovian*. A Markovian problem of minimum is described as follows (speaking imprecisely for the moment). Let t denote a continuous time parameter, and let

$$\xi(t) = (\xi_1(t), \ldots, \xi_n(t))$$

denote the state at time t of a system governed by stochastic differential equations depending on certain "control parameters" $y_1, \ldots, y_k$. Depending on the choices made for the control parameters, there is a certain probability measure on the space of paths $\xi(\cdot)$ described by the states, such that almost all paths are continuous. Moreover, the past states condition the future only through the present state (Markovian property). Such continuous-parameter Markov processes are called *diffusion processes*. Let Φ be some real-valued functional of the paths and the control parameters. The problem is to choose the control parameters to minimize the expected value $E\{\Phi\}$. In order that the problem be Markovian, we must assume that the control parameters are chosen with complete instantaneous information of the state $\xi(t)$ of the system at each instant t.

In many problems of practical interest, the controller can only partially observe the state $\xi(t)$. These problems cannot properly be called Markovian, and require different methods not well understood at present. [For partially observable discrete-parameter problems more is known; see, for example, (5, 20).]

We shall assume that the functional Φ is of the form (1.1). There is then an intimate connection between Markovian optimization problems and certain boundary problems for nonlinear second-order partial differential equations. These equations are possibly degenerate forms of parabolic equations. Our methods are based on a combination of known results for second-order parabolic equations and various estimates derived directly from the stochastic differential equations describing the control system.

Using this relationship between control problems and parabolic equations, some results have been proved about the Cauchy problem and initial-boundary problems for degenerate nonlinear parabolic equations (Sections III–VI). These results are somewhat like ones obtained by Freĭdlin (2, 9) for degenerate linear elliptic and parabolic equations by probabilistic methods.

I. Deterministic Control Problems

Let us begin with a short review of some optimal-control problems which are deterministic (in other words, without random effects). These problems can be formulated in a way similar to the problem of Lagrange in the calculus of variations. We seek to minimize the integral

$$\int_s^T L[t, \xi(t), y(t)] \, dt, \tag{1.1}$$

where

$$\xi(t) = (\xi_1(t), \ldots, \xi_n(t))$$

belongs to Euclidean space R^n for every t and the vector function $\xi(\cdot)$ satisfies the system of ordinary differential equations

$$\dot{\xi} = f[t, \xi(t), y(t)], \qquad t \geqslant s, \tag{1.2}$$

together with initial data

$$\xi(s) = x \tag{1.3}$$

and terminal data

$$(T, \xi(T)) \in \Sigma, \tag{1.3'}$$

where $\Sigma \subset R^{n+1}$ is a certain closed set (called the *terminal set*). The vector $\xi(t)$ is called the *state* of the system at time t. The vector

$$y(t) = (y_1(t), \ldots, y_k(t))$$

belongs to K for every t, where the set K is fixed in advance. The vector $y(t)$ is called the *control* at time t and K is the *control region*. If $K = R^k$ and $y(t) = \dot{\xi}(t)$, the problem is the simplest one, that of the calculus of variations. In classical calculus of variations K was an open set, but in control theory K is frequently compact.

General existence theorems are known for this problem. For instance, let f and L be of class $C^{(2)}$. Let f_x be bounded. Let f be linear in y and L convex in y. Let K be compact and convex, and let T be bounded on Σ. Then there exists a measurable vector function $y(\cdot)$ with values in K minimizing (1.1). The minimizing function $y(\cdot)$ satisfies as a necessary condition the minimum principle of Pontryagin (*17*). If L is strictly convex in y, then $y(\cdot)$ is a continuous function.

The Hamilton-Jacobi Equation

For every s, $x = (x_1, \ldots, x_n)$, $p = (p_1, \ldots, p_n)$, let

$$H(s, x, p) = \min_{y \in K} [L(s, x, y) + f(s, x, y) \cdot p]. \tag{1.4}$$

The function H is concave in the variable p. In case $f(s, x, y) = y$, the function H is dual in the sense of convex functions to the function L.

Let us now think not just of one $(n+1)$-tuple of initial data (s, x), but of all possible such $(n+1)$-tuples. Then the minimum value of (1.1) can be considered as a function $\phi(s, x)$ of the initial data:

$$\phi(s, x) = \min \left\{ \int_s^T L[t, \xi(t), y(t)] \, dt \, \big| \, \xi(s) = x \right\}. \tag{1.5}$$

This point of view has been emphasized by Bellman (*1*).

If the function ϕ is of class $C^{(1)}$ in an open set G, then ϕ satisfies in G the Hamilton-Jacobi equation:

$$\phi_s + H(s, x, \phi_x) = 0, \tag{1.6}$$

where $\phi_x = (\phi_{x_1}, \ldots, \phi_{x_n})$ denotes the gradient in the "space" variables. Moreover, ϕ satisfies the boundary data

$$\phi(s, x) = 0 \qquad \text{for} \quad (s, x) \in \Sigma. \tag{1.7}$$

Unfortunately, as is well known from the method of characteristics, the problem (1.6)–(1.7) generally has a solution of class $C^{(1)}$ only in the small.

However, in some cases a generalized solution of the problem exists. If T is fixed and Σ is the hyperplane $s = T$ in (s, x)-space (Cauchy problem for 1.6), then Theorem 3 below gives as a special case the existence of a generalized solution $\phi(s, x)$. This solution is the limit as $\epsilon \to 0$ of $\phi^\epsilon(s, x)$ satisfying the parabolic equation

$$\phi_s^\epsilon + \frac{\epsilon^2}{2} \Delta \phi^\epsilon + H(s, x, \phi_x^\epsilon) = 0, \qquad \phi^\epsilon(T, x) = 0.$$

Under rather stringent assumptions at the boundary, similar results have been obtained for generalized solutions in cylindrical domains (Section IV).

The generalized solution ϕ is not necessarily unique. However, in some special cases additional conditions have been found which assure uniqueness (*12, 16*).

II. Diffusion Processes

Let us next review a few facts about diffusion processes given by a system of stochastic differential equations (*3, 4*). Let $b(\cdot, \cdot)$, $\sigma(\cdot, \cdot)$ be Hölder continuous functions on R^{n+1}. The values of b are in R^n and those of σ are $n \times n$ matrices. Suppose that

$$\begin{aligned} |\sigma(t, 0)| &\leqslant M_1, & |\sigma(t, \xi) - \sigma(t, \xi')| &\leqslant M_1 |\xi - \xi'|, \\ |b(t, 0)| &\leqslant M, & |b(t, \xi) - b(t, \xi')| &\leqslant M |\xi - \xi'|, \end{aligned} \qquad (2.1)$$

where M_1 and M are positive constants. Consider a Brownian-motion process in R^n, whose paths are denoted by $w(\cdot)$. Then a diffusion process, with paths $\xi(\cdot)$, satisfies the system of stochastic differential equations.

$$d\xi = b(t, \xi(t)) \, dt + \sigma(t, \xi(t)) \, dw \qquad (2.2)$$

with initial data $\xi(s) = x$ if with probability 1 the paths $\xi(\cdot)$ satisfy the system of integral equations

$$\xi(t) = x + \int_s^t b[\tau, \xi(\tau)] \, d\tau + \int_s^t \sigma[\tau, \xi(\tau)] \, dw(\tau). \qquad (2.2')$$

The last integral in (2.2') must be defined as a stochastic integral, because almost none of the Brownian paths have finite length.

For every (s, x) consider the symmetric nonnegative definite matrix

$$a(s, x) = \tfrac{1}{2}\sigma(s, x)\,\sigma^*(s, x), \tag{2.3}$$

where * denotes the adjoint. Let

$$A\phi = \phi_s + a(s, x)\cdot\phi_{xx} + b(s, x)\cdot\phi_x,$$

where

$$a\cdot\phi_{xx} = \sum_{i,j=1}^{n} a_{ij}\phi_{x_i x_j}.$$

The linear operator A is parabolic if all the characteristic values of $a(s, x)$ are positive. When some of the characteristic values are 0, we call A a degenerate parabolic operator.

Let us consider the Cauchy problem

$$A\phi + g(s, x) = 0 \qquad \text{for} \quad 0 \leqslant s \leqslant T, \quad x \in R^n, \quad \phi(T, x) = 0,$$

where T is fixed and the operator A can be degenerate. This problem has the unique solution

$$\phi(s, x) = E\left\{\int_s^T g[t, \xi(t)]\,dt \,\big|\, \xi(s) = x\right\}, \tag{2.4}$$

the function ϕ being of class $C^{(k)}$ if a, b, g are of class $C^{(k+1)}$, $k \geqslant 2$ (2). If the operator A is uniformly parabolic, then such strong assumptions about a, b, g are not needed (4, 10). Freĭdlin (9) has also proved by probabilistic methods results about the corresponding degenerate elliptic boundary problem

$$a(x)\cdot\phi_{xx} + b(x)\cdot\phi_x = g(x) \quad \text{in } D,$$
$$\phi(x) = 0 \qquad \text{on } \partial D,$$

under certain rather strong hypotheses at the boundary.

III. Markovian Control Problems, Fixed Stopping Time T

Let σ be as in Section II and let $a = \tfrac{1}{2}\sigma\sigma^*$. Let f, L be functions of class $C^{(2)}$ fatisfying

$$|f(s, x, y)| \leqslant M_2, \qquad |f(s, x, y) - f(s, x', y)| \leqslant M_2|x - x'|,$$
$$|L(s, x, y)| \leqslant M_2, \qquad |L(s, x, y) - L(s, x', y)| \leqslant M_2|x - x'|. \tag{3.1}$$

Let the control region K be compact and convex.

To begin with, let us admit controls of the following sort. Let $Y = Y(\cdot, \cdot)$ be a function from the strip $[0, T] \times R^n$ into K which is Hölder-continuous and satisfies a uniform Lipschitz condition

$$| Y(s, x) - Y(s, x')| \leqslant M_Y |x - x'|.$$

Given such an admissible control Y let

$$b(t, \xi) = f[t, Y(t, \xi)].$$

Then the diffusion process determined by the stochastic integral equation (2.2') is called the *response* of the system to the control Y. The problem is to select a control Y such that the expected value

$$E\left\{\int_s^T L[t, \xi(t), Y(t, \xi(t))]\, dt \,|\, \xi(s) = x\right\} \tag{3.2}$$

is minimum.

Theorem 1. Let $\sum\limits_{i,j=1}^{n} a_{ij}(s, x)\lambda_i\lambda_j \geqslant m_1 |\lambda|^2$ for all λ, where $m_1 > 0$. Let f be linear in y, and let $\sum\limits_{i,j=1}^{k} L_{y_i y_j}\mu_i\mu_j \geqslant m_2 |\mu|^2$ for all μ, where $m_2 > 0$. Then there exists an admissible control Y^* optimal with respect to every $(n+1)$-tuple (s, x) of initial data, $0 \leqslant s \leqslant T$. In fact, if $\phi(s, x)$ is the minimum value of (3.2), then ϕ, ϕ_s, ϕ_x, ϕ_{xx} are bounded, Hölder-continuous, and satisfy the parabolic equation

$$\phi_s + a(s, x) \cdot \phi_{xx} + H(s, x, \phi_x) = 0, \qquad 0 \leqslant s \leqslant T \tag{3.3}$$

with terminal data

$$\phi(T, x) = 0. \tag{3.4}$$

For every (s, x), $Y^*(s, x)$ is the unique $y \in K$ such that

$$L(s, x, y) + f(s, x, y) \cdot \phi_x(s, x) = \text{minimum}.$$

The function H is defined by (1.4). Theorem 1 is an easy consequence of (1.4), (2.4), the maximum principle, and Schauder-type estimates for parabolic equations (10).

Some observations are in order regarding Theorem 1. By existence theorems for parabolic equations the function ϕ in (3.3)–(3.4) exists without assuming linearity of f or strict convexity of L in y. But these hypotheses are needed to ensure the existence of an optimal admissible Y^*.

By admitting controls Y of the above type, we are in effect supposing that the controller knows the state of the system at any time t. If the controller has only partial information about the state of the system, then the problem is no longer Markovian and must be treated by other methods.

To study the problem without the strong hypotheses of Theorem 1, the following *a priori* estimate for the gradient is useful.

Theorem 2. Let the matrices $a(s,x)$ be uniformly positive definite as in Theorem 1, and f, L be as in (3.1). Let ϕ satisfy (3.3)–(3.4). Then there exists $N > 0$ such that $|\phi_x| \leqslant N$. The number N depends only on M_1, M_2, and T.

This theorem was proved in (7), by first establishing the corresponding estimate for discrete time-parameter problems with gap $\delta = T/r$ between successive times, and then by taking limits as $r \to \infty$. In the proof it is useful to consider controls depending explicitly on complete past history. By the Markovian nature of the problem, the minimum in this class of controls is the same as among controls depending only on the states (i.e., of type Y above). The proof of Theorem 2 is then in effect reduced to the following estimate of Doob, which depends on his martingale inequality. Let $\xi(\cdot)$ and $\xi'(\cdot)$ denote paths for diffusion processes satisfying a system of stochastic differential equations of the type

$$d\xi = b(t, \xi(t), \pi_t w) \, dt + \sigma(t, \xi(t)) \, dw,$$

where $\pi_t w$ is the past of the Brownian motion up to t, with initial data $\xi(s) = x$, $\xi'(s) = x'$. Then if M and M_1 are as in (2.1),

$$E\left\{ \max_{s \leqslant t \leqslant T} |\xi(t) - \xi'(t)|^2 \right\} \leqslant C|x' - x|^2,$$

where C depends only on M, M_1, and T.

If the matrices $a(s, x)$ are not uniformly positive definite, then we shall consider in place of (2.2) perturbed systems

$$d\xi = b(t, \xi(t)) \, dt + \sigma^\epsilon(t, \xi(t)) \, dw \qquad (2.2^\epsilon)$$

depending on a small positive parameter ϵ such that for each $\epsilon > 0$ the corresponding matrices $a^\epsilon(s, x)$ are uniformly positive definite.

For simplicity, let us take the case when there exists ν, $0 \leqslant \nu < n$, such that $\sigma_{ij} = 0$ for $i = 1, 2, \ldots, \nu$ and that

$$a(s, x) = \begin{pmatrix} 0 & 0 \\ 0 & \hat{a}(s, x) \end{pmatrix},$$

where the $(n - \nu) \times (n - \nu)$ matrices $\hat{a}(s, x)$ are uniformly positive definite. Let

$$\sigma_{ij}^{\epsilon} = \begin{cases} \epsilon \delta_{ij} & \text{for } i = 1, \ldots, \nu, \\ \sigma_{ij} & \text{for } i = \nu + 1, \ldots, n. \end{cases}$$

Then the Cauchy problem corresponding to (3.3)–(3.4) is

$$\phi_s^{\epsilon} + \frac{\epsilon^2}{2} \sum_{i=1}^{\nu} \phi_{x_i x_i}^{\epsilon} + \sum_{i,j=\nu+1}^{n} a_{ij}(s, x) \phi_{x_i x_j}^{\epsilon} + H(s, x, \phi_x^{\epsilon}) = 0, \qquad (3.3^{\epsilon})$$

$$\phi^{\epsilon}(s, x) = 0, \qquad (3.4)$$

and by Theorem 2 there is an estimate $|\phi_x^{\epsilon}| \leqslant N$. The functions ϕ^{ϵ} also satisfy a uniform Hölder estimate in s with exponent $1/2$.

Theorem 3. $\phi^{\epsilon}(s, x)$ tends to a limit $\phi(s, x)$ as $\epsilon \to 0$, uniformly on compact sets. The function ϕ satisfies (3.3) for almost all (s, x) under either of the following two additional conditions:

(a) $\sigma \equiv 0$ (deterministic case), or
(b) $\sigma = \sigma(s, x_{\nu+1}, \ldots, x_n)$, $f_i = f_i(s, x)$ for $i = 1, \ldots, \nu$.

The last assumption states that only the last $n - \nu$ components of the system (2.2) can be controlled directly. This theorem was proved in (7). Like Theorem 2, the proof that $\phi^{\epsilon}(s, x)$ tends to $\phi(s, x)$ depends on rather simple estimates based on the martingale inequality.

It seems reasonable that $\phi(s, x) = \inf_Y$ [expression in (3.2)], but no detailed proof has been given. However, if for $r = 1, 2, \ldots$ we let $\phi_r(s, x)$ denote the value of the minimum for the corresponding time-discrete problem with gap T/r between successive times, then it has been proved (7) that $\phi_r(s, x) \to \phi(s, x)$ uniformly on compact sets as $r \to \infty$.

IV. Markovian Control Problems, Variable Stopping Time

Let $D \subset R^n$ be an open set whose boundary ∂D can be represented locally in the form $x_i = \psi(x_1, \ldots, x_{i-1}, x_{i+1}, \ldots, x_n)$, where ψ has Hölder continuous second derivatives. Let $T_0 > 0$. Consider the following problem: minimize

$$E\left\{ \int_s^T L[t, \xi(t), Y(t, \xi(t))] \, dt \,\middle|\, \xi(s) = x \right\},$$

$$T = \min\{T_0, \text{ first exit time from } D\}.$$

Consider the cylinder $Q = (0, T_0) \times D$, and the "terminal set"

$$\Sigma = [0, T_0] \times \partial D \cup \{T_0\} \times D.$$

In place of the terminal data (3.4) we now consider (3.3) in Q with the data

$$\phi(s, x) = 0 \qquad \text{for} \quad (s, x) \in \Sigma. \tag{4.1}$$

Theorems 2 and 3 remain true, provided we know in addition an estimate of the type

$$|\phi(s, x)| \leqslant N_1 \, d(x), \tag{4.2}$$

where $d(x)$ is the distance from x to ∂D and N_1 depends only on M_1, M_2, T_0, and D. Such an estimate (4.2) will hold, for example, if $L \geqslant 0$ and $\delta(x) \leqslant Cd(x)$, where $\delta(x)$ is the minimum mean exit time from D starting at x.

The Autonomous Case. Let $f(x, y)$, $L(x, y)$, $\sigma(x)$ be independent of s, and admit controls $Y(x)$ satisfying a Lipschitz condition. Let D be bounded. For $x \in D$, let

$$\phi(x) = \inf_Y E\left\{ \int_0^\tau L[\xi(t), Y(\xi(t))] \, dt \,\middle|\, \xi(0) = x \right\},$$

where $\tau = $ first exit time from D. Under the hypotheses of Theorem 1, ϕ has Hölder continuous second derivatives and satisfies the elliptic equation corresponding to (3.3):

$$a \cdot \phi_{xx} + H(x, \phi_x) = 0$$

with data $\phi(x) = 0$ on ∂D. Moreover, as in Theorem 1, there is an admissible Y^* which is optimal for every starting position $x \in D$. To prove analogs of

Theorems 2 and 3 it is necessary to make some additional assumption about the speed with which trajectories of the $\xi(\cdot)$-processes reach ∂D, as was done by Freĭdlin (9) in case of degenerate linear elliptic equations.

V. Stochastic Differential Games

In this section we shall summarize some results from (7) about control problems in which there are two controllers. Speaking imprecisely, the first controller chooses a control Y and the second a control Z, which are functions with values in their respective (compact) control regions K_1 and K_2. The states of the game are to be determined from a system of stochastic differential equations

$$d\xi = f[t, \xi(t), Y(t, \xi(t)), Z(t, \xi(t))]\, dt + \sigma(t, \xi(t))\, dw \qquad (5.1)$$

with initial data $\xi(s) = x$. The first controller wishes to minimize the payoff

$$E\left\{\int_s^T L[t, \xi(t), Y(t, \xi(t)), Z(t, \xi(t))]\, dt \,|\, \xi(s) = x\right\} \qquad (5.2)$$

and the second controller wishes to maximize it. In the deterministic case ($\sigma \equiv 0$) such a problem is a differential game in the sense of Isaacs (11).

It is difficult to formulate precisely for stochastic differential games such ideas as mixed strategy and the kind of information each controller has. However, we can discretize time with gap T/r between successive times (for simplicity we consider fixed stopping time T). The equations (5.1) are replaced by corresponding stochastic difference equations and the integral in (5.2) by the corresponding Riemann sum. At each instant $t = jT/r$, $j = 0, 1, \ldots, r$, both controllers know the state $\xi(t)$ of the game. Let us also assume that the second controller knows the control y chosen by the first controller at time t before choosing his control z at time t.

Let $\phi_r(s, x)$ be the value (in the sense of game theory) of this game, if the initial time is s and $\xi(s) = x$. Because of the completeness of information available it is unnecessary to use mixed strategies.

Let us make the same assumptions about σ, f, and L as in Section III. Then $\phi_r(s, x)$ tends to a limit $\phi(s, x)$ as $r \to \infty$. Let [compare with (1.4)]

$$H(s, x, p) = \min_{y \in K_1} \max_{z \in K_2} [L(s, x, y, z) + p \cdot f(s, x, y, z)]. \qquad (5.3)$$

If the matrices $a(s,x)$ are uniformly positive definite, then ϕ solves the Cauchy problem (3.3)–(3.4). Moreover, the estimate $|\phi_x| \leqslant N$ in Theorem 2 again holds. If as in Section III we define ϕ^ϵ by (3.3$^\epsilon$)–(3.4), then Theorem 3 remains valid. The proofs of these facts are virtually the same as for the case of one controller.

VI. Generalized Solutions of Degenerate Parabolic Equations

Let us consider Cauchy problems of the type

$$\phi_s + a(s, x) \cdot \phi_{xx} + F(s, x, \phi, \phi_x) = 0, \qquad 0 \leqslant s \leqslant T, \tag{6.1}$$

$$\phi(T, x) = 0. \tag{6.2}$$

Although (6.1) may arise in some completely different context, we can sometimes find a generalized solution by control-theory methods.

For simplicity, let us first suppose that $F = F(s, x, p)$. If we can find a control region K and functions $L(s, x, y)$, $f(s, x, y)$ such that $F = H$ in (1.4), then Theorem 3 can be applied. Since (1.4) defines a concave function of p, this will be possible only if F is concave in p.

If we seek instead of a problem with one controller a stochastic differential game, then we must find $L(s, x, y, z)$, $f(s, x, y, z)$, K_1 and K_2 such that F is given by (5.3). When the operator "min" in (1.4) is replaced by "min max," no concavity or convexity condition is imposed on F. However, since K_1 and K_2 are to be compact sets, from (3.1) any F representable by (5.3) must satisfy the inequalities

$$|F(s, x, 0)| \leqslant M_2, \qquad |F_x(s, x, p)| \leqslant M_2(1 + |p|), \qquad |F_p(s, x, p)| \leqslant M_2. \tag{6.3}$$

Now let F be of class $C^{(2)}$ and satisfy (6.3) with some constant M_2. The following choices are convenient:

$$K_1 = \{y \in R^n : |y| \leqslant N_1\}, \qquad K_2 = \{z \in R^n : |z| \leqslant N_2\},$$

$$L(s, x, y, z) = \frac{F(s, x, y)}{1 + |y|^2} - y \cdot z, \qquad f(s, x, y, z) = \frac{F(s, x, y) y}{1 + |y|^2} + z.$$

Lemma. If N_2 is suitably chosen (depending only on M_2), then

$$F(s,x,p) = \min_{y \in N_1} \max_{z \in N_2} [L + p \cdot f]$$

whenever $|p| \leqslant N_1$.

But inequalities (3.1) hold, with some constant M_2'; and hence for some N_1 there is an *a priori* estimate $|\phi_x^\epsilon| \leqslant N_1$ for the solutions of the Cauchy problem (3.3^ϵ)–(3.4). Hence

$$\phi_s^\epsilon + a(s,x) \cdot \phi_{xx}^\epsilon + F(s,x,\phi_x^\epsilon) = 0,$$

and if the further assumptions in Theorem 3 are satisfied, we get when $\epsilon \to 0$ a generalized solution ϕ of problem (6.1)–(6.2).

If $F = F(s,x,u,p)$, then we consider stochastic differential games with payoffs of the slightly more general form

$$E\left\{ \int_s^T L \exp\left(\int_s^t h \, d\tau \right) dt \,\middle|\, \xi(s) = x \right\}, \tag{6.4}$$

where L and h are functions of s, x, y, and z, or more precisely discrete-time stochastic games in which (6.4) is replaced by the corresponding finite sum.

In fact, the following theorem was proved in (7).

Theorem 4. Let $F(s,x,u,p)$ be of class $C^{(1)}$ and satisfy for some M

$$|F(s,x,0,0)| \leqslant M, \quad |F_x| \leqslant M(1+|u|+|p|), \quad |F_u| \leqslant M, \quad |F_p| \leqslant M. \tag{6.5}$$

Then the problem (6.1)–(6.2) has a generalized solution ϕ in each of the following cases:

(a) $a \equiv 0$.

(b) $a(s,x) = \frac{1}{2}\sigma(s,x)\sigma^*(s,x)$, where σ is as in Theorem 3, and

$$F(s,x,u,p) = \sum_{i=1}^{\nu} g_i(s,x) p_i + \hat{F}(s,x,u,p_{\nu+1},\ldots,p_n).$$

The inequalities (6.3) imply that $F(s,x,p)$ grows no faster than $|p|$ as $|p| \to \infty$. When F grows more rapidly, we can in certain cases obtain a generalized solution by exploiting the idea of duality between convex and concave functions. Let us assume that $F(s,x,p)$ is of class $C^{(2)}$ and satisfies

(1) $|F| \geqslant C_1|p|^\beta - C_2, \quad \beta > 1, \quad C_1 > 0,$

(2) $\displaystyle\sum_{i,j=1}^{n} F_{p_i p_j}\mu_i\mu_j \leqslant -m|\mu|^2 \quad$ for all μ, where $m > 0,$ $\qquad$ (6.6)

(3) $|F_x| \leqslant C_3|F - p \cdot F_p| + C_4,$

(4) $|F_p| \leqslant C(N) \qquad$ if $|p| \leqslant N$, for $N = 1, 2, \ldots.$

Let L be the function, strictly convex in y, which is dual to the function F:

$$L(s, x, y) = \max_{p \in R^n} [F(s, x, p) - p \cdot y]. \qquad (6.7)$$

The dual formula

$$F(s, x, y) = \min_{y \in R^n} [L(s, x, y) + p \cdot y] \qquad (6.7')$$

holds. Let

$$f(s, x, y) = y, \qquad K_B = \{y \in R^n : |y| \leqslant B\},$$

where $B = 1, 2, \ldots.$ For $\epsilon > 0$ let ϕ_B^ϵ be the solution of the Cauchy problem (3.3^ϵ)–(3.4) with control region $K = K_B$.

Lemma. Let σ be a constant matrix. Then there exists $N_0 > 0$, depending only on C_3, C_4, and T, such that $|(\phi_B^\epsilon)_x| \leqslant N_0$.

The minimum in $(6.7')$ is attained when $L_y = -p$, $F_p = y$. Let $B \geqslant C(N_0)$. If $|p| \leqslant N_0$, then

$$F(s, x, p) = \min_{y \in B} [L(s, x, y) + p \cdot y].$$

Taking $p = \phi_x^\epsilon$ and applying Theorem 3, we get

Theorem 5. Let F be of class $C^{(2)}$ and satisfy (6.6). Then the Cauchy problem (6.1) with $\phi(T, x) = 0$ has a generalized solution in either of the following cases:

(a) $a \equiv 0;$

(b) $a = \frac{1}{2}\sigma\sigma^*$, where σ is a constant matrix with $\sigma_{ij} = 0$ for $i \leqslant \nu$, and

$$F(s, x, p) = \sum_{i=1}^{\nu} g_i(s, x)p_i + F(s, x, p_{\nu+1}, \ldots, p_n).$$

The assumptions in (b) are probably unduly restrictive, and it is an interesting problem to weaken them. Just as in Theorem 3, the function ϕ

is the limit of ϕ^ϵ satisfying (3.3$^\epsilon$)–(3.4) with H replaced by F. The limit exists without the special assumptions (a) or (b), which are used to prove that ϕ satisfies (6.1) almost everywhere.

When $a \equiv 0$, inequality (2) in (6.6) states that the first-order equation (6.1) is "genuinely nonlinear" in Lax's terminology (*15*).

VII. An Existence Theorem for Optimal Controls

In this section we summarize some recent joint work of Nisio and the author (*8*). The objective is to provide a setting for proving the existence of solutions to rather general stochastic control problems.

Let C^n be the space of all continuous functions from $(-\infty, \infty)$ into R^n. We put on C^n a metric compatible with uniform convergence on compact subsets of $(-\infty, \infty)$. Let C_+^n, C_-^n be the spaces of all continuous functions from $[0, \infty)$, $(-\infty, 0]$ into R^n, similarly metrized.

Let ξ be a stochastic process on $(-\infty, \infty)$ with continuous paths in R^n; there is a probability measure space Ω such that ξ is a function from $(-\infty, \infty) \times \Omega$ into R^n with $\xi(\cdot, \omega)$ continuous with probability 1 and $\xi(t, \cdot)$ measurable for each t. Let $B_{uv}(\xi)$ be the least σ-algebra with respect to which $\xi(t, \cdot)$ is measurable whenever $u \leqslant t \leqslant v$. As is customary we omit further explicit reference to $\omega \in \Omega$, writing for instance $\xi(t)$ instead of $\xi(t, \omega)$. For each fixed s, let $\pi_s \xi$ be the process defined by

$$(\pi_s \xi)(t) = \xi(s+t), \qquad -\infty < t \leqslant 0. \tag{7.1}$$

It is called the past of the process ξ up to time s.

It is useful to introduce an idea of distance between stochastic processes. Let us use the L-distance of Prohorov (*18*). It has the property that $L(\xi, \tilde{\xi}) = 0$ if and only if ξ and $\tilde{\xi}$ are processes with the same probability law. If we regard any two such processes as equivalent, then L becomes a metric on the space of all processes on $(-\infty, \infty)$ with continuous paths in R^n.

Let w be a k-dimensional Brownian-motion process with $w(0) = 0$. Let $B_{uv}(dw)$ denote the least σ-algebra with respect to which the differences $w(t) - w(s)$ are measurable whenever $u \leqslant s$, $t \leqslant v$.

Let ξ_- be a process on $(-\infty, 0]$ with continuous paths in R^n, such that $E\{|\xi_-(t)|^4\}$ is bounded. Let $K \subset R^k$ be compact and convex (as above, K is the "control region"). Let $\mathfrak{M}$ be a class of processes η on $[0, \infty)$, such that each $\eta \in \mathfrak{M}$ satisfies:

(1) η has values in R^k, and $\eta(0) = 0$.

(2) With probability 1, the paths satisfy a Lipschitz condition and $\dot{\eta}(t) \in K$ for almost all t ($\cdot = d/dt$).

(3) There exist $\check{\xi}_-$, $\tilde{w}$ defined on the same probability space as η, such that $L(\xi_-, \check{\xi}_-) = L(w, \tilde{w}) = 0$ and $B_{-\infty 0}(\check{\xi}_-) \vee B_{0t}(\eta) \vee B_{-\infty t}(\tilde{w})$ is independent of $B_{t\infty}(d\tilde{w})$ for every $t \geqslant 0$.

In (3), $B_1 \vee B_2 \vee B_3$ is the least σ-algebra containing B_1, B_2, and B_3. This condition in effect says that the control process η does not anticipate future values of the Brownian-motion process. It is technically slightly more convenient to consider the η-process, rather than the $\dot{\eta}$-process, since the former has continuous paths.

Given a process $\eta \in \mathfrak{M}$ let us consider a system of stochastic differential equations of the form

$$d\xi = \alpha(t, \pi_t \xi) \, d\eta + \beta(t, \pi_t \xi) \, dw, \qquad t \geqslant 0, \tag{7.2}$$

together with initial data

$$\pi_0 \xi = \check{\xi}_-, \qquad \text{where} \quad L(\xi_-, \check{\xi}_-) = 0, \tag{7.3}$$

and the condition for every $t \geqslant 0$,

$$B_{-\infty t}(\xi) \subset B_{-\infty 0}(\check{\xi}) \vee B_{0t}(\eta) \vee B_{-\infty t}(\tilde{w}), \tag{7.4}$$

where $L(w, \tilde{w}) = 0$. Let us assume that the matrix-valued functions α and β are continuous on $[0, \infty) \times C_-^n$, and that there exist bounded measures Γ_1, and Γ_2 on $(-\infty, 0]$ such that

$$|\alpha(t,f) - \alpha(t,\tilde{f})|^2 + |\beta(t,f) - \beta(t,\tilde{f})|^2 \leqslant \int_{-\infty}^{0} |f(s) - \tilde{f}(s)|^2 \, d\Gamma_1(s), \tag{7.5}$$

$$|\beta(t,f)|^4 \leqslant M_1(t) + \int_{-\infty}^{0} |f(s)|^4 \, d\Gamma_2(s) \tag{7.6}$$

for every $t \geqslant 0$ and $f, \tilde{f} \in C_-^n$. Then there is a process ξ satisfying (7.2)–(7.4). Moreover, this process is unique in the sense that if $\check{\xi}$ is any solution of (7.2)–(7.4), then $L(\xi, \check{\xi}) = 0$.

Now let Φ be some real-valued functional on $C_+^n \times C_+^k$. Let us consider the following:

Problem. Find a process $\eta \in \mathfrak{M}$ which minimizes the expected value $E\{\Phi(\xi, \eta)\}$.

Theorem 6. Let $\mathfrak{M}$ be closed under L-sequential limits. Let Φ be lower semicontinuous and $\Phi \geqslant 0$. Then the minimum is attained for some $\eta_0 \in \mathfrak{M}$.

The proof proceeds as follows. Consider the set $\mathfrak{A}$ of all pairs (ξ, η) of processes such that (7.2)–(7.4) are satisfied. Then $\mathfrak{A}$ is L-totally bounded. To show this we use a criterion of Prohorov and an estimate

$$E\{|\xi(t) - \xi(s)|^4\} \leqslant C_j|t - s|^{3/2}$$

when $0 \leqslant t,\, s \leqslant j$, where C_j does not depend on the choice of $\eta \in \mathfrak{M}$. Similar reasoning was used in (*21*). Now let $\eta_1, \eta_2, \ldots$ be a minimizing sequence and $\xi_1, \xi_2, \ldots$ the sequence of corresponding solutions of (7.2)–(7.4). By taking subsequences we may assume that the sequence (ξ_1, η_1), (ξ_2, η_2), $\ldots$ is L-Cauchy. By a theorem of Skorokhod (*19*) there exist processes $\tilde{\xi}_m$ and $\tilde{\eta}_m$ on the Lebesgue interval $[0, 1]$ such that $L(\xi_m, \tilde{\xi}_m) = L(\eta_m, \tilde{\eta}_m) = 0$, for $m = 1, 2, \ldots$ and ξ_0, η_0 such that, with probability 1,

$$\tilde{\xi}_m(\cdot) \to \xi_0(\cdot), \qquad \tilde{\eta}_m(\cdot) \to \eta_0(\cdot)$$

uniformly on compact subsets of $(-\infty, \infty)$. Moreover, $(\xi_0, \eta_0) \in \mathfrak{A}$. By Fatou's lemma $E\{\Phi\}$ is lower semicontinuous, and hence η_0 minimizes.

As an example, let $A \subset R^n$ be closed, and let

$$\Phi(\xi, \eta) = \int_0^{\tau_A} L[t, \xi(t), \dot{\eta}(t)]\, dt,$$

where $\tau_A =$ first time $t \geqslant 0$ when $\xi(t) \in A$. If L is continuous, $L \geqslant 0$, and $L(t, x, \cdot)$ is convex for each t, x, then Φ is lower semicontinuous and $\Phi \geqslant 0$.

Theorem 6 is not completely satisfactory, for the following reason. In many stochastic-control problems one is allowed to observe not the process ξ itself, but only some function of it. Only controls should then be admitted which are "functions of the observed past data." The space $\mathfrak{M}$ of such controls is usually not closed, and Theorem 6 then gives only the existence of "generalized solutions" in the L-closure of $\mathfrak{M}$. It is an interesting open problem to find fairly broad conditions under which the generalized solution actually belongs to $\mathfrak{M}$.

For problems which have enough linearity the existence of a minimum can be proved more easily using weak convergence in the space of bounded measurable functions on $(-\infty, \infty) \times \Omega$ *(13)*. Some necessary variational conditions for a minimum in stochastic optimization problems have been derived in *(14)*.

REFERENCES

1. R. Bellman, "Dynamic Programming," Princeton Univ. Press, Princeton, New Jersey, 1957.
2. Yu. N. Blagoveščenskiĭ and M. I. Freĭdlin, Certain Properties of Diffusion Processes Depending on a Parameter, *Dokl. Akad. Nauk SSSR* **138**, 508–511 (1962); *Soviet Math.* **2**, 633–636.
3. J. L. Doob, "Stochastic Processes." Wiley, New York, 1953.
4. E. B. Dynkin, "Markov Processes" (English transl.). Springer, Berlin, 1965.
5. E. B. Dynkin, Controlled Stochastic Processes—Discrete Parameter, *Teoriya Veroyatnostei i ee Primeneniya* **10**, 3–18 (1965).
6. W. H. Fleming, Some Markovian Optimization Problems, *J. Math. Mech.* **12**, 131–140 (1963).
7. W. H. Fleming, The Cauchy Problem for Degenerate Parabolic Equations, *J. Math. Mech.* **13**, 987–1008 (1964).
8. W. H. Fleming and M. Nisio, On the Existence of Optimal Stochastic Controls, *J. Math. Mech.* **15**, 777–794 (1966).
9. M. I. Freĭdlin, A Priori Estimates of Solutions of Degenerating Elliptic Equations, *Dokl. Akad. Nauk SSSR* **158**, 281–283 (1964).
10. A. Friedman, "Partial Differential Equations of Parabolic Type," Prentice-Hall, Englewood Cliffs, New Jersey, 1964.
11. R. Isaacs, "Differential Games," Wiley, New York, 1965.
12. S. N. Kruzhkov, The Cauchy Problem in the Large for Nonlinear Equations and Some Quasilinear Systems of First Order in Many Variables, *Dokl. Akad. Nauk SSSR* **155**(4), 743–746 (1964).
13. H. J. Kushner, On the Existence of Optimal Stochastic Controls, preprint.
14. H. J. Kushner, On Stochastic Extremum Problems: Calculus, *J. Math. Anal. Appl.* **10**, 354–367 (1965); pt. 2, Calculus of Variations, *Ibid.* **11**, 78–92 (1965).
15. P. D. Lax, Hyperbolic Systems of Conservation Laws II, *Commun. Pure Appl. Math.* **10**, 537–566 (1957).
16. O. A. Oleĭnik, On Discontinuous Solutions of Non-Linear Differential Equations, *Dokl. Akad. Nauk SSSR* **109**, 1098–1101 (1956).

17. L. S. Pontryagin, V. G. Baltyanskii, R. V. Gamkrelidze, and E. F. Mishchenko, "The Mathematical Theory of Optimal Processes," Wiley (Interscience), New York, 1962.
18. Yu. V. Prohorov, Convergence of Random Processes and Limit Theorems in Probability Theory, *Theory Probability Appl. USSR* (English transl.) **1956**(2), 157–214.
19. A. V. Skorokhod, Limit Theorems for Stochastic Processes, *Theory Probability Appl.* (English transl.) (**1956**), 261–290.
20. W. M. Wonham, Some Applications of Stochastic Differential Equations to Optimal Non-Linear Filtering, *J. SIAM Control* **A2** (1965).
21. K. Ito and M. Nisio, On Stationary Solutions of a Stochastic Differential Equation, *J. Math. Kyoto* **4**, 1–75 (1964).

Convexity and Control Theory

Hubert Halkin[1]

Bell Telephone Laboratories
Whippany, New Jersey

In the present paper we are interested in some problems of the theory of convex sets which are not considered in the classical literature but which have interesting applications in control theory. The first section of this paper is devoted to some generalizations of the well-known theorem of Lyapounov on the convexity of the range of a vector measure. In Section II we consider some properties of classes of nonlinear differential equations. In Section III, we combine the results of the first two sections to obtain some interesting applications to nonlinear control theory. Section IV is independent of the preceding sections and contains some new results pertaining to convex sets and their separations. In Section V we study some geometric aspects of nonlinear optimal control problems with the help of the four preceding sections.

I. Theorems of the Lyapounov Type

Notations and Assumptions

We shall denote by $\mathscr{B}$ the class of all Borel subsets of $[0,1]$ and by $\mathscr{A}$ the class of all subsets of $[0,1]$ which are the union of a finite number of intervals. Note that $\mathscr{B}$ is a σ-algebra and that $\mathscr{A}$ is an algebra but not a σ-algebra. The Lebesgue measure will be denoted by μ. For any positive integer k we define the sets

$$\Lambda_k = \left\{ \alpha = (\alpha_1, \alpha_2, \ldots, \alpha_k) : \alpha_i \geqslant 0, \sum_{i=1}^{k} \alpha_i = 1 \right\}, \qquad (1.1)$$

[1]*Present address:* Department of Mathematics, University of California, San Diego, La Jolla, California.

$$\mathscr{L}_k = \Big\{ A = (A_1, A_2, \ldots, A_k) : A_i \cap A_j = \phi \text{ if } i \neq j,$$

$$A_i \in \mathscr{B}, \bigcup_{i=1}^{k} A_i = [0, 1] \Big\}, \quad (1.2)$$

$$\mathscr{N}_k = \Big\{ A = (A_1, A_2, \ldots, A_k) : A_i \cap A_j = \phi \text{ if } i \neq j,$$

$$A_i \in \mathscr{A}, \bigcup_{i=1}^{k} A_i = [0, 1] \Big\}. \quad (1.3)$$

We shall endow Λ_k with the metric

$$\sigma(\alpha', \alpha'') = \sum_{i=1}^{k} |\alpha_i' - \alpha_i''| \quad (1.4)$$

and we shall endow $\mathscr{L}_k$ and $\mathscr{N}_k$ with the metric

$$d(A', A'') = \sum_{i=1}^{k} \mu(A_i' \varDelta A_i''), \quad (1.5)$$

where $A_i' \varDelta A_i''$ denotes the symmetric difference of the sets A_i' and A_i''.

In the present section we shall give six propositions which can be divided in two groups of three. The first group (Propositions 1.1, 1.2, and 1.3) is related to the σ-algebra $\mathscr{B}$. The second group (Propositions 1.1a, 1.2a, and 1.3a) is related to the algebra $\mathscr{A}$.

Proposition 1.1. If f is an integrable function from $[0, 1]$ into E^n, then there exists a mapping $D(t)$ from $[0, 1]$ into $\mathscr{B}$ such that

(a) $D(t') \subset D(t'')$ $\quad$ if $t' < t''$, $\qquad\qquad$ (1.6)

(b) $\mu(D(t)) = t$ $\quad$ for all $t \in [0, 1]$, $\qquad\qquad$ (1.7)

(c) $\displaystyle\int_{D(t)} f \, d\mu = t \int_0^1 f \, d\mu$ $\quad$ for all $t \in [0, 1]$. $\qquad$ (1.8)

Proposition 1.2. Let $f_1, f_2, \ldots, f_k$ be integrable functions from $[0, 1]$ into E^n. Then there exists a continuous mapping $A(\alpha)$ from Λ_k into $\mathscr{L}_k$ such that for all $\alpha \in \Lambda_k$,

(a) $\mu(A_i(\alpha)) = \alpha_i,$ $\qquad\qquad\qquad\qquad\qquad$ (1.9)

(b) $\displaystyle\alpha_i \int_0^1 f_i \, d\mu = \int_{A_i(\alpha)} f_i \, d\mu.$ $\qquad\qquad\qquad$ (1.10)

Proposition 1.3. If f is an integrable function from $[0,1]$ into E^n, then the set $\left\{\int_D f\,d\mu : D \in \mathscr{B}\right\}$ is convex.

Proposition 1.1a. If f is an integrable function from $[0,1]$ into E^n, then for any $\epsilon > 0$ there exists a mapping $D(t)$ from $[0,1]$ into $\mathscr{A}$ such that

$$\text{(a)} \quad D(t') \subset D(t'') \quad \text{if } t' < t'', \tag{1.11}$$

$$\text{(b)} \quad \mu(D(t)) = t \quad \text{for all } t \in [0,1], \tag{1.12}$$

$$\text{(c)} \quad \left|\int_{D(t)} f\,d\mu - t\int_0^1 f\,d\mu\right| \leqslant \epsilon \quad \text{for all } t \in [0,1]. \tag{1.13}$$

Proposition 1.2a. Let $f_1, f_2, \ldots, f_k$ be integrable functions from $[0,1]$ into E^n. Then for any $\epsilon > 0$ there is a continuous mapping $A(\alpha)$ from Λ_k into $\mathscr{N}_k$ such that for all $\alpha \in \Lambda_k$,

$$\text{(a)} \quad \mu(A_i(\alpha)) = \alpha, \tag{1.14}$$

$$\text{(b)} \quad \left|\sum_{i=1}^k \alpha_i \int_0^1 f_i\,d\mu - \sum_{i=1}^k \int_{A_i(\alpha)} f_i\,d\mu\right| \leqslant \epsilon. \tag{1.15}$$

Proposition 1.3a. If f is an integrable function from $[0,1]$ into E^n, then the set $\left\{\int_D f\,d\mu : D \in \mathscr{A}\right\}$ is convex.

Propositions 1.1 and 1.3 are proved in Halkin (*1*, Propositions 8.8 and 8.9, p. 68). Propositions 1.1a and 1.3a are proved in Halkin (*2*, Proposition I and Theorem I*, p. 273). The proof of Proposition 1.2 is implicitly contained in Halkin (*1*) but will be given below for completeness. The proof of Proposition 1.2a is the exact analog of the proof of Proposition 1.2 but with Proposition 1.1a replacing Proposition 1.1.

Proof of Proposition 1.2. We define f as the function $(f_1, f_2, \ldots, f_k)$ from $[0,1]$ into $E^{k \times n}$. We apply Proposition 1.1 to the function f and we obtain a mapping $D(t)$ from $[0,1]$ into $\mathscr{B}$ which satisfies the conditions (1.6), (1.7), and (1.8). We shall now construct the function $A(\alpha) = (A_1(\alpha), A_2(\alpha), \ldots, A_k(\alpha))$ from Λ_k into $\mathscr{L}_k$ by the following procedure:

$$A_1(\alpha) = D(\alpha_1), \tag{1.16}$$

$$A_{i+1}(\alpha) = D\left(\sum_{j=1}^{i+1} \alpha_j\right) \sim D\left(\sum_{j=1}^{i} \alpha_j\right), \tag{1.17}$$

where, according to our previous notations, the components of α are denoted $\alpha_1, \alpha_2, \ldots, \alpha_k$. It is a trivial matter to verify that this mapping $A(\alpha)$ satisfies all the conclusions of Proposition 1.2.

II. Alternated Integration of Classes of Nonlinear Differential Equations

Notations and Assumptions

We are given k functions $f_i(x,t)$, $i = 1, 2, \ldots, k$ from $E^n \times [0,1]$ into E^n. These functions are measurable with respect to t and have continuous second partial derivatives with respect to x which are uniformly bounded over any bounded subset of $E^n \times [0,1]$. We recall the definition of the set

$$\mathcal{L}_k = \left\{ A = (A_1, A_2, \ldots, A_k) : A_i \in \mathcal{B}, A_i \cap A_j = \phi \text{ if } i \neq j, \right.$$
$$\left. \bigcup_{i=1}^{k} A_i = [0,1] \right\}, \tag{2.1}$$

where $\mathcal{B}$ is the class of all Borel subsets of $[0,1]$. We have defined over $\mathcal{L}_k$ the metric

$$d(A', A'') = \sum_{i=1}^{k} \mu(A_i' \Delta A_i'') \tag{2.2}$$

where $A_i' \Delta A_i''$ denotes the symmetric difference of the sets A_i' and A_i'' and where μ is the Lebesgue measure on $\mathcal{B}$. For all $A \in \mathcal{L}_k$ we assume that the system[2]

$$\dot{x} = \sum_{i=1}^{k} \mathcal{X}(A_i) f_i(x,t), \tag{2.3}$$

$$x = 0 \qquad \text{at } t = 0 \tag{2.4}$$

has a bounded absolutely continuous solution denoted $x(t; A)$ and defined over $[0, 1]$. We shall assume, moreover, that the functions $x(t; A)$ are uniformly bounded for all $A \in \mathcal{L}_k$.

Proposition 2.1. There exists an $M < +\infty$ such that

[2] In (2.3) the characteristic function of the set A_i is denoted $\mathcal{X}(A_i)$.

$$|x(t; A') - x(t; A'')| \leqslant M d(A', A'') \tag{2.5}$$

for all $t \in [0, 1]$ and for all A' and $A'' \in \mathscr{L}_k$.

Proposition 2.2. Let us assume that $f_1(0, t) = 0$ and $(\partial/\partial x) f_1(x, t)|_{x=0} = 0$ for all $t \in [0, 1]$ and let us define $\overset{+}{x}(t; A)$ as the solution of the system

$$\dot{x} = \sum_{i=1}^{k} \mathscr{X}(A_i) f_i(0, t), \tag{2.6}$$

$$x = 0 \qquad \text{at } t = 0; \tag{2.7}$$

i.e., we have

$$\overset{+}{x}(t; A) = \int_0^t \sum_{i=1}^{k} \mathscr{X}(A_i) f_i(0, \tau) \, d\tau. \tag{2.8}$$

Then there is a $K < +\infty$ such that

$$\left| \overset{+}{x}(1; A) - x(1; A) \right| \leqslant K \left(\sum_{i=2}^{k} \mu(A_i) \right)^2 \tag{2.9}$$

for all $A \in \mathscr{L}_k$.

Proof of Proposition 2.1. We have

$$|x(0; A') - x(t; A'')| = 0 \tag{2.10}$$

and

$$\frac{d}{dt} |x(t; A') - x(t; A'')|$$

$$\leqslant \left| \sum_{i=1}^{k} f_i(x(t; A'), t) \mathscr{X}(A_i') - \sum_{i=1}^{k} f_i(x(t; A''), t) \mathscr{X}(A_i'') \right|, \tag{2.11}$$

$$\frac{d}{dt} |x(t; A') - x(t; A'')|$$

$$\leqslant \left| \sum_{i=1}^{k} f_i(x(t; A'), t) \mathscr{X}(A_i') - \sum_{i=1}^{k} f_i(x(t; A''), t) \mathscr{X}(A_i') \right|$$

$$+ \left| \sum_{i=1}^{k} f_i(x(t; A''), t) \mathscr{X}(A_i') - \sum_{i=1}^{k} f_i(x(t; A''), t) \mathscr{X}(A_i'') \right|, \tag{2.12}$$

$$\frac{d}{dt} |x(t; A') - x(t; A'')|$$

$$\leqslant L_1 |x(t; A') - x(t; A'')| + L_2 \mathscr{X} \left(\bigcup_{i=1}^{k} (A_i' \varDelta A_i'') \right) \tag{2.13}$$

for some L_1 and $L_2 < +\infty$. These constants L_1 and L_2 are independent of t, A', and A''. We apply Gronwall's inequality to relations (2.10) and (2.13) and we obtain the required result.

Proof of Proposition 2.2. We have

$$|x(1;A) - \overset{+}{x}(1;A)| \leqslant \int_0^1 |g(t;A)| \, dt, \tag{2.14}$$

where $g(t;A)$ is defined by

$$g(t;A) = \sum_{i=1}^k f_i(x(t;A),t)\mathscr{X}(A_i) - \sum_{i=1}^k f_i(0,t)\mathscr{X}(A_i). \tag{2.15}$$

From the assumptions made previously it is easy to prove that there exists a $K^* < +\infty$ such that for all $A \in \mathscr{L}_k$ we have

(a) $|g(t;A)| \leqslant K^* |x(t;A)|^2$ if $t \in A_1$,   (2.16)

(b) $|g(t;A)| \leqslant K^* |x(t;A)|$ if $t \in [0,1] \sim A_1$.   (2.17)

We have then

$$|x(1;A) - \overset{+}{x}(1;A)|$$

$$\leqslant K^* \left(\max_{t \in A_1} |x(t;A)|^2 \mu(A_1) + \max_{t \in [0,1] \sim A_1} |\dot{x}(t;A)| \mu([0,1] \sim A_1) \right). \tag{2.18}$$

From Proposition 2.1 we have for all $A \in \mathscr{L}_k$,

$$|x(t;A)| \leqslant M \left(\sum_{i=1}^k \mu(A_i) \right). \tag{2.19}$$

The proof of Proposition 2.2 then follows immediately from relations (2.18) and (2.19).

III. Convexity and Nonlinear Control Theory

Let $f_i(x,t)$, $i = 1, 2, \ldots, k$, be k given functions satisfying the assumptions stated in Section II, including the supplementary assumptions given in Proposition 2.2. Moreover, we shall assume that the vectors $\int_0^1 f_i(0,t) \, dt$, $i = 2, 3, \ldots, k$ are linearly independent.

Proposition 3.1. There exists a continuous mapping $A(\alpha)$ from Λ_k into $\mathscr{L}_k$ and a $L < +\infty$ such that for all $a \in \Lambda_k$,

$$\text{(a)} \quad \mu(A_i(\alpha)) = \alpha_i, \tag{3.1}$$

$$\text{(b)} \quad x(1; A(\alpha)) \text{ is continuous with respect to } \alpha, \tag{3.2}$$

$$\text{(c)} \quad \overset{+}{x}(1; A(\alpha)) = \sum_{i=1}^{k} a_i \int_0^1 f_i(0, t)\, dt, \tag{3.3}$$

$$\text{(d)} \quad |x(1; A(\alpha)) - \overset{+}{x}(1; A(\alpha))| \leqslant L|\overset{+}{x}(1; A(\alpha))|^2. \tag{3.4}$$

Proposition 3.1a. For any $\epsilon > 0$ there exists a continuous mapping $A(\alpha)$ from Λ_k into $\mathscr{N}_k$ and a $L < +\infty$ such that for any $\alpha \in \Lambda_k$,

$$\text{(a)} \quad \mu(A_i(\alpha)) = \alpha_i, \tag{3.5}$$

$$\text{(b)} \quad x(1; A(\alpha)) \text{ is continuous with respect to } \alpha, \tag{3.6}$$

$$\text{(c)} \quad \left| \overset{+}{x}(1; A(\alpha)) - \sum_{i=1}^{k} \alpha_i \int_0^1 f_i(0, t)\, dt \right| \leqslant \epsilon, \tag{3.7}$$

$$\text{(d)} \quad \left| x(1; A(\alpha)) - \sum_{i=1}^{k} \alpha_i \int_0^1 f_i(0, t)\, dt \right| \leqslant L \left| \sum_{i=1}^{k} \alpha_i \int_0^1 f_i(0, t)\, dt \right|^2 + \epsilon. \tag{3.8}$$

Proof of Propositions 3.1 and 3.1a. We shall give only the proof of Proposition 3.1 The proof of Proposition 3.1a is completely analogous if we replace Proposition 1.2 by Proposition 1.2a. Let $A(\alpha)$ be the continuous mapping from Λ_k into $\mathscr{L}_k$ given by Proposition 1.2 for the functions $f_i(0, t)$, $i = 1, 2, \ldots, k$. Relations (3.1) and (3.3) are immediate consequences of Proposition 1.2. Relation (3.2) follows from Proposition 2.1, in which we have proved that $x(1; A)$ is continuous with respect to A. We conclude by proving relation (3.4). From Proposition 2.2 we have

$$|x(1; A(\alpha)) - \overset{+}{x}(1; A(\alpha))| \leqslant K \left(\sum_{i=2}^{k} \mu(A_i(\alpha)) \right)^2 ; \tag{3.9}$$

i.e., from relation (3.1),

$$|x(1; A(\alpha)) - \overset{+}{x}(1; A(\alpha))| \leqslant K \left(\sum_{i=2}^{k} a_i \right)^2 . \tag{3.10}$$

Since the vectors $\int_0^1 f_i(0,t)\,dt,\ i=2,\ \ldots,\ k$ are independent and since the coefficients $\alpha_i\, i=2,\ \ldots,\ k$ are nonnegative, then for some $M<+\infty$ we have

$$\left|\sum_{i=2}^k a_i\right| \leqslant M\left|\sum_{i=2}^k a_i\int_0^1 f_i(0,t)\,dt\right|. \tag{3.11}$$

The required result then follows immediately from relations (3.10) and (3.11).

IV. A Property of Nonseparated Convex Sets

In this section we give two propositions. Proposition 4.1 is a particular case of Proposition 4.1a. A direct proof of Proposition 4.1 is given in Halkin (4), and the proof of Proposition 4.1a is given in Halkin (5). The motivation behind these two propositions will appear clearly in Section V.

Proposition 4.1. Let K_1 and K_2 be two non-separated[3] convex sets in Euclidean space E^n. We assume that $0\in\bar{K}_1\cap\bar{K}_2$ and $0\notin K_1\cap K_2$. Let L be a positive constant. We are given a continuous mapping ϕ_1 from K_1 into E^n and a continuous mapping ϕ_2 from K_2 into E^n. We assume that for $i=1,2$ we have

$$|\phi_i(e)-e| \leqslant L|e|^2 \qquad \text{for all } e\in K_i. \tag{4.1}$$

Then the set $\phi_1(K_1)\cap\phi_2(K_2)$ is not empty.

Proposition 4.1a. Let K_1 and K_2 be two nonseparated convex sets in a Euclidean space E^n. We assume that $0\in\bar{K}_1\cap\bar{K}_2$ and $0\notin K_1\cap K_2$. Let L be a positive constant. For every $\eta>0$ we are given a continuous mapping $\phi_1{}^\eta$ from K_1 into E^n and a continuous mapping $\phi_2{}^\eta$ from K_2 into E^n. We assume that for every $\eta>0$ and for $i=1,2$ we have

$$|\phi_i{}^\eta(e)-e| \leqslant L|e|^2+\eta \qquad \text{for all } e\in K_i. \tag{4.2}$$

Then the set $\bigcup_{\eta>0}(\phi_1{}^\eta(K_1)\cap\phi_2{}^\eta(K_2))$ is not empty.

---

[3] Two sets A and B of E^n are separated if there exists a hyperplane P such that A is contained in one of the closed half-spaces determined by P and B is contained in the other closed half-space determined by P.

V. Geometric Aspects of Nonlinear Optimal-Control Theory

In this section we shall consider classes of nonlinear differential equations of the type

$$\dot{x} = f(x, t), \tag{5.1}$$

where x is an element of the n-dimensional Euclidean space E^n, t is the time restricted to the interval $[0, 1]$, $\dot{x} = dx/dt$, and $f(x, t)$ is a given function from $E^n \times [0, 1]$ into E^n. We shall assume that the function $f(x, t)$ is measurable with respect to t and has continuous second partial derivatives with respect to x which are uniformly bounded over any bounded subset of $E^n \times [0, 1]$. We shall assume further that (5.1) has a bounded absolutely continuous solution which is defined over $[0, 1]$ and equal to zero at $t = 0$. Moreover, for all classes of equations of the type (5.1) considered in this section we shall assume that the corresponding solutions are uniformly bounded over the class.

We shall now define a terminal manifold

$$M = \{x : g_i(x) = 0, i = 1, 2, \ldots, l\} \tag{5.2}$$

and an objective function $g_0(x)$. We shall assume that the given functions $g_0(x)$, $g_1(x)$, ..., $g_l(x)$ are twice continuously differentiable and that the vectors $(\partial/\partial x)g_0(x)$, $(\partial/\partial x)g_1(x)$, ..., $(\partial/\partial x)g_l(x)$ are linearly independent for all $x \in E^n$.

The optimal-control problem is then the following: Given a class F of differential equations, a manifold M, and an objective $g_0(x)$, all satisfying the assumptions stated above, find an absolutely continuous solution $x(t)$ of

$$\dot{x}(t) = f(x(t), t) \qquad \text{a.e. } t \in [0, 1] \tag{5.3}$$

for some $f \in F$ such that $x(0) = 0$, $x(1) \in M$, and $g_0(x(1))$ is maximum. We shall denote by $\hat{x}(t)$ the solution of this optimal-control problem and by $\hat{f}$ the function in the class F corresponding to this solution.

Let W be the set of all points $x(1)$ corresponding to all solutions $x(t)$ with $x(0) = 0$ for all functions f in the class F. The set W is the set of all points reachable from the origin at $t = 1$.

For any $x \in M$ let $S(x)$ be the set

$$\{y : g_i(y) = 0, i = 1, 2, \ldots, l, g_0(y) > g_0(x)\}. \tag{5.4}$$

The set $S(x)$ is then the set of all points of M which are "better" than x with respect to the objective function g_0.

From the definition of the optimality of a solution we have immediately the two following results:

Proposition 5.1. If $\hat{x}(t)$ is optimal, then $\hat{x}(1) \in \partial W$, where ∂W is the boundary of the set W.

Proposition 5.2. If $\hat{x}(t)$ is optimal, then the sets W and $S(\hat{x}(1))$ are disjoint.

To obtain deeper results for our problem we have to add some structure to the class F.

We recall that $\mathscr{B}$ denotes the set of all Borel subsets of $[0, 1]$ and that $\mathscr{A}$ denotes the set of all subsets of $[0, 1]$ which are the union of a finite number of intervals.

A class F of differential equations of the type (5.1) is said to be $\mathscr{B}$-convex if it satisfies the following condition: If f' and $f'' \in F$ and if $A \in \mathscr{B}$ then the function f defined by

$$f(x, t) = f'(x, t) \qquad \text{if } t \in A, \tag{5.5}$$

$$f(x, t) = f''(x, t) \qquad \text{if } t \in [0, 1] \sim A \tag{5.6}$$

belongs to the class F. Similarly, a class F is said to be α-convex if it satisfies the preceding condition with $\mathscr{A}$ replacing $\mathscr{B}$.

An optimal-control problem will be called linear if (a) the functions f in the class F can be represented by

$$f(x, t) = A(t)x + \phi(t), \tag{5.7}$$

where $A(t)$ is the same matrix for all functions in the class F, but where the functions $\phi(t)$ are not necessarily the same, and if (b) the functions $g_0(x)$, $g_1(x)$, ..., $g_l(x)$ are linear.

Proposition 5.3. If the problem is linear and if the class F is $\mathscr{B}$-convex, then the set W is convex.

Proposition 5.3a. If the problem is linear and if the class F is $\mathscr{A}$-convex, then the set W is convex.

The proof of Propositions 5.3 and 5.3a are easy applications of Propositions 1.3 and 1.3a [see Halkin (*1*, Proposition 8.11, p. 70)].

We see immediately that for a linear problem the set $S(\hat{x}(1))$ is convex. Combining Proposition 5.2 with Propositions 5.3 and 5.3a we obtain the two following results.

Proposition 5.4. If the problem is linear and if the class F is $\mathcal{B}$-convex, then the sets W and $S(\hat{x}(1))$ are separated.[4]

Proposition 5.4a. If the problem is linear and if the class F is $\mathcal{A}$-convex, then the sets W and $S(\hat{x}(1))$ are separated.

The separation of the sets W and $S(\hat{x}(1))$ implies the Pontryagin maximum principle for linear systems (including the transversability condition).

To solve the given *nonlinear* problem we shall introduce the following linearization around the solution $\hat{x}(t)$:

$$g_i(x) \text{ becomes } g_i(\hat{x}(1)) + (\partial/\partial x \, g_i(x)|_{x=\hat{x}(1)})(x - \hat{x}(1)),$$

$$f(x,t) \text{ becomes } f(\hat{x}(t),t) + (\partial/\partial x \hat{f}(x,t)|_{x=\hat{x}(t)})(x - \hat{x}(t)).$$

We note immediately that the function $\hat{x}(t)$ constitutes a solution (but not necessarily an optimal solution) for the linearized problem defined above. We now define the sets $\hat{W}(\hat{x}(1))$ and $\hat{S}(\hat{x}(1))$ in the same way as the sets W and $S(\hat{x}(1))$ defined earlier but with respect to the linearized problem defined above and not with respect to the initial nonlinear problem which was used in the definition of W and $S(\hat{x}(1))$. As we saw earlier, for the linear problem the sets $\hat{W}(\hat{x}(1))$ and $\hat{S}(\hat{x}(1))$ are convex. We are now in a position to state some of the most useful results in the theory of optimal control of nonlinear systems.

Proposition 5.5. If the class F is $\mathcal{B}$-convex and if $\hat{x}(1) \in \partial W$, then $\hat{x}(1) \in \partial W(\hat{x}(1))$.

Proposition 5.5a. If the class F is $\mathcal{A}$-convex and if $\hat{x}(1) \in \partial W$, then $\hat{x}(1) \in \partial \hat{W}(\hat{x}(1))$.

Proposition 5.6. If the class F is $\mathcal{B}$-convex and if the sets W and $S(\hat{x}(1))$ are disjoint, then the sets $\hat{W}(\hat{x}(1))$ and $\hat{S}(\hat{x}(1))$ are separated.

---

[4] Two sets A and B of E^n are separated if there exists a hyperplane P such that A is contained in one of the closed half-spaces determined by P and B is contained in the other closed half-space determined by P. There exist disjoint sets which are not separated and separated sets which are not disjoint.

Proposition 5.6a. If the class F is $\mathscr{A}$-convex and if the sets W and $S(\hat{x}(1))$ are disjoint, then the sets $\hat{W}(\hat{x}(1))$ and $\hat{S}(\hat{x}(1))$ are separated.

Propositions 5.5 and 5.5a imply the Pontryagin maximum principle for nonlinear systems *without the transversability conditions*, whereas Propositions 5.6 and 5.6a imply the Pontryagin maximum principle for nonlinear systems *including the transversability conditions*. The proofs of these four propositions are very similar. The proof of Proposition 5.5 is given in Halkin (*1*, Theorem III, p. 77). In the present paper we shall give the proof of Proposition 5.6. The proof of Proposition 5.6a is very similar but is based on the corresponding "a" propositions, for instance, Proposition 1.3a instead of Proposition 1.3.

Proof of Proposition 5.6. We shall assume that the sets $\hat{W}(\hat{x}(1))$ and $\hat{S}(\hat{x}(1))$ are not separated and show that this implies that the sets W and $S(\hat{x}(1))$ are not disjoint. There is no loss of generality[5] by assuming that for all $t \in [0, 1]$ we have

$$\hat{x}(t) = 0, \tag{5.8}$$

$$\hat{f}(0, t) = 0, \tag{5.9}$$

$$\frac{\partial}{\partial x} \hat{f}(x, t)\bigg|_{x=0} = 0. \tag{5.10}$$

$$G(1) = I, \qquad \dot{G}(t) = -G(t)\frac{\partial}{\partial x} f(x, t)\bigg|_{x = \hat{x}(t)}$$

If the convex sets $\hat{W}(\hat{x}(1))$ and $\hat{S}(\hat{x}(1))$ are not separated, then there exists a finite number of linearly independent vectors $\hat{x}_2(1)$, $\hat{x}_3(1)$, ..., $\hat{x}_k(1)$ in $\hat{W}(\hat{x}(1))$ such that the set

$$K_1 = \text{convex hull } \{\hat{x}(1) = \hat{x}_1(1) = 0, \hat{x}_2(1), \hat{x}_3(1), ..., \hat{x}_k(1)\}$$

and some bounded subsets K_2 of $\hat{S}(\hat{x}(1))$ are not separated.

From Proposition 3.1 there exists a continuous mapping $\phi_1 \colon K_1 \to W$ and a $L_1 < +\infty$ such that

$$|\phi_1(e) - e| \leqslant L_1 |e|^2 \qquad \text{for all } e \in K_1. \tag{5.11}$$

---

[5] This result can be achieved by defining a new state variable $y = G(t)(x - \hat{x}(t))$, where $G(t)$ is the solution of the matrix differential system.

Since the functions $g_i(x)$ are twice continuously differentiable, there exists a continuous mapping $\phi_2: K_2 \to S(\hat{x}(1))$ and a $L_2 < +\infty$ such that

$$|\phi_2(e) - e| \leqslant L_2 |e|^2 \qquad \text{for all } e \in K_2. \tag{5.12}$$

We now apply Proposition 4.1 to relations (5.11) and (5.12) and we obtain that the sets $\phi_1(K_1)$ and $\phi_2(K_2)$ are not disjoint, which implies *a fortiori* that the sets W and $S(\hat{x}(1))$ are not disjoint. This contradiction concludes the proof of Proposition 5.6.

REFERENCES

1. H. Halkin, On the Necessary Condition for Optimal Control of Nonlinear Systems, *J. Anal. Math.* **12**, 1–82 (1964).
2. H. Halkin, Some Further Generalizations of a Theorem of Lyapounov, *Arch. Rat. Mech. Anal.* **17**, 272–277 (1964).
3. A. Lyapounov, Sur les fonctions vecteurs complètement additives, *Bull. Acad. Sci. USSR* **4**, 465–478 (1940) (in Russian with a French résumé).
4. H. Halkin, A Maximum Principle of the Pontryagin Type for Systems Described by Nonlinear Difference Equations, *J. SIAM Control.* **4**, 90–111 (1966).
5. H. Halkin, A Property of Nonseparated Convex Sets, *Proc. Am. Math. Soc.* (in press).

Non-Well-Set Problems and the Method of Quasi Reversibility

ROBERT LATTÉS

Groupe Metra-International (SEMA—Société d'Informatique Appliquée)
Paris, France

I. The Problem

Let $A(t)$, t in $(0, t)$, be a family of unbounded operators in a Hilbert space H. We assume that $A(t) + kI$ (I, the identity operator) is, for k large enough, uniformly accretive; therefore, the following boundary-value problem is well set:

$$A(t) u(t) + d/dt\, u(t) = 0, \qquad t \in (0, T),$$

$$u(t) \in \text{domain of } A(t), \qquad (1.1)$$

$$u(0) = \xi \qquad \xi \text{ given in } H.$$

Now let X be given in H, and set

$$J(\xi) = \|u(T) - X\|, \qquad (1.2)$$

where $\|f\|$ stands for the norm of f in H.

Under quite general circumstances (see articles by J. L. Lions) one can prove that

$$\inf_{\xi \in H} J(\xi) = 0. \qquad (1.3)$$

Therefore, given $\eta > 0$, there exists a ξ_η in H such that

$$J(\xi_\eta) \leqslant \eta. \qquad (1.4)$$

Remark 1.1. The obvious solution, i.e., solving the backward problem,

$$A(t) v(t) + \frac{d}{dt} v(t) = 0 \qquad v(t) = X, \qquad (1.5)$$

then taking $\xi = v(0)$ is generally meaningless, since (1.5) is a non-well-set problem and consequently has no solution for an arbitrary X.

99

II. The Quasi-Reversibility Method

The proof of (1.3) is not constructive, and we here propose a systematic way of finding ξ_η satisfying (1.4). We shall explain the method in the particular case where the domain of A does not depend on t. We also can always assume that the $A(t)$ are strictly positive. We shall set

$$\lambda_0 = \inf R[\lambda(A)], \qquad t \in (0, T), \quad \lambda_0 > 0 \tag{2.1}$$

(λ is the spectrum of A). We now choose a family of unbounded operators $B(t)$ such that

$$\text{domain of } B(t) = \text{domain of } A(t), \qquad t \in (0, T),$$
$$\|B(t)\,v\| \geqslant c\|A(t)\,v\|, \qquad\qquad \forall v \in D(A), \tag{2.2}$$

where c is a suitable constant.

Remark 2.1. Such a family of operators exists [for example, $B(t) = A(t)$]. In the numerical applications, $B(t)$ has to be chosen so as to make (2.3) the simplest possible problem.

Let us consider now the problem of finding u_ϵ satisfying

$$A(t)\,u_\epsilon(t) + d/dt\,u_\epsilon(t) - \epsilon B^*(t)\,B(t)\,u_\epsilon(t) = 0,$$
$$u_\epsilon(t) \in D[B^*(t)\,B(t)], \tag{2.3}$$
$$u_\epsilon(T) = X.$$

Here ϵ is positive, fixed, and arbitrarily "small."[1] The term $-\epsilon B^*(t)\,B(t)$ may be held as a viscosity term, playing a smoothing role leading to reversibility.

One can prove, under very mild hypotheses, that the problem (2.3) admits a unique solution.

We conjecture that by choosing ϵ such that

$$[1 - \exp(-\epsilon c^2 \lambda_0{}^2 T)]\|X\| \leqslant \eta, \tag{2.4}$$

one can take

$$\xi = u_\epsilon(0).$$

---

[1] In fact, for numerical reasons, there exists a lower bound to the admissible ϵ.

Remark 2.2. The preceding conjecture is actually proved in the particular case when

$$A(t) = A^*(t) = A$$

by using the spectral decomposition of A.

But this conjecture can be understood in the following heuristic way. Consider

$$\frac{du}{dt} + \lambda u = 0, \qquad u(0) \text{ given} \tag{2.5}$$

and solve instead

$$(du_\epsilon/dt) + \lambda u_\epsilon - \epsilon \lambda^2 u_\epsilon = 0, \qquad u_\epsilon(t) = \chi. \tag{2.6}$$

One has

$$u_\epsilon(0) = \chi \exp(\lambda - \epsilon \lambda^2) T.$$

Now returning to (2.5) with

$$u(0) = u_\epsilon(0)$$

one finds

$$u(T) = \chi \exp(-\epsilon \lambda^2 T). \tag{2.7}$$

Thus $u(T)$ is close to χ when one takes $u_\epsilon(0)$ for ξ. One even can estimate the error, and one is led to the conjecture (2.4) with constant c because of (2.2).

Remark 2.3. The principle of the method is closely related to the summability procedures. For instance, if (λ_j, w_j) are the associate eigenvalues and eigenfunctions of A, one knows that

$$u(x, 0) = \sum (\chi, w_j) \exp(\lambda_j T) w_j \qquad\qquad \text{diverges}$$

when

$$u_\epsilon(x, 0) = \sum_j (\chi, w_j) \exp[(\lambda_j - \epsilon \lambda_j^2) T] w_j \qquad \text{obviously converges.}$$

In fact, one has:

Theorem. If in (1.1),

$$\xi(x) = u_\epsilon(x, 0), \tag{2.8}$$

where $u_\epsilon(x,0)$ is given by (2.3), then

$$\|u_\xi(x, T) - X(x)\| \leqslant [1 - \exp(-\epsilon\, c^2 \lambda_0^2 T)]\|X\|. \tag{2.9}$$

Remark 2.4. In practice, one solves (2.3), one computes $u_\epsilon(x,0)$, then one solves the initial problem (1.1) to verify the results, that is, (1.4). Obviously ϵ must be not too small [see $u_\epsilon(x,0)$ in Remark 2.3]; in fact, with $\epsilon = 0$ one is immediately led to high numerical instabilities; one has to take, in the chosen integration schemes,

$$\frac{\Delta t'}{(\Delta x)^2} \leqslant K,$$

but K is a function of ϵ and goes to zero with ϵ.

III. Monodimensional Examples

One seeks $\xi(x)$ on $(0,1)$ such that, $X(x)$ and η being given, if $u(x,t)$ satisfies

$$\frac{\partial u}{\partial t} - \frac{\partial}{\partial x}\left[a(x)\frac{\partial u}{\partial x}\right] = 0,$$

$$u(0,t) = u(1,t) = 0, \tag{3.1}$$

$$u(x,0) = \xi(x),$$

then one has

$$\left\{\int_0^1 [u(x, T) - X(x)]^2\, dx\right\}^{1/2} \leqslant \eta. \tag{3.2}$$

By taking

$$B = \frac{\partial^2}{\partial x^2},$$

one is led to solve

$$\frac{\partial U}{\partial t} - \frac{\partial}{\partial x}\left[a(x)\frac{\partial U}{\partial x}\right] - \epsilon\frac{\partial^4 U}{\partial x^4} = 0,$$

$$U(0,t) = U(1,t) = 0,$$

$$\frac{\partial}{\partial x}\left[a(x)\frac{\partial U}{\partial x}\right](0,t) = \frac{\partial}{\partial x}\left[a(x)\frac{\partial U}{\partial x}\right](1,t) = 0, \tag{3.3}$$

$$U(x,T) = X(x).$$

Remark 3.1. Only in a purpose of verification, one solves after (3.3) the problem (3.1) with the initial condition

$$\xi(x) = U(x, 0), \tag{3.4}$$

and one verifies condition (3.2).

Remark 3.2. To solve (3.3) one has to rely on a different scheme which introduces truncation errors; one has verified that integrating this system is numerically impossible for $\epsilon = 0$ (one is immediately faced with high numerical instabilities which lead to meaningless values, even if the steps Δt and Δx are considerably decreased).

Remark 3.3. ϵ is defined by condition (2.4) with

$$c = \inf_u \frac{\|u''\|}{\|a(x)u'' + u'\|}, \tag{3.5}$$

$$\lambda_0 = \inf_u \frac{\int_0^1 au'^2 \, dx}{\int_0^1 u^2 \, dx}. \tag{3.6}$$

Remark 3.4. There exists numerically a lower bound ϵ_0 to the admissible ϵ, that is, $X(x)$ and η being given, the problem is possible only if

$$T \leqslant \frac{-\log(1 - \eta/\|X\|)}{c^2 \lambda_0^2 \epsilon_0}, \tag{3.7}$$

which has been verified numerically $[\Delta t/(\Delta x)^2$ being given, one is led to divergence if one tries to solve the problem for too great values of T].

Remark 3.5. Let $U(x, t)$ be the exact solution of (3.3) and $\tilde{U}(x, t)$ the approximate solution (obtained through a stable scheme). Let us assume that the discretization steps are chosen such that:

$$\|\tilde{U}(x, 0) - U(x, 0)\| \leqslant \eta_1. \tag{3.8}$$

Let now $u(x, t)$ be the exact solution of (3.1) for

$$\xi(x) = U(x, 0)$$

and $\tilde{u}(x, t)$ the solution corresponding to

$$\tilde{\xi}(x) = \tilde{U}(x, 0). \tag{3.9}$$

Then $w = u - \tilde{u}$ satisfies to

$$\frac{\partial w}{\partial t} - \frac{\partial}{\partial x}\left[a(x)\frac{\partial w}{\partial x}\right] = 0,$$

$$w(0, t) = w(1, t) = 0,$$

$$w(x, 0) = \xi(x) - \tilde{\xi}(x),$$

(3.10)

which leads to

$$d/dt\,\|w(t)\|^2 + 2\int_0^1 a(x)[\partial w/\partial x]^2\,dx = 0.$$

But

$$\int_0^1 a(x)(\partial w/\partial x)^2\,dx \geqslant \lambda_0\|w(t)\|^2;$$

thus

$$d/dt\,\|w(t)\|^2 + 2\lambda_0\|w(t)\|^2 \leqslant 0,$$

$$\|w(t)\|^2 \leqslant \|\xi - \tilde{\xi}\|^2 \exp(-2\lambda_0 t),$$

and, finally,

$$\|u(T) - \tilde{u}(T)\| \leqslant \|\xi - \tilde{\xi}\| \exp(-\lambda_0 T).$$

Thus, if one has (3.9), one has also

$$\|\tilde{u}(T) - X\| \leqslant \|\tilde{u}(T) - u(T)\| + \|u(T) - X\|$$

$$\leqslant \eta_1 \exp(-\lambda_0 T) + \|u(T) - X\|.$$

As one seeks

$$\eta_1 \exp(-\lambda_0 T) + \|u(T) - X\| \leqslant \eta,$$

it is normal to choose ϵ such that

$$\|u_\epsilon(T) - X\| \leqslant \theta\eta, \qquad 0 < \theta < 1$$

and then the steps Δx, Δt in numerical integration such that

$$\eta_1 \exp(-\lambda_0 T) \leqslant (1 - \theta)\eta.$$

IV. Numerical Results[2]

The integration schemes for (3.3) and (3.1) are of the Crank-Nicolson type; we have not actually considered that we had to devote particular effort to the integration procedure. Computations have been made for $a(x)=1$, $a(x)=1+x$, many values of ϵ, and different $X(x)$: $X(x)=x(1-x)$; $X(x)$ "hat" function; $X(x)$ constant with discontinuities at both ends (results are much better by smoothing X at both ends); $X(x)$ step function (here again it is worth while to smooth at discontinuity points).

All results have proved very satisfactory.

Remark 4.1. One solves (3.3), then (3.1) for the purpose of verification, for many different values ϵ_j of ϵ; then one compares $u_{\epsilon_j}(x,T)$ with $X(x)$. One thus has a linear application

$$\xi_{\epsilon_j} = \phi_j \rightarrow u_{\epsilon_j}(x,T) = L\phi_j.$$

One can improve the quality of results by taking as "control" in (3.1)

$$\xi(x) = \sum_{j=1}^{n} \lambda_j \phi_j \tag{4.1}$$

and by choosing the λ_j so as to minimize, in a norm at our disposal,

$$\left\| L\left(\sum_{1}^{n} \lambda_j \phi_j\right) - X(x) \right\|. \tag{4.2}$$

V. Multidimensional Examples

One has considered the domain $K \times (0,T)$, where K is the square of side equal to 1 in the (x,y) plane, $X(x,y)$ and η are given, and one seeks $\xi(x,y)$ such that if $u(x,y,t)$ satisfies

$$\frac{\partial u}{\partial t} - \frac{\partial}{\partial x}\left[a(x,y)\frac{\partial u}{\partial x}\right] - \frac{\partial}{\partial y}\left[b(x,y)\frac{\partial u}{\partial y}\right] = 0,$$

$$u(x,0,t) = u(x,1,t) = u(0,y,t) = u(1,y,t) = 0, \tag{5.1}$$

$$u(x,y,0) = \xi(x,y),$$

[2] All numerical computations were processed on a Control Data 3600 computer.

then

$$\|u(x, y, T) - X(x, y)\| \leqslant \eta. \tag{5.2}$$

The quasi-reversibility method consists here of adding

$$- \epsilon \Delta(\Delta u)$$

in the first equation (5.1), where Δ is the Laplacian, and the boundary conditions

$$\frac{\partial}{\partial x}\left[a(x, y)\frac{\partial u}{\partial x}\right](0, y, t) = \frac{\partial}{\partial x}\left[a(x, y)\frac{\partial u}{\partial x}\right](1, y, t) = \frac{\partial}{\partial y}\left[b(x, y)\frac{\partial u}{\partial y}\right](x, 0, t)$$

$$= \frac{\partial}{\partial y}\left[b(x, y)\frac{\partial u}{\partial y}\right](x, 1, t) = 0.$$

Computations have been made for various $X(x, y)$, especially

$$X(x, y) = xy(1 - x)(1 - y),$$

$$X(x, y) \qquad \text{piecewise linear.}$$

All results again have proved very satisfactory.

VI. Control of Boundary Conditions

A. THE PROBLEM

One considers an open Ω in R^n of boundary Γ and the cylinder $Q = \Omega \times (0, T)$ of lateral boundary $\Sigma = \Gamma \times (0, T)$.

Let $u = u(x, t, g)$ be the solution, for g given on Σ, of

$$\frac{\partial u}{\partial t} - \Delta u = 0 \qquad \text{in } Q,$$

$$(u)_\Sigma = g, \tag{6.1}$$

$$u(x, 0) = 0.$$

Let now X be given in $L_2(\Omega)$, and set

$$J(g) = \|u(T) - X\|. \tag{6.2}$$

One can prove that

$$\inf_{g \in L_2(\Sigma)} J(g) = 0. \tag{6.3}$$

Therefore, given $\eta > 0$, there exists a g_η in $L_2(\Sigma)$ such that

$$J(g_\eta) \leqslant \eta. \tag{6.4}$$

B. THE QUASI-REVERSIBILITY METHOD

The method consists here of introducing an operator Δ_ϵ which approximates Δ, with a singular coefficient vanishing at the boundary, to precisely suppress the boundary conditions on Σ. Then one considers the problem

$$\frac{\partial u_\epsilon}{\partial t} - \Delta_\epsilon u_\epsilon - \epsilon \frac{\partial^2 u_\epsilon}{\partial t^2} = 0,$$

$$u_\epsilon(x, 0) = 0, \tag{6.5}$$

$$u_\epsilon(x, T) = X(x).$$

Because of the choice of Δ_ϵ there is no condition on Σ.

Remark 6.1. Under quite general and suitable hypotheses on Δ_ϵ, the problem (6.5) admits a unique solution; then one takes

$$g = u_\epsilon/\Sigma \tag{6.6}$$

(u_ϵ is not singular on Σ).

Remark 6.2. Practical problems concern the choices of Δ_ϵ and ϵ, the numerical computation of u_ϵ, then of g, then the verification of results.

C. CHOICE OF Δ_ϵ

One can take

$$\Delta_\epsilon u = \sum_i \frac{\partial}{\partial x_i}\left[\rho_\epsilon^2(x)\frac{\partial u}{\partial x_i}\right], \tag{6.7}$$

where ρ_ϵ is a function defined in Ω in the following way: If $d(x, \Gamma)$ is the distance from x to the boundary Γ, one takes

$$\rho_\epsilon(x) = 1 \qquad \text{if} \quad d(x, \Gamma) \geqslant \phi(\epsilon),$$

$$\rho_\epsilon(x) = 0 \qquad \text{on} \quad \Gamma, \tag{6.8}$$

$$\left|\frac{\partial \rho_\epsilon}{\partial x_i}\right| \leqslant \frac{c'}{d(x, \Gamma)} \qquad \text{if} \quad d(x, \Gamma) \leqslant \phi(\epsilon).$$

Remark 6.3. In fact, the actual quasi-reversibility method leads here to problems of elliptic type. [It is seen through variational formulation used to prove existence and uniqueness of the solution of (6.5).]

D. EXAMPLES

If one takes $\Omega = \,]0, 1[$, one can take ρ_ϵ as in Fig. 1. The method allows for computing the solution $u_\epsilon(x, t)$ in a domain

$$Q' = \Omega' \times (0, T) \qquad \text{where} \quad \Omega' \subset \Omega.$$

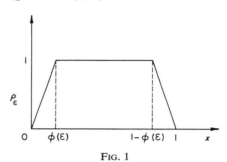

FIG. 1

To obtain u_ϵ on Σ, one has to extrapolate $u_\epsilon(x, T)$ in Q. In the case of the actual example, one has to extrapolate the solution on the vertical boundaries of the integration domain.

Computations have been made to study the influence of ϵ, $\phi(\epsilon)$, and of the shape of $\rho(x)$. One has equally taken many integration schemes with variable steps to study the behavior near boundaries.

The Analytical Solution Is Known

Consider the problem

$$\frac{\partial u}{\partial t} - \frac{\partial^2 u}{\partial x^2} = 0, \qquad x \in (0, 1), \quad t \in (0, T),$$

$$u(0, t) = u(1, t) = 2(T - t), \tag{6.9}$$

$$u(x, 0) = 2T + x(1 - x).$$

The solution of (6.9) is

$$u(x, t) = 2(T-t)+x(1-x). \tag{6.10}$$

By taking

$$\xi(x) = 2T+x(1-x)$$

and

$$X(x) = x(1-x),$$

the method leads to two functions, $g_0^*(t)$ and $g_1^*(t)$, and to a very good approximation $X^*(x)$ of $X(x)$; g_0^* and g_1^* are quite different from the values in (6.9). This result comes from the fact that there is no uniqueness for the g_i of the problem under consideration.

$X(x)$ Is a Numerical Solution of the Problem under Consideration

Consider the problem

$$\frac{\partial u}{\partial t} - \frac{\partial^2 u}{\partial x^2} = 0,$$

$$u(1, t) = u(0, t) = t/T, \tag{6.11}$$

$$u(x, 0) = 0.$$

The numerical integration of (6.11) leads to a function $X(x)$ taken as terminal for $t = T$, and to attain by taking $\xi(x) = 0$. Here again $X^*(x)$ is quite satisfactory but the $g_i(t)$ quite different from their values in (6.11).

VII. Generalizations of the Terminal Condition

For obvious practical reasons, it appears useful to solve the problem ξ with the condition (1.4) replaced by conditions of the form

$$\text{minimize} \int_{T-\tau}^{T+\tau} \int_{\Omega} |u(x, t) - X(x)|^2 \, dx \, dt, \qquad t > 0, \quad x \in \Omega \tag{7.1}$$

or

$$\int_{T-\tau}^{T+\tau} \int_{\Omega} |u(x, t) - X(x)|^2 \, dx \, dt \leqslant \eta, \tag{7.2}$$

where η, T, and τ are given, τ being "small." Here the quasi-reversibility method consists of solving

$$\frac{\partial u}{\partial t} - \Delta u - \epsilon \Delta^2 u - \epsilon u(x, t+2\tau) = 0, \qquad x < T-\tau,$$

$$u(x, t) \, X = (x) \qquad\qquad \text{for} \quad t \in [T-\tau, T+\tau], \qquad\qquad (7.3)$$

$$u(x, t) = 0 \quad \Delta u(x, t) = 0 \qquad \text{for } x \in \Gamma \quad t < T-\tau, \ (\Gamma \text{ boundary of } \Omega).$$

Remark 7.1. One can prove that problem (7.3) admits a unique solution; then one has to solve numerically (7.3) and take $u_\epsilon(x, 0)$ as the control $\xi(x)$. Of course, it is also possible to solve such a problem by controlling the boundary conditions.

Remark 7.2. It is worth noting that (7.3) is a "delay problem."

VIII. Generalization to Other Equations

The quasi-reversibility method can be applied to problems of the type

$$\frac{du}{dt} + Au + Ku = 0,$$

where K is a linear continuous operator (for example, an integrodifferential operator; and thus one can consider Boltzmann equations).

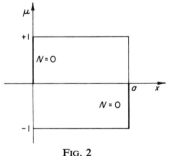

FIG. 2

Example. The transport equation in the monodimensional case (see Fig. 2). Consider the following problem:

$$\frac{\partial N}{\partial t} + \mu \frac{\partial N}{\partial x} + \sigma N - \frac{c}{2} \int_{-1}^{+1} N(x, \mu, t)\, d\mu = 0, \qquad (8.1)$$

with the usual boundary conditions: no reentering neutrons, i.e.,

$$N = 0 \quad \text{if } \mathbf{v} \cdot \mathbf{n} = 0, \tag{8.2}$$

where $\mathbf{v}$ is the neutronic speed and $\mathbf{n}$ the outer normal. One has thus

$$N = 0 \quad \text{for} \begin{cases} x = 0 & 0 < \mu < 1, \\ x = a & -1 < \mu < 0. \end{cases}$$

The problem is: Let $X(x,\mu)$ be given in $L_2[(0,a) \times (\mu \in (-1,+1))]$, and let η and T be given (both positive). Find a control

$$\xi = \xi(x,\mu) = \xi_\eta(x,\mu)$$

such that the solution of

$$\frac{\partial N}{\partial t} + \mu \frac{\partial N}{\partial x} + \sigma N - \frac{c}{2} \int_{-1}^{+1} N(x,\mu,t)\, d\mu = 0, \tag{8.1a}$$

$$N(x,\mu,0) = \xi(x,\mu)$$

satisfies

$$\left\{ \int_0^a \int_{-1}^{+1} |N(x,\mu,T) - X(x,\mu)|^2\, dx\, d\mu \right\}^{1/2} \leqslant \eta. \tag{8.3}$$

Let us set

$$AN = \mu \frac{\partial N}{\partial x} \qquad BN = \sigma N - \frac{c}{2} \int_{-1}^{+1} N(x,\mu)\, d\mu. \tag{8.4}$$

The application of the quasi-reversibility method leads us to solve

$$\frac{\partial N}{\partial t} + AN + BN - \epsilon A^* AN = 0,$$

$$N(x,\mu,T) = X(x,\mu), \tag{8.5}$$

$$N \in \text{domain of } A,$$

$$AN \in \text{domain of } A^*,$$

Thus one has

$$\mu \frac{\partial N}{\partial x} = 0 \quad \text{for} \begin{cases} x = 0 & -1 < \mu < 0 \\ x = a & 0 < \mu < +1 \end{cases}$$

and the first of equations (8.5) is

$$\frac{\partial N}{\partial t} + AN + BN + \epsilon \mu^2 \frac{\partial^2 N}{\partial x^2} = 0.$$

Remark 8.1. The problem (8.1a), by reverting the time and taking

$$N(x, \mu, T) = X(x, \mu)$$

as the initial condition, is not well set. But the quasi-reversibility method can be applied and the problem (8.5) solved.

Remark 8.2. Now one must solve numerically problem (8.5); it is a parabolic problem depending on a parameter μ; it seems possible to solve it for a series of values μ_1, μ_2, ..., μ_p of μ, then interpolating with respect to the numerical μ_i.

IX. Concluding Remarks

The quasi-reversibility method has allowed us up to now to solve many "non-well-set" problems, even in intricate cases, with very satisfactory numerical precision.

Other generalizations[3] than those mentioned are actually attacked.

(1) Submit the controls to constraints, for instance,

$$|\xi(x)| \leq M \tag{9.1}$$

or

$$\xi(x) > 0, \tag{9.2}$$

the last condition ensuring that the solution u remains positive (maximum principle for parabolic equations). In this case it seems that one has to rely on the boundary conditions as controls.

(2) Stationary problems.

---

[3] All results, both theoretical and numerical, will be developed in a book by R. Lattés and J. L. Lions, "Méthode de Quasi-Reversibilité et Applications". Dunod, Paris; Academic Press, New York, 1967.

(3) Various problems in the field of analytical continuation.

(4) Inverse problems.

On the other hand, one has begun to study the influence of perturbations on the controls (sensitivity analysis).

Also in the case where $\xi(x)$ and $X(x)$ are given (one controls the boundary conditions), one can expect that there exists a lower bound T^* for T, and that for $T < T^*$, the problem becomes impossible. Of course,

$$\inf T = T^* = T^*(\xi, X; \epsilon). \tag{9.3}$$

ACKNOWLEDGMENT

This work is sponsored by the French DRME (Direction des Recherches et Moyens d'Essais).

On Some Optimization Problems for Linear Parabolic Equations

J. L. LIONS

Department of Mathematics
Institut Henri Poincaré, Paris, France

Introduction

We consider here some optimization problems for evolution equations,

$$A(t)u + \frac{\partial u}{\partial t} = f, \qquad u(0) \text{ given,}$$

where the operators $A(t)$ are *unbounded* in a *Hilbert* space H [we could extend some results to the "Banach case," using $(8, 9)$]. We assume that the $A(t)$ span a set $\mathscr{B}$ of operators, and that f and u_0 span sets F and U_0. We take the optimization when $A(t), f, u_0$ vary in $\mathscr{B}$, F, U_0 (and therefore the controls can also be in the coefficients of the operators).

We give in Sections IV and VI sufficient conditions for an optimal control to *exist*; these conditions are shown to be satisfied in the examples of Sections III and V. Our existence results seem to contain all similar results previously given in $(3, 4, 6, 20)$ (but this does not mean that our paper contains all the results of these papers!). The uniqueness problem (7) is not considered here.

Many variants and extensions are possible:

(1) Our results immediately apply to the *elliptic* case; we shall show that they also extend to some *nonlinear elliptic families* (for the elliptic situation, we shall quote here from the interesting paper (15)).

(2) We shall partially extend the results of this paper to some families of nonlinear parabolic type.

(3) We shall also consider other types of equations: hyperbolic, Schrödinger, well set in the sense of Petrowsky.

(4) We shall also study similar problems for variational *inequalities*.

115

The plan is as follows:

I. A Closure Result

A. EVOLUTION PROBLEMS

Let V and H be two Hilbert spaces, $V \subset H$ (which means inclusion with continuous injection), V dense in H, V separable. If u, $v \in V$ (resp. $f, g \in H$), $((u, v))$ (resp. (f, g)) denotes their scalar product in V (resp. H), we shall set $\|u\| = ((u, u))^{1/2}$, $|f| = (f, f)^{1/2}$. We shall denote by V' the antidual of V; if we identify H with its antidual, we have

$$V \subset H \subset V'.$$

If $v' \in V'$, $v \in V$, (v', v) denotes their scalar product (antilinear in v).

If X denotes a Banach space, $L_p(0, T; X)$ denotes the space of (classes of) strongly measurable functions v from $(0, T)$ to X, such that $\|v(t)\|_X$ belongs to $L_p(0, T)$, $1 \leqslant p \leqslant \infty$.

Let $A(t)$ be a family of operators, $A(t) \in \mathscr{L}(V; V')$, $t \in (0, T)$. We assume that [if A denotes the function[1] $t \to A(t)$]

$$A \in L_{\infty, s}(0, T; \mathscr{L}(V; V')) \tag{1.1}$$

and that

$$\operatorname{Re}(A(t)v, v) \geqslant c\|v\|^2, \qquad v \in V, \quad c > 0, \quad t \in (0, T). \tag{1.2}$$

Remark 1.1. In the applications, the operators $A(t)$ are partial differential operators. See Section III.

If $u \in L_2(0, T; V)$, then one can take its derivative $du/dt = u'$ in the sense of distributions on $]0, T[$ with values in V [cf. (*17*)]. The following result is known (*10*): under hypotheses (1.1), (1.2), there exists a function u and only one, which satisfies

$$A(t)u + u' = f \tag{1.3}$$

[f being given in $L_2(0, T; V')$],

$$u \in L_2(0, T; V), \qquad u' \in L_2(0, T; V'), \tag{1.4}$$

$$u(0) = u_0 \qquad (u_0 \text{ given in } H). \tag{1.5}$$

Note that condition (1.5) makes sense; indeed (*12*) every function u which satisfies (1.4) is a.e. equal to a continuous function from $[0, T] \to H$.

---

[1] $L_{\infty, s}(0, T; \mathscr{L}(V; V'))$ is the space of functions $t \to A(t)$ from $(0, T) \to \mathscr{L}(V; V')$, such that

    (a) for every $u \in V$, $v \in V$, $t \to (A(t)u, v)$ is measurable.
    (b) $\|A(t)\|_{\mathscr{L}(V; V')}$ is essentially bounded.

Since V is separable, it amounts to the same as saying that $t \to A(t)u$ is (strongly) measurable from $(0, T) \to V$ [this does not imply that $A(t)$ is measurable for the norm of $\mathscr{L}(V; V')$; a simple counter example was shown to me by J. Dixmier].

B. The Set $H(\mathscr{B}, F, U_0; \tau)$

We are now given the following sets:

$\mathscr{B}$ = bounded set of $L_{\infty,s}(0, T; \mathscr{L}(V; V'))$, every $A \in \mathscr{B}$ satisfying
(1.2) with the same constant c,   (1.6)

F (resp. U_0) bounded and weakly closed set of $L_2(0, T; V')$ (resp. H).
                                                                                    (1.7)

Let τ be given $\epsilon[0, T]$. *We define* $H(\mathscr{B}, F, U_0; \tau)$ *as the subset of H described by* $u(\tau)$ [*u a solution of* (1.3), (1.4), *and* (1.5)], *when* A, f, u_0 *span* $\mathscr{B}$, F, U_0.

Our first result gives a sufficient condition for $H(\mathscr{B}, F, U_0; \tau)$ to be *weakly closed in H*.

C. The Closure Theorem

Let $A^*(t)$ be the adjoint of $A(t)$; $A^*(t) \in \mathscr{L}(V; V')$; if A^* denotes the function $t \rightarrow A^*(t)$, $A^* \in L_{\infty,s}(0, T; \mathscr{L}(V; V'))$. We denote by $\mathscr{B}^*$ the set spanned by A^* when A spans $\mathscr{B}$. We shall make the following hypothesis: There exists two Hilbert spaces W_1, W_2 such that

(a) $W_1 \subset V \subset W_2 \subset H$, each space being dense in the following one, and the injection $V \rightarrow W_2$ being compact;

(b) if W_2' denotes the antidual of W_2 (then $W_2 \subset H \subset W_2'$ $\subset V'$), we assume that $\mathscr{B}^*$ is bounded[2] in $L_{\infty,s}(0, T; \mathscr{L}(W_1; W_2'))$;

(c) from every sequence $A_n^* \in \mathscr{B}^*$, one can extract a subsequence A_μ^* such that $A_\mu^* \rightarrow A^*$ in $L_{\infty,s}(0, T; \mathscr{L}(V; V'))$ weakly[3] and $A^* \in \mathscr{B}^*$.   (1.8)

(In Section III we shall give examples of cases in which this condition is satisfied.) We shall prove in the next section the

Theorem 1.1. *Under hypotheses* (1.1), (1.2), (1.6), (1.7), *and* (1.8), *the set* $H(\mathscr{B}, F, U_0; \tau)$ *is bounded and weakly closed in H*.

---

[2] That is, $(A^*(t) w_1 w_2)$ is measurable $\forall w_i \in W_i$, and $\|A^*(t)\|_{\mathscr{L}(W_1; W_2')} \leq$ constant.

[3] Following the Dunford-Pettis theorem, $L_{\infty,s}(0, T; \mathscr{L}(V; V))$ [which is isomorphic to $L_{\infty,s}(0, T; \mathscr{L}(V; V'))$] is the dual of a Banach space (see the proof of Lemma (2.1) and "weakly" means for the corresponding weak star topology.

II. Proof of Theorem 1.1

A. Lemmas

Lemma 2.1. *From every sequence $A_n \in \mathscr{B}$ one can extract a subsequence A_v such that*

$$\forall v \in V, \qquad \forall \phi \in L_2(0, T), \qquad \forall u \in L_2(0, T; V)$$

one has

$$\int_0^T (A_v(t) u(t), v) \phi(t) \, dt \to \int_0^T (A(t) u(t), v) \phi(t) \, dt, \tag{2.1}$$

where $A \in \mathscr{B}$.

Proof. (1) Let J be the canonical isomorphism from V' into V; when A(resp. A^*) spans $\mathscr{B}$(resp. $\mathscr{B}^*$), JA(resp. JA^*) spans $J\mathscr{B}$(resp. $J\mathscr{B}^*$) and (2.1) is equivalent to

$$\int_0^T ((JA_v(t) u(t), v)) \phi(t) \, dt \to \int_0^T ((JA(t) u(t), v)) \phi(t) \, dt. \tag{2.2}$$

(2) Let us recall now (5) that $\mathscr{L}(V; V)$ is the dual of the space $\mathscr{L}^1(V; V)$ of trace operators. If $A \in \mathscr{L}(V; V)$, $K \in \mathscr{L}^1(V; V)$, their scalar product is

$$\langle\langle A, K \rangle\rangle = \text{tr}(AK) = \text{tr}(KA).$$

Then, by Dunford-Pettis, the dual of $L_1(0, T; \mathscr{L}^1(V; V))$ is the space of functions $B(t) \in \mathscr{L}(V; V)$ such that

(a) $\forall K \in \mathscr{L}^1(V; V)$, $\quad \langle\langle B(t), K \rangle\rangle$ is measurable;

(b) $\|B(t)\|_{\mathscr{L}(V; V)}$ is bounded.

But (a) is equivalent to assuming that $B(t) v$ is measurable $\forall v \in V$ (separable); hence $L_{\infty,s}(0, T; \mathscr{L}(V; V))$ is the dual of $L_1(0, T; \mathscr{L}^1(V; V))$; the duality can be written

$$\int_0^T \text{tr}(B(t) K(t)) \, dt = \int_0^T \text{tr}(K(t) B(t)) \, dt.$$

Therefore, using (1.8)(c), we see that we can extract A_v such that $JA_v^* \to JA^*$ in $L_{\infty,s}(0, T; \mathscr{L}(V; V))$, weak star topology, $A^* \in \mathscr{B}^*$. Therefore,

$$\int_0^T \text{tr}(K(t) JA_v^*(t)) \, dt \to \int_0^T \text{tr}(K(t) JA^*(t)) \, dt, \qquad \forall K \in L_1(0, T; \mathscr{L}^1(V; V)). \tag{2.3}$$

(3) Now choose K by

$$K(t) w = ((w, u(t))) v\overline{\phi(t)},$$

$$K \in L_1(0, T; \mathscr{L}^1(V; V)),$$

and

$$\mathrm{tr}(K(t) J A_v^*(t)) = ((J A_v^*(t) v, u(t))) \overline{\phi(t)} = (v, A_v(t) u(t)) \overline{\phi(t)}, \quad (2.4)$$

and this, together with (2.3), implies (2.1).

Lemma 2.2. *Let u_n be a sequence such that u_n (resp. u_n') belong to a bounded set of $L_2(0, T; V)$ (resp. $L_2(0, T; V')$). One can extract a subsequence u_v such that*

$$u_v \rightarrow u \qquad in \ L_2(0, T; V) \ weakly,$$
$$u_v' \rightarrow u' \qquad in \ L_2(0, T; V') \ weakly, \tag{2.5}$$

$$u_v \rightarrow u \qquad in \ L_2(0, T; W_2) \ strongly. \tag{2.6}$$

Proof. For (2.6), we use Prop. 4.2 of Lions (*10*, p. 60). [See also Aubin (*2*) for a more general result.]

B. PROOF OF THEOREM 1.1

(1) Let $\xi_n \in H(\mathscr{B}, F, U_0; \tau)$, $\xi_n \rightarrow \xi$ in H weakly. We have to show that $\xi \in H(\mathscr{B}, F, U_0; \tau)$, therefore that

$$\xi = u(\tau), \tag{2.7}$$

u being the solution of (1.3)–(1.5) for suitable A, f, u_0, elements of $\mathscr{B}, F, U_0$. By hypothesis, for each n there exists $A_n \in \mathscr{B}, f_n \in F, u_{0n} \in U_0$ such that

$$A_n(t) u_n + u_n' = f_n,$$
$$u_n(0) = u_{0n} \tag{2.8}$$

and

$$u_n(\tau) = \xi_n. \tag{2.9}$$

From (2.8) and hypothesis (1.6), it follows that

$$c \int_0^T \|u_n(t)\|^2 \, dt + \tfrac{1}{2} |u_n(T)|^2 - \tfrac{1}{2} |u_{0n}|^2 \leqslant \int_0^T \|f_n(t)\|_* \|u_n(t)\| \, dt$$

(where $\| \ \|_*$ denotes the norm in V'), whence (u_{0n} being bounded in H),

$$u_n \text{ belongs to a bounded set of } L_2(0, T; V). \tag{2.10}$$

Since $\mathscr{B}$ is bounded in $L_{\infty, s}(0, T; \mathscr{L}(V; V'))$, it follows that

$$A_n u_n \text{ belongs to a bounded set of } L_2(0, T; V'). \tag{2.11}$$

But then (2.8) implies [writing $u_n' = f_n - A_n(t) u_n$] that

$$u_n' \text{ is bounded in } L_2(0, T; V'). \tag{2.12}$$

Therefore, one can extract a subsequence u_ν such that (2.5) and (2.6) hold true and that

$$f_\nu \rightharpoonup f \qquad \text{in } L_2(0, T; V') \text{ weakly,} \qquad f \in F, \tag{2.13}$$

$$u_{0\nu} \rightharpoonup u_0 \qquad \text{in } H \text{ weakly,} \qquad u_0 \in V_0, \tag{2.14}$$

$$A_\nu u_\nu \rightharpoonup g \qquad \text{in } L_2(0, T; V') \text{ weakly.} \tag{2.15}$$

It remains to show that

$$g = Au, \text{ for a suitable } A \text{ in } \mathscr{B}. \tag{2.16}$$

Admitting this for a moment, it follows that

$$A(t) u + u' = f, \qquad u(0) = u_0,$$

and since $u_\nu(\tau) \rightharpoonup u(\tau)$ in H weakly, and since $\xi_\nu \rightharpoonup \xi$ in the same sense, we see that $\xi = u(\tau)$; hence (2.7) follows.

(3) *Proof of* (2.16). Since W_1 is dense in V, it is enough to check that

$$\int_0^T (g(t), v) \phi(t) \, dt = \int_0^T (A(t) u(t), v) \phi(t) \, dt,$$

$\forall v \in W_1$, $\phi \in L_2(0, T)$, and for a suitable A in $\mathscr{B}$. By Lemma 2.1, we can assume that (2.1) holds true.

We have then to show that

$$X_\nu = \int_0^T (A_\nu(t) u_\nu, v) \phi(t) \, dt \to X = \int_0^T (A(t) u, v) \phi(t) \, dt. \tag{2.17}$$

But

$$X_v = Y_v + Z_v,$$

$$Y_v = \int_0^T (A_v(t)(u_v - u), v)\,\phi(t)\,dt = \int_0^T (u_v - u, A_v{}^*(t)\,v)\,\phi(t)\,dt,$$

$$Z_v = \int_0^T (A_v(t)\,u, v)\,\phi(t)\,dt.$$

And, using (1.8)(b),

$$|Y_v| \leqslant (\text{constant})\|v\|_{W_1} \int_0^T \|u_v(t) - u(t)\|_{W_2}|\phi(t)|\,dt,$$

and therefore $Y_v \to 0$, using (2.6).

Next, $Z_v \to X$, thanks to Lemma 2.1, and (2.17) follows. This completes the proof of Theorem 2.1.

III. The Case of Differential Operators

We give some simple examples where the hypotheses of Theorem 1.1 are satisfied.

A. Spaces $H^s(\Omega)$[4]

We denote by $H^s(\mathbf{R}^n)$ the space of tempered (16) distributions u such that

$$\|(1 + \xi_1{}^2 + \cdots + \xi_n{}^2)^{s/2}\,\mathscr{F}u\|_{L_2(\mathbf{R}^n)} < \infty$$

($\mathscr{F}u = $ Fourier transform of u), $s \in \mathbf{R}$ (of arbitrary sign); the above quantity is a norm and for this norm $H^s(\mathbf{R}^n)$ is a Hilbert space. When $s = m = $ integer, then

$$H^s(\mathbf{R}^n) = H^m(\mathbf{R}^n) = \{u \,|\, D^\alpha u \in L_2(\mathbf{R}^n), \quad |\alpha| \leqslant m\}$$

[Sobolev space (18)].

Let now Ω be a bounded set of $\mathbf{R}^n$, with a Lipschitz boundary Γ. We set, for $s \in \mathbf{R}$, $s \geqslant 0$,

---

[4] See, e.g., Lions (12); Lions and Magenes (13).

$H^s(\Omega) = \{u | u = \text{restriction to } \Omega \text{ of some element of } H^s(\mathbf{R})^n\}$, provided with the natural quotient structure.

We next define

$H_0^s(\Omega)$ = closure in $H^s(\Omega)$ of functions with compact support in Ω,

$H^{-s}(\Omega)$ = dual of $H_0^s(\Omega)$.

B. SPACES V, W_1, W_2

We shall take

$H = L_2(\Omega)$,

V = closed subspace of $H^m(\Omega)$, $\qquad H_0^m(\Omega) \subset V \subset H^m(\Omega)$. $\qquad$ (3.1)

We choose

$$W_1 = V \cap H^{m+\epsilon}(\Omega) \qquad \epsilon > 0 \text{ fixed with } 0 < \epsilon < \tfrac{1}{2}, \qquad (3.2)$$

$$W_2 = \text{closure of } V \text{ in } H^{m-\epsilon}(\Omega) \qquad (\text{same } \epsilon). \qquad (3.3)$$

It follows, for instance from Lions and Peetre (14) that $V \to W_2$ is compact, and we assume (this will be verified whenever Γ is smooth enough, V being defined by differential boundary conditions)

$$W_1 \text{ is dense in } V. \qquad (3.4)$$

C. OPERATORS $A(t)$

Let $a_{\alpha\beta} = a_{\alpha\beta}(x, t)$ be a family of given functions in $\Omega \times (0, T)$, $|\alpha|, |\beta| \leqslant m$, satisfying

$$|a_{\alpha\beta}(x, t)| \leqslant c_2, \qquad x, t \in \Omega \times (0, T). \qquad (3.5)$$

For u, $v \in V$, we set

$$a(t; u, v) = \sum_{|\alpha|, |\beta| \leqslant m} \int_\Omega a_{\alpha\beta}(x, t) D^\alpha u \overline{D^\beta v} \, dx. \qquad (3.6)$$

The (antilinear) form $v \to a(t; u, v)$ is continuous on V, therefore

$$a(t; u, v) = (A(t)u, v),$$

$$A(t)u \in V'. \qquad (3.7)$$

Remarks 3.1. The space V' is not [except in the case $V = H_0{}^m(\Omega)$] a space of distributions on Ω. The boundary conditions are contained in "$u \in V$" and (3.7). For details, see Lions (*10, 11*).

Note that (3.5) implies that $A \in L_{\infty,s}(0, T; \mathscr{L}(V; V'))$. We are now going to check:

Proposition 3.1. *Let $\mathscr{B}$ be a set of operators $A(t)$ defined by (3.6) and (3.7), when the $a_{\alpha\beta}$ vary subject to (3.5) and*

$$\left| \frac{\partial}{\partial x_i} a_{\alpha\beta}(x, t) \right| \leq c_3, \qquad \forall i, \alpha, \beta. \tag{3.8}$$

Then, if we assume also that

$$\operatorname{Re} a(t; v, v) \geq c\|v\|^2, \qquad \forall v \in V, \quad t \in (0, T), \quad c > o \text{ fixed}, \tag{3.9}$$

the set $\mathscr{B}$ satisfies (1.8), with W_1 and W_2 chosen by (3.2) and (3.3) (ϵ being arbitrarily fixed with $0 < \epsilon < \frac{1}{2}$).

Proof. Property (1.8)(c) is immediate. The only point that remains to be checked is (1.8)(b); i.e.,

$$|a(t; u, v)| \leq c_4 \|u\|_{W_1} \|v\|_{W_2}, \qquad u \in W_1, \quad v \in V. \tag{3.10}$$

It is enough to check that

$$\left| \int_\Omega a_{\alpha\beta}(x, t)\, D^\alpha u \overline{D^\beta v}\, dx \right| \leq c_5 \|D^\alpha u\|_{H^\epsilon(\Omega)} \|D^\beta v\|_{H^{-\epsilon}(\Omega)}. \tag{3.11}$$

But since $0 < \epsilon < \frac{1}{2}$, one has (*13*)

$$\left| \int_\Omega a_{\alpha\beta}\, D^\alpha u \overline{D^\beta v}\, dx \right| \leq \|a_{\alpha\beta}\, D^\alpha u\|_{H^\epsilon(\Omega)} \|D^\beta v\|_{H^{-\epsilon}(\Omega)},$$

and (3.11) follows if $a_{\alpha\beta}$ is a *multiplier* on $H^\epsilon(\Omega)$ and

$$\|a_{\alpha\beta}(x,t)\|_{\mathscr{L}(H^\epsilon(\Omega);\, H^\epsilon(\Omega))} \leq c_5. \tag{3.12}$$

But (3.8) is a sufficient condition for (3.12) to hold. Hence the result follows.

Remark 3.2. We actually proved a little more: Proposition 3.1 is still true under the more general (but more awkward to handle) condition (3.12).

IV. An Optimization Problem

A. SETTING OF THE PROBLEM

To each $u \in L_2(0,T;V)$ such that $u' \in L_2(0,T;V')$, we associate a real number $J(u)$ such that

if $u_n \to u$ in $L_2(0,T;V)$ weakly, if $u_n' \to u'$ in $L_2(0,T;V')$ weakly, then $J(u) \leqslant \inf \lim J(u_n)$. (4.1)

Since the data of the triple $\{A, f, u_0\}$ uniquely defines u, we can also set

$$J(u) = \mathscr{J}(A, f, u_0). \tag{4.2}$$

Let X be a bounded weakly closed subset of H. We assume (with the notations of Section I) that

$$H(\mathscr{B}, F, U_0; \tau) \cap X \neq \phi. \tag{4.3}$$

We then set

$$J_0 = \inf J(u) = \inf \mathscr{J}(A, f, u_0), A \in \mathscr{B}, f \in F, u_0 \in U_0,$$
$$\text{whenever } u(\tau) \in X. \tag{4.4}$$

We want to prove:

Theorem 4.1. *We assume the conditions of Theorem 1.1 and conditions (4.1) and (4.3) to be satisfied. Then, there exists $A \in \mathscr{B}, f \in F, u_0 \in V_0$, such that*

$$\mathscr{J}(A, f, u_0) = J_0.$$

B. PROOF OF THEOREM 4.1

Let $A_n, f_n, u_{0n} \in \mathscr{B} \times F \times U_0$, such that

$$\mathscr{J}(A_n, f_n, u_{0n}) \to J_0.$$

One can extract from u_n [solution of $A_n(t)u_n + u_n' = f_n$, $u_n(0) = u_{0n}$] a sequence u_ν such that $u_\nu \to u$ in $L_2(0,T;V)$ weakly, $u_\nu' \to u'$ in $L_2(0,T;V')$ weakly [and then $u_\nu(\tau) \to u(\tau)$ in H weakly] and, using Theorem 1.1, such that u is the solution of (1.3)–(1.5) for $(A, f, u_0) \in \mathscr{B} \times F \times U_0$. Since X is weakly closed, $u(\tau) \in X$ and $J(u) \leqslant \inf \lim J(u_\nu) = J_0$. Since $J(u) < J_0$ is impossible, $J(u) = J_0$ and the theorem follows.

V. Examples

We give here only very simple examples.

A. Example 1

Control in the Coefficients (I)
We take for $\mathscr{B}$ the set of operators $A(t)$ defined by

$$a(t;u,v) = \sum_{i=1}^{n} (2-q(t)) \int_{\Omega} \frac{\partial u}{\partial x_i} \frac{\overline{\partial v}}{\partial x_i} dx \qquad u, v \in H_0^1(\Omega), \qquad (5.1)$$

where $q(t)=q$ spans the set of measurable functions on $[0,T]$ such that

$$|q(t)| \leqslant 1. \qquad (5.2)$$

Theorems 1.1 and 4.1 apply.

B. Example 2

Control in the Coefficients (II)
Again take $V = H_0^1(\Omega)$, and take the set $\mathscr{B}$ defined by

$$a(t;u,v) = \sum_{i=1}^{n} \int_{\Omega} (2-q(x,t)) \frac{\partial u}{\partial x_i} \frac{\overline{\partial v}}{\partial x_i} dx, \qquad (5.3)$$

where $q(x,t)=q$ spans the set of measurable functions on $\Omega \times (0,T)$ which satisfy

$$|q(x,t)| \leqslant 1,$$
$$\left| \frac{\partial}{\partial x_i} q(x,t) \right| \leqslant 1. \qquad (5.4)$$

According to Proposition 3.1, we can again apply Theorems 1.1 and 4.1.

C. Example 3

Control in the Coefficients of Boundary Conditions
We take $V = H^1(\Omega)$ and for $\mathscr{B}$ the set of operators defined by

$$a(t;u,v) = \sum_{i=1}^{n} \int_{\Omega} \frac{\partial u}{\partial x_i} \frac{\overline{\partial v}}{\partial x_i} dx + \int_{\Gamma} q(x,t) u\bar{v} \, d\Gamma, \qquad (5.5)$$

where $\Gamma =$ boundary of Ω. Here q spans the set of measurable functions on $\Gamma \times (0, T)$ such that

$$|q(x, t)| \leqslant 1, \qquad x \in \Gamma, \quad t \in (0, T). \tag{5.6}$$

The boundary-value problems which correspond to (1.3)–(1.5) are then

$$\frac{\partial u}{\partial t} - \Delta u = f \qquad \text{on } \Omega \times (0, T), \tag{5.7}$$

$$\frac{\partial u}{\partial n} + qu = 0 \qquad \text{on } \Gamma \times (0, T) \tag{5.8}$$

$(\partial / \partial n =$ normal derivative to Γ), and

$$u(x, 0) = u_0(x), \qquad x \in \Omega. \tag{5.9}$$

By changing u in $e^{\lambda t} u$, we can always replace $a(t; u, v)$ by $a(t; u, v) + \lambda(u, v)$, $(u, v) = \int_{\Omega} u \bar{v} \, dx$. But

$$\left| \int_{\Gamma} q u \bar{v} \, d\Gamma \right| \leqslant \|u\|_{L_2(\Gamma)} \|v\|_{L_2(\Gamma)}, \tag{5.10}$$

and, for every $\eta > 0$, there exists $c_1(\eta)$ such that

$$\|v\|_{L_2(\Gamma)} \leqslant \eta \|v\| + c_1(\eta) |v|$$

$(\| \ \| =$ norm in V, $| \ | =$ norm in H). Therefore, for every $\eta > 0$ there exists $c_2(\eta)$ such that

$$\left| \int_{\Gamma} q u \bar{v} \, d\Gamma \right| \leqslant \eta \|u\| \|v\| + c_2(\eta) |u| \, |v|, \tag{5.11}$$

and therefore, one can choose λ in such a way that

$$\text{Re } a(t; v, v) + \lambda |v|^2 \geqslant c \|v\|^2, \qquad c > 0, \quad v \in H^1(\Omega) = V$$

and this for every q which satisfies (5.6).

Therefore, to prove that one can apply Theorems 1.1 and 6.1 to the present situation, it remains to check (1.8). As in Section III, we take $W_1 = H^{1+\epsilon}(\Omega)$, $W_2 = H^{1-\epsilon}(\Omega)$, ϵ fixed with $0 < \epsilon < \frac{1}{2}$. But (5.10) implies

$$\left| \int_{\Gamma} q u \bar{v} \, d\sigma \right| \leqslant c' \|u\|_{W_1} \|v\|_{W_2},$$

since
$$\|u\|_{L_2(\Gamma)} \leqslant c''\|u\|_{W_2} \leqslant c'''\|u\|_{W_1};$$
hence the result follows.

VI. A Time-Optimal Problem

A. Setting of the Problem

Let $\mathscr{B}$, F, U_0 be given as in Section I, and let X be a given subset of H, satisfying

$$X \text{ is weakly closed in } H. \tag{6.1}$$

We assume

there exist $A \in \mathscr{B}$, $f \in F$, $u_0 \in U_0$, $\tau \in [0, T]$ such that the corresponding solution u of (1.3)–(1.5) satisfies $u(\tau) \in X$. (6.2)

We set

$$\tau_0 = (\text{optimal time}) = \inf \tau, \text{ when (6.2) holds true.} \tag{6.3}$$

We are going to prove:

Theorem 6.1. *We assume the hypothesis of Theorem 1.1 and conditions (6.1) and (6.2) to be satisfied. Then, there exists* $(A, f, v_0) \in \mathscr{B} \times F \times U_0$ *such that, for the corresponding solution u of (1.3)–(1.5) one has*

$$u(\tau_0) \in X. \tag{6.4}$$

B. Proof of Theorem 6.1

(1) Let $\tau_n \to \tau_0$, such that for every τ_n there exists $(A_n, f_n, u_{0n}) \in \mathscr{B} \times F \times U_0$, satisfying

$$u_n' + A_n(t) u_n = f_n,$$
$$u_n(0) = u_{0n}, \tag{6.5}$$
$$u_n(\tau_n) \in X. \tag{6.6}$$

Since F and U_0 are bounded, we see that

$$u_n \text{ remains in a bounded set of } L_2(0, T; V)$$
$$u_n' \text{ remains in a bounded set of } L_2(0, T; V'), \tag{6.7}$$

and

$$A_n u_n \text{ remains in a bounded set of } L_2(0, T; V'). \tag{6.8}$$

But (6.7) and (12) imply that u_n remains in a bounded set of $L_\infty(0, T; H)$ and therefore that

$$|u_n(\tau_n)| \leqslant \text{constant.} \tag{6.9}$$

It follows from the proof of Theorem 1.1 that we can extract a sequence u_v such that

$$u_v \to u \text{ weakly in } L_2(0, T; V),$$
$$u_v' \to u' \text{ weakly in } L_2(0, T; V'), \tag{6.10}$$
$$A_v u_v \to Au \text{ weakly in } L_2(0, T; V'),$$

and, due to (6.9), we can also assume that

$$u_v(T_v) \to x \text{ weakly,} \qquad x \in X. \tag{6.11}$$

We can assume that $f_v \to f$ in $L_2(0, T; V')$ weakly, $u_{0v} \to u_0$ in H weakly, and then u satisfies

$$A(t)u + u' = f, \qquad u(0) = u_0. \tag{6.12}$$

It only remains to check that

$$u(T_0) = x. \tag{6.13}$$

(2) Let us introduce

$$W_n = \begin{cases} u_n & \text{in} & (0, \tau_n) \\ 0 & \text{in} & (\tau_n, T) \end{cases} \qquad g_n = \begin{cases} f_n & \text{in} & (0, \tau_n) \\ 0 & \text{in} & (\tau_n, T). \end{cases}$$

Then, the derivatives being taken in the sense of vector-valued distributions on $]0, T[$, one has

$$W_n' + A_n(t) W_n = g_n - u_n(\tau_n)\delta(t - \tau_n),$$
$$W_n(0) = u_{0n}, \tag{6.14}$$

where $\delta(t-\tau_n)=$ mass 1 at point τ_n.

We use (6.14) with $n=v$. Since $u_v \to u$ weakly in $L_2(0,T;V)$ and $\tau_v \to \tau_0$, one has

$$w_v \to w = \begin{cases} u & \text{in} & (0,\tau_0) \\ 0 & \text{in} & (\tau_0,T) \end{cases} \text{ weakly in } L_2(0,T;V), \qquad (6.15)$$

and therefore $w_v' \to w'$ in the distributions' sense.

Analogously, $A_v w_v \to Aw$ weakly in $L_2(0,T;V')$ and

$$g_v \to g = \begin{cases} f & \text{in} & (0,\tau_0) \\ 0 & \text{in} & (\tau_0,T) \end{cases} \text{ weakly in } L_2(0,T;V').$$

Therefore,

$$w_v' + A_v(t)w_v - g_v \to w' + A(t)w - g \text{ in the sense of distributions}$$
$$\text{in }]0,T[\text{ with values in } V'. \qquad (6.16)$$

But according to (6.14), $w_v' + A_v(t)w_v - g_v = -u_v(\tau_v)\delta(t-\tau_v)$ and, by (6.11), since $\tau_v \to \tau_0$, one has

$$-u_v(\tau_v)\delta(t-\tau_v) \to -\chi\delta(t-\tau_0)$$

in the sense of distributions with values in H; by comparison with (6.16), we obtain

$$w' + A(t)w = g - \chi\,\delta(t-\tau_0).$$

But according to the definition of $w=u$ in $(0,\tau_0)$, $=0$ in (τ_0,T), one has

$$w' + A(t)w = g - u(\tau_0)\delta(t-\tau_0);$$

hence (6.13) follows.

Remark 6.1. Theorem 6.1 applies, in particular, to the examples of Section V.

Remark 6.2. We already used [Lions (*11*)] reasoning similar to that of (2) to prove a regularity theorem. See also Artola (*1*), Torelli (*19*), and Vallee (*20*).

REFERENCES

1. M. Artola, to appear.
2. J. P. Aubin, Un Théorème de compacité, *Compt. Rend*, **256**, 5042–5044 (1963).
3. A. V. Balakrishnan, Semi-Group Theory and Control Theory, IFIP, New York, May, 1965.

4. A. V. Balakrishnan, Optimal Control Problems in Banach Spaces, *J. SIAM Control* 3, (1965).

5. J. Dixmier, Les Fonctionnelles linéaires sur l'ensemble des opérateurs bornés d'un espace de Hilbert, *Ann. Math.* (2) **51**, 387–408 (1950).

6. Yu. V. Egorov, Conditions nécessaires d'optimalité dans les espaces de Banach, *Mat. Sb.* **106**, 79–101 (1964) (in Russian).

7. H. P. Fattorini, Time Optimal Control of Solutions of Operational Differential Equations, *J. SIAM Control* **A2**, 54–59 (1964).

8. T. Kato, Integration of the Equation of Evolutions in Banach Spaces, *J. Math. Soc. Japan* **5**, 209–304 (1953).

9. T. Kato and H. Tanabe, On the Abstract Evolution Equation, *Osaka Math. J.* **14**, 107–133 (1962).

10. J. L. Lions, "Equations différentielles opérationnelles et problèmes aux limites," Vol. 111. Springer (Collection Jaune), Berlin, 1961.

11. J. L. Lions, Cours CIME, Varenna, May 1963.

12. J. L. Lions, Espaces intermédiaires entre espaces hilbertiens et applications, *Bull. Math. R.P.R., Bucarest* **2**, 419–432 (1958).

13. J. L. Lions and E. Magenes, Problèmes aux limites non homogenes, *Ann. Scuola Norm. Sup. Pisa* **14**, 259–308 (1960).

14. J. L. Lions and J. Peetre, Sur une classe d'espaces d'interpolation. *Publ. Institut des Hautes Etudes Sc., Paris*, No. 19, pp. 5–68, 1964.

15. C. Pucci, Un Problema variazionale, *Ann. Scuola Norm. Sup. Pisa*, **16**, 160–172 (1962).

16. L. Schwartz, "Théorie des distributions," Vol. 2. Hermann, Paris, 1951.

17. L. Schwartz, Théorie des distributions à valeurs vectorielles, *Ann. Inst. Fourier* (I)7, 1–139 (1957); II(8), 1–209 (1958).

18. S. L. Sobolev, "Applications de l'analyse fonctionnelle à la physique mathématique." Leningrad, 1950.

19. G. Torelli, Rend. Sem. Mat. Padova, (1964) XXXIV, 224–241.

20. A. Vallee, *Ann. Scuola Norm. Sup. Pisa* (1965).

NOTE ADDED IN PROOF

Others existence theorems for partial differential equations optimization problems are given in L. Cesari, "Existence theorems for multidimensional problems of optimal control," The Univ. of Michigan Report, March, 1966. The result alluded to in (2) of the Introduction appeared in J. L. Lions, *Ann. di Matematica* LXXII 275–294 (1966).

Controllability and Observability

Institute of Technology, Center for Control Science
Minneapolis, Minnesota

I. Examples of Linear Autonomous Control Processes in Finite- and Infinite-Dimensional Spaces

Consider a linear autonomous control process

$$\mathcal{L}) \quad x(t) = \Phi(t)\,x(0) + \int_0^t \Phi(t-s)\,Bu(s)\,ds.$$

Here $x(t)$ is the state, a point in a vector space $\mathcal{X}$, at each time $t \geqslant 0$, and $u(s)$ is a control value in a vector space $\mathcal{U}$, for each $0 \leqslant s \leqslant t$. The linear dynamics of the process are expressed by the semigroup $\Phi(t)$

$$\Phi(t_1 + t_2) = \Phi(t_1)\,\Phi(t_2) \quad \text{for} \quad t_1 \geqslant 0, \quad t_2 \geqslant 0,$$

of linear transformations of $\mathcal{X}$ into $\mathcal{X}$; see (2, 4). Also B is a linear transformation from $\mathcal{U}$ into $\mathcal{X}$.

For example, the linear differential process

$$\frac{dx}{dt} = Ax + Bu,$$

where $x \in \mathcal{X} = R^n$ and $u \in \mathcal{U} = R^m$ and A and B are constant real matrices, yields the integral description of the process

$$x(t) = e^{At}x(0) + \int_0^t e^{A(t-s)}\,Bu(s)\,ds.$$

Here the semigroup of transformations of R^n into R^n is defined by $\Phi(t) = e^{At}$.

We shall be primarily concerned with this finite-dimensional differential process (in its integral form) with controllers $u(s)$ which are piecewise

133

continuous functions from $0 \leqslant s \leqslant t$ into R^m. However, many of the definitions and results will also hold for infinite-dimensional linear autonomous processes. In this case $\mathcal{X}$ and $\mathcal{U}$ are Banach spaces, and $\Phi(t)x$ is continuous in $t \geqslant 0$ and $x \in \mathcal{X}$, and B is continuous. Also the controllers must be restricted to some class of functions for which the integral is defined; for instance, if $u(s)$ is piecewise continuous from $0 \leqslant s \leqslant t$ into $\mathcal{U}$, then the required integral exists in the sense of Riemann.

Example 1. Consider the control of the temperature $T(t, y)$ for $t \geqslant 0$ on an infinite rod $-\infty < y < \infty$ by a distributed controller $u(t, y)$. The dynamics are determined by the heat partial differential equation

$$\frac{\partial T}{\partial t} = \frac{\partial^2 T}{\partial y^2} + u(t, y).$$

In integral form (which we adopt as the basic control process) we have

$$T(t, y) = \int_{-\infty}^{\infty} H(t, y - \xi) T(0, \xi) \, d\xi + \int_{0}^{t} \int_{-\infty}^{\infty} H(t - \tau, y - \xi) u(\tau, \xi) \, d\xi \, d\tau,$$

where the heat kernel is

$$H(t, y) = (4\pi t)^{-1/2} e^{-y^2/4t} \qquad \text{for} \quad t > 0.$$

The initial temperature $T(0, y)$ is required to lie in the Banach space C_0 of real continuous functions which approach zero as $|y| \to \infty$ (with the uniform norm as usual). The control functions $u(t, y)$ are continuous in $t \geqslant 0$, $-\infty < y < \infty$, and approach zero as $|y| \to \infty$, uniformly on each compact time interval in $t \geqslant 0$.

Now define the state space to be $\mathcal{X} = C_0$, so that $x(t) \in C_0$ is the function $T(t, \cdot)$. We take the control space $\mathcal{U} = C_0$ and then each controller $u(t, y)$ defines a continuous map $t \to u(t)$ of R^1 into $\mathcal{U}$ and every such map is defined by just one controller $u(t, y)$. The semigroup of transformations of C_0 into itself is specified by

$$\Phi(t) x(0) = \int_{-\infty}^{\infty} H(t, y - \xi) T(0, \xi) \, d\xi,$$

which is strongly continuous, and also $\Phi(t)x$ is continuous in (t, x). Thus we obtain the required formula for the temperature distribution,

$$x(t) = \Phi(t)x(0) + \int_0^t \Phi(t-\tau)u(\tau)\,d\tau,$$

and the integral is computed for the continuous function $\Phi(t-\tau)u(\tau)$ from $R^1 \to C_0$, for each fixed $t \geqslant 0$.

Let us note that not every state x_1 is attainable from the initial state $x_0 = 0$ in a finite time, since x_1 must be a C'-differentiable function of y. However, there is a dense set $C_0^\infty \subset C_0$, consisting of C^∞ functions with compact supports, such that each pair $\hat{x}_0$ and $\hat{x}_1$ in C_0^∞ can be joined by a controlled path in C_0^∞. Namely, let $\hat{T}(t, y) = (1-t)\hat{x}_0 + t\hat{x}_1$ and define the required controller by

$$\hat{u}(t, y) = \frac{\partial \hat{T}}{\partial t} - \frac{\partial^2 \hat{T}}{\partial y^2}.$$

Example 2. Consider the linear autonomous functional-differential equation (3)

$$\dot{x}(t) = f(x_t),$$

where f is a continuous linear map of $C([-1, 0], R^n)$ into R^n; that is, for each real n-vector continuous function $x_t(\theta)$ on $-1 \leqslant \theta \leqslant 0$, $f(x_t)$ is a real n-vector.

Let $x(t)$ on $-1 \leqslant t \leqslant t_1$ for $t_1 > 0$ be any vector function. Then $x_t(\theta)$, for $0 \leqslant t \leqslant t_1$, denotes the "unit segment of $x(t)$ ending at t"; that is,

$$x_t(\theta) = x(t+\theta) \qquad \text{on} \quad -1 \leqslant \theta \leqslant 0.$$

A continuous n-vector function $X(t)$ on $-1 \leqslant t \leqslant t_1$ is a solution of the functional-differential equation in case

$$\dot{X}(t) = f(X_t) \qquad \text{on} \quad 0 < t \leqslant t_1,$$

$$X_0(\theta) = \phi(\theta) \qquad \text{on} \quad -1 \leqslant \theta \leqslant 0$$

is a prescribed initial function in $C([-1, 0], R^n)$.

It follows that the differential-difference equation

$$\dot{x}(t) = \sum_{k=1}^p A_k x(t-\tau_k)$$

for constant coefficient matrices A_k and constant delays $0 \leqslant \tau_k \leqslant 1$, and also the differential-renewal equation

$$\dot{x}(t) = \int_{-1}^{0} A(\theta) x(t + \theta) \, d\theta$$

for integrable $A(\theta)$, are special cases of linear autonomous functional-differential equations.

A linear autonomous functional-differential equation

$$\dot{x}(t) = f(x_t)$$

with initial function $\phi(\theta)$ has a unique solution $X(t)$ on $-1 \leqslant t < \infty$. Furthermore, $X_t(\theta) = X(t + \theta)$ is determined from the initial data $X_0 = \phi$ by the bounded linear transformation $\mathscr{J}(t)$ of the Banach space $C([-1,0], R^n)$ into itself,

$$X_t(\cdot) = \mathscr{J}(t) X_0(\cdot) \qquad \text{for} \quad t \geqslant 0.$$

Also $\mathscr{J}(t)$ is strongly continuous for each $t \geqslant 0$ [even $\mathscr{J}(t)\phi$ is continuous in (t, ϕ)] and the family of transformations $\{\mathscr{J}(t)\}$ is a semigroup.

Now consider the linear autonomous functional control process

$$\partial x(0, t)/\partial t = f(x(\cdot, t)) + Bu(t),$$

where $x(\theta, t) \in C([-1,0], R^n)$ for each $t \geqslant 0$ is the state, $u(t) \in R^m$ is a continuous controller vanishing for $t \leqslant 0$, and B is a real constant matrix. Again f is a continuous linear map from $C([-1,0], R^n)$ into R^n, and the initial state is $x(\theta, 0) = \phi(\theta)$. Then a solution $x(\cdot, t)$ is defined by

$$x(\cdot, t) = \mathscr{J}(t)\phi + \int_{0}^{t} \mathscr{J}(t-s) Bu_s(\cdot) \, ds,$$

which we now use as the primary description of the control process. Note that the integrand $\mathscr{J}(t-s) Bu_s(\cdot)$ is a continuous function of s with values in the Banach space $C([-1,0], R^n)$, for each fixed $t \geqslant 0$. Thus $x(\cdot, t)$ is a continuous function of t with values in $C([-1,0], R^n)$ and $x(\cdot, 0) = \phi$.

To verify this formula for the solution $x(\cdot, t)$ note that

$$X(t) = \mathscr{J}(t)\phi \qquad \text{at} \quad \theta = 0$$

is the solution of the homogeneous functional-differential equation

$$\dot{x}(t) = f(x_t).$$

Therefore, for $t \geqslant 0$ (with a right derivative at $t=0$),

$$\partial/\partial t[\mathscr{J}(t)\phi]_{\theta=0} = f(\mathscr{J}(t)\phi_0).$$

Similarly, for $t-s \geqslant 0$,

$$\partial/\partial t[\mathscr{J}(t-s)Bu_s(\cdot)]_{\theta=0} = f(\mathscr{J}(t-s)Bu_s(\cdot)).$$

Thus we compute, after fixing $\theta=0$,

$$\frac{\partial}{\partial t}x(0,t) = f(\mathscr{J}(t)\phi_0) + \int_0^t f(\mathscr{J}(t-s)Bu_s(\cdot))\,ds + \mathscr{J}(0)Bu_t(0)$$

or

$$\frac{\partial}{\partial t}x(0,t) = f(x(\cdot,t)) + Bu(t).$$

Thus the function control process is

$$x(\cdot,t) = \mathscr{J}(t)x(\cdot,0) + \int_0^t \mathscr{J}(t-s)Bu_s(\cdot)\,ds,$$

where the state space $\mathscr{X} = C([-1,0], R^n)$ and the control space $\mathscr{U} = C([-1,0], R^m)$. The semigroup $\{\mathscr{J}(t)\}$ describes the dynamics of the process.

We note finally that the control function $t \rightarrow u_t(\cdot)$ need not be selected from the segments of an m-vector function $u(t)$, and furthermore the response $x(\cdot,t)$ does not arise from the segments of an n-vector function. That is, in general,

$$x(\theta,t) \neq x(0,t+\theta),$$

and the functional control process does not coincide with any nonhomogeneous functional-differential equation.

Not every state $\psi(\theta) \in C([-1,0], R^n)$ is necessarily attainable from some initial $\phi(\theta)$ after a time $t = t_1 > 1$; for instance, if $B=0$, then every attainable state $\psi(\theta)$ is in $C^1([-1.0], R^n)$.

II. Controllability and Observability for Finite-Dimensional
Linear Autonomous Processes

In this section we consider the qualitative features of a control process described by an ordinary linear autonomous differential system in R^n,

$$\mathscr{L}) \quad \dot{x} = Ax + Bu$$

or

$$x(t) = e^{At}x_0 + \int_0^t e^{A(t-s)} Bu(s)\, ds,$$

where A is a real constant $n \times n$ matrix and B is a real constant $n \times m$ matrix. The control functions $u(t)$ will be piecewise continuous m-vectors on finite time intervals.

Definition. The linear control process in R^n,

$$\mathscr{L}) \quad \dot{x} = Ax + Bu$$

is (completely) controllable in case: For each pair of points x_0 and $x_1 \in R^n$ there is a controller $u(t)$ on some finite time duration $0 \leqslant t \leqslant t_1$ which steers the response $x(t)$ on $0 \leqslant t \leqslant t_1$ from $x(0) = x_0$ to $x(t_1) = x_1$.

It is known (7) that $\mathscr{L}$ is controllable if and only if the $n \times nm$ controllability matrix has maximal rank, i.e.,

$$\text{rank}[B, AB, A^2B, \ldots, A^{n-1}B] = n.$$

In this case the origin of R^n can be steered to every point of R^n by a continuous controller in a unit time interval.

Definition. The linear control process in R^n,

$$\mathscr{L}) \quad \dot{x} = Ax + Bu,$$

with the output specified by

$$\omega = Hx$$

for an $r \times n$ real constant matrix H, is (completely) observable in case: With the null control $u(t) \equiv 0$, two outputs $\omega_0(t)$ and $\omega_1(t)$ coincide on $t \geqslant 0$ just in case the corresponding states $x_0(t)$ and $x_1(t)$ coincide on $t \geqslant 0$.

Thus the process $\mathscr{L}$, with the output observation $\omega = Hx$, is observable if and only $He^{At}x_0 \equiv 0$ for $t \geqslant 0$ implies that $x_0 = 0$.

It is known (6) that the observed process $\mathscr{L}$ is observable if and only if the $n \times nm$ observability matrix has maximal rank, that is,

$$\operatorname{rank}[H', A'H', A'^2 H', \ldots, A'^{n-1}H'] = n,$$

where A' and H' are the transposes of A and H, respectively.

Consider the linear observed process in R^n,

$$\mathscr{L})\quad \dot{x} = Ax + Bu$$

and output

$$\omega = Hx.$$

Consider the real linear space $\mathscr{I}$ of all piecewise continuous controllers or inputs $u(t)$ in R^m, which vanish outside some compact interval $-t_1 \leqslant t \leqslant 0$. For each such input $u(t) \in \mathscr{I}$ there is an output $\omega(t)$ on $0 \leqslant t < \infty$, corresponding to a response $x(t)$ initiating at $x(-\infty) = 0$. Thus the correspondence

$$u(t) \rightarrow \omega(t)$$

determines a linear transformation τ of $\mathscr{I}$ into the real vector space $C([0, \infty), R^n)$.

Definition. Consider the linear observed process in R^n,

$$\mathscr{L})\quad \dot{x} = Ax + Bu$$

and output

$$\omega = Hx.$$

The linear transformation

$$\tau \colon \mathscr{I} \rightarrow C([0, \infty), R^n)$$

is the input-output relation of $\mathscr{L}$.

The input-output relation τ of $\mathscr{L}$ is a form of transfer function and it describes the experimentally observable aspects of $\mathscr{L}$. The following theorem, which has been proved in a slightly different form (6), shows that the transfer function τ characterizes the process $\mathscr{L}$.

Theorem 1. *Consider the linear observed process in R^n,*

$$\mathscr{L}) \quad \dot{x} = Ax + Bu$$

and output

$$\omega = Hx,$$

with input-output relation

$$\tau : \mathscr{I} \to C([0, \infty), R^n).$$

Then there exists a unique linear observed process in R^n,

$$\hat{\mathscr{L}}) \quad \dot{\hat{x}} = \hat{A}\hat{x} + \hat{B}u$$

and output

$$\omega = \hat{H}\hat{x}$$

such that

(1) *$\hat{\mathscr{L}}$ is completely controllable and observable, and*

(2) *$\hat{\mathscr{L}}$ has the same input-output relation τ.*

Proof. First let $C \subset R^n$ be the linear subspace of all points of R^n to which the origin can be steered by a continuous controller in a finite time. Then, as it is easy to show, C is an invariant subspace (any response meeting C lies in C for all times) and we consider the restriction of $\mathscr{L}$ to C.

$$\mathscr{L}_c) \quad \dot{x}_c = A_c x_c + B_c u$$

with the same output,

$$\omega = Hx_c.$$

Then $\mathscr{L}_c$ is controllable on C and has the prescribed input-output relation τ.

Now consider the free system $\mathscr{L}_c$ with $u(t) \equiv 0$ and let $C_0 \subset C$ consist of those initial states for which $\omega(t) = 0$ on $t \geq 0$. Then C_0 is a linear subspace of C and we identify two states of C in case their difference lies in C_0; that is, consider the factor space C/C_0. Let us partition the coordinates of x_c by a direct sum decomposition of C into $\binom{x_a}{x_b}$, where $x_b = 0$ on C_0. Then, after an appropriate linear coordinate change in C, the controllable process can be written

$$\mathscr{L}_c) \quad \dot{x}_a = A_{aa} x_a + A_{ab} x_b + B_a u,$$

$$\dot{x}_b = A_{bb} x_b + B_b u,$$

and

$$\omega = H_b x_b.$$

Suppose $(x_1 - x_2) \in C_0$ and consider the corresponding responses $x_1(t)$ and $x_2(t)$ for an arbitrary piecewise continuous controller $u(t)$ on $0 \leqslant t \leqslant t_1$. Then

$$\dot{x}_{1b}(t) - \dot{x}_{2b}(t) = A_{bb}(x_{1b}(t) - x_{2b}(t))$$

and so

$$x_{1b}(t) - x_{2b}(t) \equiv 0$$

and

$$x_1(t) - x_2(t) \in C_0.$$

This means that the cosets of C_0, or the points of the factor space C/C_0, are respected by the responses of $\mathscr{L}_c$ to arbitrary controllers.

Hence we can consider the quotient system

$$\mathscr{L}) \quad \dot{x}_b = A_{bb}x_b + B_b u$$

and

$$\omega = H_b x_b.$$

The quotient space $R^{\hat{n}} = C/C_0$ admits the coordinates $\hat{x} = x_b$ and the projected control system is $\mathscr{L}$ (after the indicated change of notation). Of course, the zero coset of C/C_0 can be steered to an arbitrary coset and so $\mathscr{L}$ is controllable on $R^{\hat{n}}$. By the identifications introduced in C/C_0, the process $\mathscr{L}$ is observable. Since ω depends only on x_b for the process $\mathscr{L}_c$, the input-output relation of $\mathscr{L}$ is just τ.

We next prove the uniqueness of the observable, controllable process $\mathscr{L}$ with input-output relation τ. Of course, the uniqueness of $\mathscr{L}$ is required only up to an automorphism, or nonsingular linear coordinate transformation, in the state space $R^{\hat{n}}$.

Let another observable controllable process be

$$\overline{\mathscr{L}}) \quad \dot{\bar{x}} = \bar{A}\bar{x} + \bar{B}u,$$

$$\omega = \bar{H}\bar{x}$$

in the state space $R^{\bar{n}}$, with input-output relation τ. For both $\mathscr{L}$ and $\overline{\mathscr{L}}$ we use the input-output relation τ to define the quotient space $\mathscr{I}/\mathscr{I}_0$, where $\mathscr{I}_0$ consists of those controllers on finite intervals $-t_1 \leqslant t \leqslant 0$ for which the output $\omega(t) \equiv 0$ on $t \geqslant 0$. Since $\mathscr{L}$ and $\overline{\mathscr{L}}$ are both controllable and observable, $\mathscr{I}/\mathscr{I}_0$ is isomorphic with $R^{\hat{n}}$ and with $R^{\bar{n}}$. Hence $\hat{n} = \bar{n}$ and we use the above isomorphisms to denote $R^{\hat{n}}$ and $R^{\bar{n}}$ as the same state space $\mathscr{I}/\mathscr{I}_0$. But the action of a controller $\tilde{u}(t)$ on $0 \leqslant t \leqslant \bar{t}$ on a point $\{u_0(t)\} \in \mathscr{I}/\mathscr{I}_0$ can be computed to be the (coset of the) concatenation

$$u_0(t+\bar{t}) \qquad \text{on} \quad -t_0 - \bar{t} \leqslant t \leqslant -\bar{t},$$

$$\tilde{u}(t+\bar{t}) \qquad \text{on} \quad -\bar{t} \leqslant t \leqslant 0.$$

Since this action coincides with the response movement in the state spaces $R^{\hat{n}}$ and $R^{\bar{n}}$, we conclude that $\mathscr{L}$ and $\bar{\mathscr{L}}$ are identical after the above isomorphism of state spaces has been introduced.

Q.E.D.

III. Controllability of Finite-Dimensional Nonlinear Autonomous Processes

We consider a nonlinear control process

$$\mathscr{S}) \qquad \dot{x} = f(x,u)$$

with $f(x,u)$ in C' for all $x \in R^n$ and u in R^m. We seek to steer an initial state $x_0 \in R^n$ to the origin $x_1 = 0$ by a continuous controller $u(t)$ on a finite time duration $0 \leqslant t \leqslant t_1$. It is easy to prove the following result.

Theorem 2. *Consider the control process in* R^n,

$$\mathscr{S}) \quad \dot{x} = f(x,u) \qquad in \ C' \quad in \ R^{+m} \ .$$

Assume

(1) $f(0,0) = 0$,

(2) $\text{rank}[B, AB, A^2 B, \ldots, A^{n-1} B] = n$,

where $A = \partial f(0,0)/\partial x$ *and* $B = \partial f(0,0)/\partial u$. *Then for each neighborhood* U *of* $u = 0$ *in* R^m *there is a neighborhood* N *of* $x_1 = 0$ *in* R^n *such that each initial state* $x_0 \in N$ *can be steered to* $x_1 = 0$ *by a continuous controller* $u(t)$ *in* U *on* $0 \leqslant t \leqslant 1$.

The demonstration of Theorem 2 follows the methods utilized in the nonlinear bang-bang theorem, 3, which is proved elsewhere (8).

Theorem 3. *Consider the control process in* R^n,

$$\mathscr{S}) \quad \dot{x} = f(x,u) \qquad in \ C' \quad in \ R^{n+m}$$

with

$$f(0,0) = 0$$

and

$$\text{rank}[B, AB, \ldots, A^{n-1} B] = n.$$

Let π be a fixed convex polytope about the origin in R^m. Then there exists an $\epsilon > 0$ and a neighborhood N of $x_1 = 0$ in R^n such that: Each initial state $x_0 \in N$ can be steered to $x_1 = 0$ by a measurable controller $u(t)$ on $0 \leqslant t \leqslant 1$ with values only in the finite set of vertices of the similar polytope $\epsilon\pi$.

The proof of this theorem uses the result of A. Liapounov on the convexity of the range of a vector measure, and combines this bang-bang theorem for linear processes with standard approximation and continuity techniques for nonlinear differential systems.

ACKNOWLEDGMENT

This research was supported by NONR Grant 3776-(00).

REFERENCES

1. A. Balakrishnan, Optimal Control Problems in Banach Spaces, *J. SIAM Control* **3**, 152–180 (1965).
2. A. Balakrishnan, Semigroup Theory and Control Theory, *Proc. IFIP*, Spartan Books, Washington, D.C., 1965.
3. J. Hale, Linear Functional-Differential Equations with Constant Coefficients. *Contrib. Differential Eqs.* **2**, 291–317 (1963).
4. E. Hille and R. Phillips, Functional Analysis and Semigroup Theory, AMS Colloq. Publ., 1957.
5. R. Kalman, On the General Theory of Control Systems, *Proc. IFAC*, 481–492 (1960).
6. R. Kalman, Canonical Structure of Linear Dynamical Systems, *Proc. Natl. Acad. Sci.* **48**, 596–600 (1962).
7. R. Kalman, Y. Ho, and K. Narenda, Controllability of Linear Dynamical Systems, *Contrib. Differential Eqs.* **1**, 189–213 (1962).
8. L. Markus, Controllability of Nonlinear Processes, *J. SIAM Control* **3**, 78–90 (1965).
9. W. Miranker, Approximate Controllability for Distributed Linear Systems. *J. Math. Anal. Appl.* **10**, 378–387 (1965).

Convexity and Duality

J. J. Moreau

Faculté des Sciences, University of Montpellier
Montpellier, France

I. Introduction

A. Duality

Let us first explain, by a simple example, how the consideration of *duality* in some convex optimization problems may lead to a localization of the unknowns, possibly useful in numerical treatments.

B. The Two-Cones Theorem

Let H be a real Hilbert space; the scalar product of two elements x and y of H will be denoted $(x|y)$.

Let $P \subset H$ be a *closed convex cone* (with vertex at the origin). As this set is convex, it is equivalent to say it is closed with respect to the strong or weak topology.

The *polar cone* of P will be denoted by Q; i.e.,

$$Q = \{y \in H : (x|y) \leqslant 0 \quad \text{for every } x \in P\},$$

and it is well known that P is, conversely, the polar cone of Q. This symmetry of the relationship between P and Q results from the fact that in H and, more generally, in any locally convex Hausdorff linear space, every closed convex set equals the intersection of the closed half-spaces containing it.

Let z be an arbitrary point of H. It is known that the distance $\|z - u\|$, for u ranging over a closed convex set such as P, always attains its infimum for a unique u, usually called the *projection* of z on the set. Denote by

$$x = \text{proj}_P z \tag{1.1}$$

145

this proximal point of z in P and, similarly, put

$$y = \text{proj}_Q z. \tag{1.2}$$

Then it is proved in Moreau (*1, 17*) that

$$z = x+y, \tag{1.3}$$

$$(x|y) = 0, \tag{1.4}$$

and, conversely, the properties (1.3) and (1.4) imply (1.1) and (1.2); i.e., the projections x and y embody the unique decomposition of z into the sum of two *orthogonal* elements belonging to P and Q, respectively. In particular, if z lies in P or Q, its projection on the other cone is the origin.

This result may be regarded as a generalization of the classical decomposition of the Hilbert space H into the direct sum of two orthogonal complementary subspaces. For, if the convex cone P is a closed subspace of H, the polar cone is in fact the orthogonal complementary subspace.

The reader may construct simple examples of the preceding situation by taking as H the usual tridimensional Euclidean vector space. On the other hand, a functional example will be given later.

The idea of duality in convex optimization problems in now classical. Here and in Section V the specific feature is that the elements of two problems essentially belong to the same self-dual space; so the pair of dual problems turns to be equivalent to a *decomposition problem*.

C. LOCALIZATION OF THE UNKNOWNS

The preceding duality-decomposition theory involves two optimization problems. Let us consider the first one: given z in H, to find x in P where the numerical function $u \to \|z-u\|$ attains its minimum (equivalently, the square $\|z-u\|^2$ may be considered, so that the problem appears as a quadratic programming problem).

In some applications, computation of only the minimal value $\|z-x\|$ is required. Clearly, for every $u \in P$, the distance $\|z-u\|$ gives an upper estimate of this numerical unknown. To test how good this estimate is, a lower estimate is needed. Now, for every $v \in Q$, the distance $\|z-v\|$ gives an upper estimate of $\|z-y\|$. And, from the orthogonality relation (1.4) follows the Pythagorean equality

$$\|z-x\|^2 + \|z-y\|^2 = \|z\|^2,$$

by which any upper estimate of $\|z-y\|$ leads to a lower estimate of $\|z-x\|$.

In other applications, the very localization of the proximal point x is needed. Then one remarks that the projection mapping $z \to \text{proj}_P z$ is contractive; i.e., if z_1 is another point of H and $x_1 = \text{proj}_P z_1$, one has

$$\|x-x_1\| \leqslant \|z-z_1\|.$$

If z_1 and x_1 are known, this inequality localizes the unknown x in the ball of center x_1 with the known radius $\|z-z_1\|$. The practical problem is to find a point z_1 whose projection x_1 is known. By the two-cones theorem this problem reduces to that of finding two orthogonal elements x_1 and y_1, respectively, in P and Q and taking $z_1 = x_1 + y_1$. The functional example developed below shows that, in some cases, constructing such a pair x_1, y_1 may be easy.

In the special case of linear variational problems of mathematical physics, similar ideas were developed under the name "hypercircle method" by Prager and Synge (*1*) and Synge (*1*); in that linear case, projections are made on two orthogonal linear manifolds of the Hilbert space. Concerning the principle of this method, see also Courant and Hilbert (*1*) and Diaz (*1*).

D. A FUNCTIONAL EXAMPLE

Let us take as H the space $L^2(E_n, \mathbf{E}_n)$ of the (classes of) vector fields defined on the n-dimensional Euclidean space E_n which are measurable and whose square is summable with respect to Lebesgue measure on E_n. If x and y are two such vector fields, let us denote by $\mathbf{x}(\xi)$ and $\mathbf{y}(\xi)$ the values they take at the point ξ of E_n; these values are elements of the Euclidean vector space $\mathbf{E}_n$ associated with E_n (free vectors). The scalar product in $\mathbf{E}_n$ being denoted by $\cdot$, the scalar product of x and y in H is defined as

$$(x|y) = \int_{E_n} \mathbf{x}(\xi) \cdot \mathbf{y}(\xi) \, d\xi.$$

Denote by P_0 the subset of H whose elements are indefinitely differentiable vector fields with nonnegative divergence. Denote by Q_0 the subset of H consisting of the vector fields having the form grad p, where p is a nonnegative indefinitely differentiable numerical function with compact support. Clearly these two sets are convex cones. If $x \in P_0$ and grad $p = y \in Q_0$, an integration by parts gives

$$(x|y) = \int_{E_n} \mathbf{x} \cdot \mathbf{grad}\, p\, d\xi = -\int_{E_n} p\, \mathrm{div}\, \mathbf{x}\, d\xi \leqslant 0. \qquad (1.5)$$

So each of the two cones P_0 and Q_0 is contained in the polar of the other. Using the regularization technique (convolution with a sequence of indefinitely differentiable nonnegative functions on E_n whose integrals equal 1 and whose supports shrink to the origin) it can be proved that the (strong or weak) closures P and Q of P_0 and Q_0 form a pair of two mutually polar cones.

P is simply the set of the vector fields $x \in H$ whose divergence, in the sense of the theory of distributions, is a positive distribution (i.e., a positive measure). Interpretation of the set Q is more complicated. Every $y \in Q$ is the distribution gradient of a function p which, in the weak sense, may be said to be "positive, null at infinity." If $n \geqslant 3$ (to permit use of Sobolev's inequality) the function p belongs to L^q with $q = 2n/(n-2)$. When such a function is continuous, it is in fact nonnegative.

For a given z in H, the problem of finding its proximal point x in P and its proximal point y in Q possesses one and only one solution. These elements x and y satisfy the decomposition relation (1.3) and the orthogonality relation (1.4).

If z is sufficiently smooth, x and y form *strong solutions* of the two projection problems; i.e., x is a continuously differentiable vector field on E_n, y is the gradient of a continuously differentiable numerical function p, and this x and this p go to zero at infinity in such a way that an integration by parts similar to (1.5) holds. So the orthogonality condition (1.4) becomes

$$\int_{E_n} p\, \mathrm{div}\, \mathbf{x}\, d\xi = 0.$$

By the continuity and the nonnegativity of p and of $\mathrm{div}\, \mathbf{x}$, this is equivalent to

$$p\, \mathrm{div}\, \mathbf{x} = 0 \qquad (1.6)$$

at any point of E_n. In this property lies the interest of this functional example for hydrodynamical applications [inception of cavitation; see Moreau (*15, 18*)]. For the present purpose one remarks that the alternative form (1.6) of the orthogonality relation (1.4) permits easy construction of pairs x_1, y_1 in order to apply the localization technique of Section I.C.

E. An Alternative Optimization Problem

When the given vector field z is differentiable and so smooth that x and y yield a strong solution in the sense defined above, the couple of problems under consideration turns to be equivalent to another optimization problem of a quite different type: *constructing a hull*. By a hull of a given function f is meant the function (if it exists) which, among a given set of functions, is the greatest minorant of f.

As a matter of fact, if x and $y = \operatorname{grad} p$ form a strong solution of the preceding problems, we have the decomposition relation (1.3)

$$\mathbf{x} + \operatorname{\mathbf{grad}} p = \mathbf{z} \tag{1.7}$$

together with

$$p \geqslant 0, \tag{1.8}$$

$$\operatorname{div} \mathbf{x} \geqslant 0, \tag{1.9}$$

and, again, (1.6). Besides, we assume that p goes uniformly to zero at infinity. Let us consider a continuous function f such that

$$\Delta f = \operatorname{div} \mathbf{z}$$

(it may be constructed as a potential). Take as a new unknown function

$$\phi = f - p.$$

conditions (1.6) to (1.9) are then rewritten in the equivalent form

$$\phi \leqslant f,$$

$$\Delta \phi \geqslant 0,$$

$$(f - \phi) \Delta \phi = 0,$$

$$f - \phi \to 0 \qquad \text{at infinity.}$$

In other words, ϕ is a continuous subharmonic minorant of the known function f and this minorant is harmonic in the open set ω, where if differs from f. Let Φ be another continuous subharmonic minorant of f. The difference $\Phi - \phi$ is continuous, subharmonic in ω, nonpositive on the complement of ω; at infinity this difference becomes uniformly less than any $\epsilon > 0$. By the properties of subharmonic functions, this proves $\Phi - \phi \leqslant 0$ everywhere in E_n. So ϕ is the *greatest continuous subharmonic minorant* of f.

II. Polar of a Given Function

A. Affine Minorants of a Function

Let X be a real topological linear space and let X' be its topological dual. Any *continuous affine function* defined on X is written

$$X \ni x \to \langle x, y \rangle - \alpha \in \mathbf{R} \tag{2.1}$$

with $\alpha \in \mathbf{R}$ and $y \in X'$; the element y will be called the *slope* of the affine function.

Let f be a numerical function on X, i.e., a mapping of X into $\overline{\mathbf{R}} = [-\infty, +\infty]$ ($-\infty$ and $+\infty$ included). We are concerned with the continuous affine functions which are *minorants* of f. Clearly the affine function written in (2.1) is such a minorant if and only if

$$\alpha \geqslant \sup \{\langle x, y \rangle - f(x) : x \in X\}. \tag{2.2}$$

The values of x such that $f(x) = +\infty$ may indifferently be omitted in constructing this supremum; note that if f takes at some point of X the value $-\infty$, the supremum will be $+\infty$.

The right member of the inequality (2.2) is denoted by $f^*(y)$; the numerical function f^* defined thereby on X' is called the *polar function* of f.

f possesses continuous affine minorants of a given slope y if and only if $f^*(y) \neq +\infty$; among them the greatest one is the function

$$x \to \langle x, y \rangle - f^*(y). \tag{2.3}$$

The supremum of all the continuous affine minorants of f will be called the *Γ-regularized* of f. Clearly this supremum may be constructed by considering only the *maximal* minorant such as (2.3); thus the Γ-regularized of f is

$$f^{**}(x) = \sup \{\langle x, y \rangle - f^*(y) : y \in X'\}$$

or *bipolar* function of f.

B. The Functional Set $\Gamma(X)$

The denomination Γ-regularized comes from this general notation:

We denote by $\Gamma(X)$ the totality of the numerical functions defined on X which are equal to the supremum of a family of continuous affine functions.

Clearly f^{**} is the largest function in $\Gamma(X)$ which minores f; in particular, f belongs to $\Gamma(X)$ if and only if $f=f^{**}$.

An important fact is that if the topological linear space X is *locally convex and Hausdorff*, the set $\Gamma(X)$ consists of the following parts:

(1) The totality of the functions, taking values in $]-\infty, +\infty]$ (i.e., nowhere taking the value $-\infty$) which are *convex and lower semicontinuous*.

(2) The constant function $-\infty$ (it is the supremum of an empty family of continuous affine functions!).

This is easily proved by standard separation techniques. In the following we are only concerned with locally convex Hausdorff spaces, so that this description of the set $\Gamma(X)$ might be taken as a definition.

Example. To any subset A of X let us associate its *indicatrix function* ψ_A defined by

$$\psi_A(x) = \begin{cases} 0 & \text{if } x \in A, \\ +\infty & \text{if } x \notin A. \end{cases}$$

Then (X being assumed locally convex and Hausdorff) ψ_A belongs to $\Gamma(X)$ if and only if A is *closed and convex*.

The polar function of ψ_A,

$$\psi_A^*(y) = \sup\{\langle x, y \rangle - \psi_A(x): x \in X\}$$
$$= \sup\{\langle x, y \rangle : x \in A\},$$

is well known under the rather improper name of *support function* of the set A. Actually a continuous affine function

$$x \to \langle x, y \rangle - \alpha$$

is a minorant of ψ_A if and only if the closed half-space

$$\{x \in X: \langle x, y \rangle - \alpha \leqslant 0\}$$

contains A. For any y such that $\psi_A^*(y) \neq +\infty$, the *maximal affine minorant of ψ_A having this y as slope*, i.e., the function

$$x \to \langle x, y \rangle - \psi_A^*(y),$$

defines in this way a closed half-space which is *minimal* (with respect to the inclusion order) in the family of the closed half-spaces containing A. But such a minimal half-space is not necessarily a "supporting half-space"; i.e., its limiting closed hyperplane does not necessarily contain a point of A. In other words, this hyperplane is not necessarily a supporting hyperplane of A even if this set is closed and convex.

III. Dual Functions

A. Linear Spaces in Duality

To develop a duality theory in which two linear spaces play perfectly symmetric parts, let us slightly change our standpoint.

Let X and Y be two linear spaces *put in duality* by the bilinear form $\langle .,. \rangle$. That means that the bilinear form satisfies the following separation hypothesis: For any $x \neq 0$ in X, there exists $y \in Y$ such that $\langle x,y \rangle \neq 0$ and, symmetrically, for any $y \neq 0$ in Y, there exists $x \in X$ such that $\langle x,y \rangle \neq 0$.

It is well known that each of the two spaces, say, for instance, X, may be provided with various locally convex Hausdorff topologies which are compatible with the duality; i.e., with respect to those topologies, the totality of the continuous linear functions consists of the functions

$$X \ni x \to \langle x,y \rangle \qquad (y \in Y).$$

Then Y may be identified with the topological dual of X. Among these topologies, the weakest one is the *weak topology*, denoted by $\sigma(X, Y)$, and the strongest one is the *Mackey topology*, denoted by $\tau(X, Y)$.

Note that if a *nonreflexive Banach space* is taken as X and its dual as Y, the norm topology (or strong topology) on Y is *not* compatible with the duality. If, on the contrary, X is a *reflexive* Banach space, the Mackey topologies $\tau(X, Y)$ on X and $\tau(Y, X)$ on the dual Y are, respectively, the norm topologies on these two spaces.

From the definition of the functional sets $\Gamma(X)$ and $\Gamma(Y)$ it follows that these sets are the same for all the topologies which are compatible with the duality. So is, classically, the family of the subsets of X (resp. Y) which are closed and convex.

B. Dual Functions and Conjugate Points

If $f \in \Gamma(X)$ and $g \in \Gamma(Y)$ it follows from Section II.A that the relation $f^* = g$ is equivalent to $f = g^*$. In that symmetric case f and g are called *dual* *functions.* So the star defines a one-to-one correspondence between $\Gamma(X)$ and $\Gamma(Y)$.

From the definition of * it arises that, for any x in X and any y in Y, the inequality

$$f(x)+g(y) \geq \langle x,y \rangle \tag{3.1}$$

holds. If the equality

$$f(x)+g(y) = \langle x,y \rangle \tag{3.2}$$

is attained, x and y are said to be *conjugate* with respect to the pair of dual functions f and g. This equality may be interpreted as follows: The maximal continuous affine minorant of slope y for the function f, the affine function

$$u \rightarrow \langle u,y \rangle - g(y)$$

[note that equality (3.2) implies that $g(y)$ is finite], is also written by (3.2),

$$u \rightarrow \langle u-x,y \rangle + f(x).$$

This shows that y is the slope of a continuous affine minorant of f which takes the same value as f at the point x (minorant said to be "exact" at the point x). The set of such $y \in Y$ associated with some $x \in X$ is called the *subgradient (or subdifferential) of f at the point x* and denoted $\partial f(x)$. By writing alternatively

$$\partial f(x) = \{y \in Y : g(y) - \langle x,y \rangle \leq -f(x)\},$$

it is shown that $\partial f(x)$ is a closed convex set (possibly empty) in X, since the function

$$y \rightarrow g(y) - \langle x,y \rangle$$

is convex and lower semicontinuous.

In short, the equality (3.2) may equivalently be written $y \in \partial f(x)$ or, symmetrically, $x \in \partial g(y)$.

If the set $\partial f(x)$ is not empty, the function f is said to be *subdifferentiable* at the point x.

From the bibliographical standpoint, an early source of the idea of dual functions, for $X = Y = \mathbf{R}^n$, may be seen in the *Legendre transform*, used in the elementary theory of partial differential equations (without reference to convexity). Another classical concept is that of *Young's conjugate functions* [see, e.g., Birnbaum and Orlicz (*1*)], which are convex and increasing functions defined on $[0, +\infty[$. Similarly, for conjugate convex functions defined on **R**, see Mandelbrojt (*1*).

Conjugate convex functions in $\mathbf{R}^n$ appear in Fenchel (*1*) and are applied to convex programming theory in Fenchel (*2*), Karlin (*1*), and Rockafellar (*1*). Extension of Fenchel's ideas to topological linear spaces was initiated by Jones (*1*) and Broensted (*1*). The somewhat different standpoint presented here appears in Moreau (*2*) and has been widely developed by Rockafellar, Broensted, and the author.

Concerning conjugate functions defined on the positive orthant of $\mathbf{R}^n$, see also several papers of Bellman and Karush [e.g., (*1, 2*)].

C. SOME PROPERTIES OF THE SUBGRADIENTS

The concept of subdifferentiability appears to be interesting in convex optimization problems because of the following. From the definition of dual functions, one has

$$\inf\{g(y): y \in Y\} = -f(0),$$

and the set of the points in Y where g attains this infimum is the subgradient $\partial f(0)$. In other words, the function $g \in \Gamma(Y)$ possesses a minimum if and only if its dual f is subdifferentiable at the origin of X.

We now give a usual case of subdifferentiability: If the function $f \in \Gamma(X)$ is finite and *continuous* at the point x_0 (for some topology compatible with the duality and, therefore for the Mackey topology, which is the strongest one), then the set $\partial f(x_0)$ *is nonempty and weakly compact in* Y. This may be derived from the following property, which plays an important part in the whole theory: The function $f \in \Gamma(X)$ is finite and continuous at the origin of X for the Mackey topology $\tau(X, Y)$ if and only if its dual $g \in \Gamma(Y)$ is *weakly inf-compact*; i.e., for any $k \in \mathbf{R}$ the set

$$\{y \in Y: g(y) \leqslant k\}$$

is compact (possibly empty) with respect to the weak topology $\sigma(Y,X)$. A similar criterium is deduced, by translation, for the continuity of f at another point of X [see the proofs in Moreau (*13*)].

Among the computational rules of the subgradients, let us note that if

f_1 and f_2 are in $\Gamma(X)$, so is the sum f_1+f_2 (in the special case where one of the functions is the constant $-\infty$, the sum must be understood as $-\infty$), and the inclusion

$$\partial(f_1+f_2)(x) \supset \partial f_1(x)+\partial f_2(x) \tag{3.3}$$

holds for any $x \in X$. This simply follows from the fact that, taking continuous affine minorants of f_1 and f_2, respectively, which are both *exact* at the point x, and adding them, one obtains a continuous affine minorant of f_1+f_2 which is also exact at this point.

A sufficient condition for equality of the two members in the inclusion (3.3) is the existence of a point x_0 in X where *one of the two functions takes a finite value while the other is finite and continuous at this point* (with respect to some topology compatible with the duality); the proof will be given in Section III.B.

Among other applications, this result is used to elucidate the relationship between the subgradient of a continuous function and the *directional derivatives or Gâteaux differential* [see Moreau (*11, 13*)]: Let $f \in \Gamma(X)$ be finite and continuous at the point x. Let u be an element of X. The function of the variable $t \in \mathbf{R}$ defined by

$$t \to f(x+tu)$$

is convex, finite, and continuous on a neighborhood of zero. The following expression is found for the right derivative of this function at the point $t=0$:

$$\frac{d}{dt}f(x+tu)\bigg|_{t=0^+} = \max\{\langle u, y\rangle : y \in \partial f(x)\}.$$

In particular, if $\partial f(x)$ contains only one element y, this becomes

$$\frac{d}{dt}f(x+tu)\bigg|_{t=0^+} = \langle u, y\rangle;$$

i.e. the function is differentiable in the sense of Gâteaux at the point x, and y is its *gradient*. A usual condition in order for $\partial f(x)$ to contain no more than one element is the *strict convexity* of the function g.

D. Subgradient Mappings and Duality Mappings

Let f be a function in $\Gamma(X)$. By associating to any x in X the (possibly empty) subset $\partial f(x)$ of Y, one defines a (multivalued) mapping of X into Y.

From the convexity of f it is easily found that such a mapping is *monotone* in the sense of Minty, i.e., for any x and x' in X, any y in $\partial f(x)$, and any y' in $\partial f(x')$, the inequality

$$\langle x - x', y - y' \rangle \geqslant 0$$

holds [see Minty (2)]. A monotone mapping is said to be *maximal* if it admits no strict extension which is still monotone. It is proved in Rockafellar (4) that when X is a Banach space and $f \in \Gamma(X)$ is not everywhere infinite, the mapping $x \to \partial f(x)$ is maximal monotone. On the other hand, some *continuity* properties of the subgradient mappings are studied in Moreau (16).

Suppose now that X is a Banach space and Y its dual. Let ϕ and θ be numerical functions defined on $[0, +\infty[$, which form a pair of Young conjugates; i.e.,

$$\phi(\xi) = \sup \{\xi\eta - \theta(\eta) : \eta \in [0, +\infty[\},$$

and conversely. As proved by Aggeri and Lescarret (1, 2), the function $f : x \to \phi(\|x\|)$ and $g : y \to \theta(\|y\|)$ belong to $\Gamma(X)$ and $\Gamma(Y)$, respectively, and form a pair of dual functions. (Starting, more generally, from an arbitrary pair of spaces in duality, these authors consider, instead of the norms, the gauge functions, or equivalently the support functions, of a pair of mutually polar sets.) Then the subgradient mapping $x \to \partial f(x)$ reduces, under additional assumptions of smoothness, to a *duality mapping* as considered by Beurling and Livingston (1) and Browder (1, 2).

IV. Inf-Convolution and Γ-Convolution

A. The Functional Sets Γ as Convex Cones

Clearly, if f_1 and f_2 are two functions in $\Gamma(X)$, so is the sum $f_1 + f_2$ (in the case where f_1 or f_2 is the constant $-\infty$, the convention $\infty - \infty = -\infty$ must be used). On the other hand, if λ is a strictly positive constant, for any f in $\Gamma(X)$, the function λf also lies in $\Gamma(X)$. By these two operations the set $\Gamma(X)$ is provided with a *convex cone structure*.

Using the one-to-one mapping (*) this structure may be *transferred* to the set $\Gamma(Y)$. We have to give direct interpretation of the two operations defined thereby in $\Gamma(Y)$.

First, let g be an element of $\Gamma(Y)$ and λ a strictly positive constant; denoting by $g\lambda$ the dual function of $\lambda(g^*)$, immediate computation gives for any $y \in Y$,

$$g\lambda(y) = \lambda g\left(\frac{1}{\lambda} y\right).$$

On the other hand, if g_1 and g_2 are in $\Gamma(Y)$, the dual function of $g_1^* + g_2^*$ will be denoted by $g_1 \bigcirc g_2$. This operation, called Γ-*convolution*, is commutative and associative, since it is the image of the addition in $\Gamma(X)$, and we have the distributivity law

$$(g_1 \bigcirc g_2)\lambda = (g_1\lambda) \bigcirc (g_2\lambda).$$

The simple properties of Γ-convolution include the following. Consider an element b of Y and the indicatrix function ψ_b of the set $\{b\}$ [i.e., $\psi_b(b) = 0$ and $\psi_b(y) = +\infty$ otherwise]; for any $g \in \Gamma(Y)$, the function $\psi_b \bigcirc g = g \bigcirc \psi_b$ is the function obtained from g by the *translation* b; i.e.,

$$(\psi_b \bigcirc g)(y) = g(y - b).$$

B. Inf-Convolution

To obtain an interpretation of the Γ-convolution let us now consider two arbitrary numerical functions h_1 and h_2 defined on Y. We call *inf-convolution* the commutative and associative operation assigning to h_1 and h_2 the function, denoted by $h_1 \nabla h_2$, which is defined as follows:

$$(h_1 \nabla h_2)(y) = \inf\{h_1(y_1) + h_2(y_2) : y_1 + y_2 = y\}.$$

Here the sum $h_1(y_1) + h_2(y)$ must be taken as $+\infty$ if the case $\infty - \infty$ occurs [concerning the theory of this operation, more generally considering as Y an arbitrary semigroup, see Moreau (9, 10)].

Example 1. If A and B are two subsets of Y, the function $\psi_A \nabla \psi_B$ is the indicatrix of the set $A + B$.

Example 2. If Y is provided with a *norm* denoted by $\|\cdot\|$, the *distance* from the point $y \in Y$ to the set $A \subset Y$ is $(\psi_A \nabla \|\cdot\|)(y)$.

Now computing the *polar functions*, one easily finds

$$(h_1 \nabla h_2)^* = h_1^* + h_2^*,$$

so that, by Section II.A, the definition of the Γ-convolution gives, for any g_1 and g_2 in $\Gamma(Y)$,

$$g_1 \bigcirc g_2 = (g_1{}^* + g_2{}^*)^* = (g_1 \nabla g_2)^{**}.$$

In other words, the Γ-convolution $g_1 \bigcirc g_2$ is the Γ-*regularized* of the inf-convolution $g_1 \nabla g_2$.

C. The Practical Case

Cases where the operations $\bigcirc$ and ∇ turn to be equivalent are of practical importance. Here is the most useful: Let g_1 and g_2 lie in $\Gamma(Y)$; suppose there exists a point $x_0 \in X$ where the dual function $g_1{}^* = f_1$ is *finite*, while $g_2{}^* = f_2$ is *continuous* at this point (with respect to some topology compatible with duality). Then we can prove [see Moreau (*7, 8, 13*)] that

$$g_1 \bigcirc g_2 = g_1 \nabla g_2$$

and the inf-convolution is everywhere *exact;* i.e., for any $y \in Y$, there exist y_1 and y_2 such that

$$y = y_1 + y_2 \tag{4.1}$$

and

$$(g_1 \bigcirc g_2)(y) = (g_1 \nabla g_2)(y) = g_1(y_1) + g_2(y_2). \tag{4.2}$$

Application. As an example, let us use this property in deriving the addition rule of the subgradients stated in Section III.C. We have only to prove the reverse inclusion of (3.3). Let y be an element of the set $\partial(f_1 + f_2)(x)$; in other words, y is *conjugate* of x with respect to the pair of dual functions $f_1 + f_2$ and $g_1 \bigcirc g_2$; i.e.,

$$f_1(x) + f_2(x) + (g_1 \bigcirc g_2)(y) - \langle x, y \rangle = 0. \tag{4.3}$$

Under the previous hypothesis, there exists y_1 and y_2 in Y such that (4.1) and (4.2) hold, and thereby (4.3) becomes

$$f_1(x) + g_1(y_1) - \langle x, y_1 \rangle + f_2(x) + g_2(y_2) - \langle x, y_2 \rangle = 0. \tag{4.4}$$

But, using the general inequality (3.1), we have

$$f_1(x) + g_1(y_1) - \langle x, y_1 \rangle \geqslant 0,$$
$$f_2(x) + g_2(y_2) - \langle x, y_2 \rangle \geqslant 0.$$

Comparing with (4.4), these two inequalities turn out to be equalities, so that $y_1 \in \partial f_1(x)$ and $y_2 \in \partial f_2(x)$. Thus, by (4.1),

$$y \in \partial f_1(x) + \partial f_2(x),$$

and this achieves the proof.

V. The Case of a Hilbert Space

A. "Prox" Mappings

As in Section I, let us consider a real Hilbert space H. It is identified with its dual so that we have $X = Y = H$, and the duality bilinear form $\langle \cdot, \cdot \rangle$ turns to be the scalar product $(\cdot \mid \cdot)$ in H.

Given $f \in \Gamma(H)$ not everywhere infinite on H, and given z in H, let us consider the numerical function

$$u \to \tfrac{1}{2}\|z - u\|^2 + f(u). \tag{5.1}$$

It can be proved [Moreau (3, 17)] that this function possesses a minimum, attained at an unique point; we denote this point by $\mathrm{prox}_f z$.

Example. If $f = \psi_C$, the indicatrix function of a closed convex subset C of H, the minimum of the function

$$u \to \tfrac{1}{2}\|z - u\|^2 + \psi_C(u),$$

is necessarily attained at a point of C, since this function has the value $+\infty$ when $u \notin C$. But, for $u \in C$ the term $\psi_C(u)$ is zero, so that in this case $\mathrm{prox}_f z$ is the *projection* or proximal point $\mathrm{proj}_C z$.

So a mapping $z \to \mathrm{prox}_f z$ of H into itself is associated to any $f \in \Gamma(X)$ (provided f is not everywhere infinite). Various properties of such mappings are exposed in detail in Moreau (17). These properties result essentially from the following *decomposition theorem*:

If f and g are dual functions (not everywhere infinite), any $z \in H$ equals the sum of $x = \mathrm{prox}_f z$ and $y = \mathrm{prox}_g z$; x and y are conjugate with respect to f and g and they embody the unique decomposition of z into the sum of two conjugate elements with respect to f and g.

The two-cones theorem stated in Section I may be derived as a corollary by taking $f = \psi_P$ and $g = \psi_Q$.

Note that "prox" mappings are contractive, so that some *localization of the unknowns* may be obtained in the same way as in the two-cones case.

B. Strong and Weakened Problems

A pair of numerical functions a and b defined on H will be said to be *superdual* if, for any x and any y in H, the inequality

$$a(x) + b(y) \geqslant (x|y)$$

holds. That means that each of the two functions majores the polar function of the other.

If a and b are superdual, they possess some pairs of minorants, say

$$f \leqslant a, \qquad g \leqslant b,$$

which are dual functions. For instance, a^{**} and a^* form such a pair of *dual minorants* of the couple a, b (as well as b^* and b^{**}).

Given $z \in H$, the problem of finding x and y such that

$$z = x + y, \tag{5.2}$$

$$a(x) + b(y) = (x|y) \tag{5.3}$$

is called a *strong problem*; it does not necessarily possess a solution. But it is immediately seen, by comparing inequalities, that, if such a solution exists, it necessarily coincides with the solution of the decomposition problem

$$z = x + y, \tag{5.4}$$

$$f(x) + g(y) = (x|y), \tag{5.5}$$

where f, g denotes an *arbitrary* pair of dual minorants of the superdual functions a and b. This latter problem always has one and only one solution, by virtue of the theorem stated in Section V.A; it will be called a *weakened problem* of the initial strong problem.

Comparing inequalities one finds that, if there exists a pair x, y satisfying (5.2) and (5.3), these points minimize the two numerical functions

$$u \to \tfrac{1}{2}\|z - u\|^2 + a(u), \tag{5.6}$$

$$v \to \tfrac{1}{2}\|z - v\|^2 + b(v). \tag{5.7}$$

respectively.

Note that if $a^{**} = b^*$ (or, equivalently, $a^* = b^{**}$), the superdual functions a and b admit only one pair of dual minorants, the functions $f = b^*$ and $g = a^*$; in this case the strong problem possesses only one weakened problem.

Let us denote by $\mathcal{Q}$ the function

$$x \to \tfrac{1}{2}\|x\|^2.$$

This function belongs to $\Gamma(H)$ and easy computation yields $\mathcal{Q}^* = \mathcal{Q}$ (one proves that is the only function which equals its dual). With respect to this pair of dual functions, the conjugacy reduces to identity; i.e., for every x in H, the set $\partial\mathcal{Q}(x)$ consists of the unique point x.

On the other hand, the minimal value of the function written in (5.1) may be expressed as $(\mathcal{Q}\nabla f)(z)$ and, by the statements of Section IV.B, the inf-convolution ∇ is, in that case, equivalent to the Γ-convolution $\odot$.

This gives the key to the extension of the "prox" mappings theory to Banach spaces; replace the identity in H by a duality mapping of X into Y, as defined in Section III.D.

VI. A Functional Example

A. THE DATA

Let Ω be an open domain in E_n, supposed bounded for the sake of simplicity, and with a smooth boundary. This boundary consists of two parts: L (the "free surface," when hydrodynamics is concerned) and S (the surface of the containing vessel or of immersed bodies). A vector field $\mathbf{F}$ is given, continuous on $\bar{\Omega} = \Omega \cup L \cup S$, continuously differentiable on Ω. Two continuous numerical functions, A and P, are given on the surfaces S and L, respectively.

B. THE LINEAR (OR "BILATERAL") PROBLEM

To find a numerical function p, continuous on $\bar{\Omega}$, continuously differentiable on Ω, and a vector field w, continuous on $\bar{\Omega}$, continuously differentiable on Ω such that

$$
\begin{aligned}
\mathbf{w} + \mathbf{grad}\, p &= \mathbf{F} \\
\operatorname{div} \mathbf{w} &= 0
\end{aligned}
\right\} \quad \text{on } \Omega
\tag{6.1}\tag{6.2}
$$

with the boundary conditions

$$p = P \qquad \text{on } L \tag{6.3}$$

$$\mathbf{w} \cdot \mathbf{n} = A \qquad \text{on } S \tag{6.4}$$

$\mathbf{n}$ denotes, at any point of S or L, the normal unit vector, directed outward of Ω.

This problem reduces to a classical nonhomogeneous harmonic mixed problem for the function p: By (6.1) this function is continuously differentiable on $\bar{\Omega}$, twice continuously differentiable on Ω, and by (6.2) it satisfies

$$\Delta p = \operatorname{div} \mathbf{F} \qquad \text{on } \Omega \tag{6.5}$$

with the boundary conditions (6.3) and (6.4), the latter being rewritten

$$\frac{dp}{dn} = \mathbf{F} \cdot \mathbf{n} - A \qquad \text{on } S. \tag{6.6}$$

For comparison with further developments, it is interesting to give two *extremal characterizations* of the solution p_0, w_0 of the preceding problem (if it exists). All the competing vector fields invoked here are elements of the space $\mathscr{C}(\bar{\Omega}, \mathbf{E}_n)$ of the vector fields which are continuous on $\bar{\Omega}$; as $\bar{\Omega}$ is compact, this is a subspace of the Hilbert space $H = L^2(\Omega, \mathbf{E}_n)$.

Extremal characterization of w_0: Among all the $w \in \mathscr{C}(\bar{\Omega}, \mathbf{E}_n)$ *which are continuously differentiable on Ω and satisfy* (6.2) *and* (6.4), *the solution* w_0 *strictly minimizes the functional*

$$\mathscr{A}(w) = \tfrac{1}{2} \int_{\Omega} \mathbf{w}^2 \, d\xi - \int_{\Omega} \mathbf{w} \cdot \mathbf{F} \, d\xi + \int_{L} P \mathbf{w} \cdot \mathbf{n} \, d\sigma. \tag{6.7}$$

$d\xi$ denotes the Lebesgue measure on Ω and $d\sigma$ the superficial measure on L or S.

Proof. As p_0, w_0 form a solution of the conditions (6.1) to (6.4), the functional $\mathscr{A}$ may be rewritten

$$\mathscr{A}(w) = \tfrac{1}{2} \int_{\Omega} \mathbf{w}^2 \, d\xi - \int_{\Omega} \mathbf{w} \cdot \mathbf{w}_0 \, d\xi - \int_{\Omega} \mathbf{w} \cdot \operatorname{\mathbf{grad}} p_0 \, d\xi + \int_{L} P \mathbf{w} \cdot \mathbf{n} \, d\sigma,$$

or, integrating by parts,

$$\mathscr{A}(w) = \tfrac{1}{2} \int_{\Omega} (\mathbf{w}^2 - 2\mathbf{w} \cdot \mathbf{w}_0) \, d\xi + \int_{\Omega} p_0 \operatorname{div} \mathbf{w} - \int_{S \cup L} p_0 \mathbf{w} \cdot \mathbf{n} \, d\sigma + \int_{L} p \mathbf{w} \cdot \mathbf{n} \, d\sigma$$

$$= \tfrac{1}{2} \int_{\Omega} (\mathbf{w}^2 - 2\mathbf{w} \cdot \mathbf{w}_0) \, d\xi - \int_{S} p_0 A \, d\sigma$$

This still holds for $w = w_0$, so that

$$\mathscr{A}(w_0) = -\tfrac{1}{2} \int_\Omega \mathbf{w}_0{}^2 \, d\xi - \int_S p_0 A \, d\sigma$$

and

$$\mathscr{A}(w) - \mathscr{A}(w_0) = \tfrac{1}{2} \int_\Omega (\mathbf{w} - \mathbf{w}_0)^2 \, d\xi,$$

which is nonnegative. By the continuity assumption made, the annulation of this integral implies $w = w_0$; i.e., the minimum is strict.

Extremal characterization of p_0: Among all the numerical functions p, *continuous, with a continuous gradient on $\bar{\Omega}$ and such that $p = P$ on L, the solution p_0 strictly minimizes the functional*

$$\mathscr{B}(p) = \tfrac{1}{2} \int_\Omega \mathbf{grad}^2 \, p \, d\xi - \int_\Omega \mathbf{F} \cdot \mathbf{grad} \, p \, d\xi + \int_S p A \, d\sigma. \qquad (6.8)$$

Proof. Using the fact that p_0, w_0 is a solution of the problem, $\mathscr{B}$ is rewritten

$$\mathscr{B}(p) = \tfrac{1}{2} \int_\Omega (\mathbf{grad}^2 \, p - 2 \, \mathbf{grad} \, p \cdot \mathbf{grad} \, p_0) \, d\xi - \int_\Omega \mathbf{w}_0 \cdot \mathbf{grad} \, p \, d\xi + \int_S p A \, d\sigma$$

or, integrating by parts,

$$\mathscr{B}(p) = \tfrac{1}{2} \int_\Omega (\mathbf{grad}^2 \, p - 2 \, \mathbf{grad} \, p \cdot \mathbf{grad} \, p_0) \, d\xi + \int_\Omega p \operatorname{div} \mathbf{w}_0 \, d\xi$$

$$- \int_{S \cup L} p \mathbf{w}_0 \cdot \mathbf{n} \, d\sigma + \int_S p A \, d\sigma$$

$$= \tfrac{1}{2} \int_\Omega (\mathbf{grad}^2 \, p - 2 \, \mathbf{grad} \, p \cdot \mathbf{grad} \, p_0) \, d\xi - \int_L P \mathbf{w}_0 \cdot \mathbf{n} \, d\xi.$$

For $p = p_0$ this reduces to

$$\mathscr{B}(p_0) = -\tfrac{1}{2} \int_\Omega \mathbf{grad}^2 \, p_0 \, d\xi - \int_L P \mathbf{w}_0 \cdot \mathbf{n} \, d\xi,$$

so that

$$\mathscr{B}(p) - \mathscr{B}(p_0) = \tfrac{1}{2} \int_\Omega \mathbf{grad}^2 \, (p - p_0) \, d\xi.$$

This difference is nonnegative and, by the continuity of $\mathbf{grad}(p - p_0)$, it is null only if $\mathbf{grad}(p - p_0) = 0$ all over Ω. As $p = p_0 = P$ on L, the annulation of this gradient implies $p = p_0$ over Ω; i.e., the minimum is strict (here L is assumed nonempty).

From these two variational characterizations of the solution it is possible, in a classical way, to formulate weak problems which have one and only one solution with respect to the unknowns w and $\operatorname{grad} p$, considered as elements of the Hilbert space $H = L^2(\Omega, \mathbf{E}_n)$, for every F given in H. If this weak solution happens to satisfy the initial continuity and differentiability requirements, it is a solution of the initial problem. Actually, this weakening procedure might be achieved according to the scheme of superdual functions explained in Section V.B. We have just presented the preceding linear problem in a classical way to permit comparison with the superdual function scheme we shall now apply, to a nonclassical problem.

C. The Nonlinear (or "Unilateral") Problem

The following problem occurs in studying the inception of cavitation in a liquid flow [cf. Moreau (*15, 18*)]. The data are the same as above, but *with the additional assumption that the given function P is nonnegative on L.*

To find a numerical function p, continuous on $\bar{\Omega}$, continuously differentiable on Ω, and a vector field w, continuous on $\bar{\Omega}$, continuously differentiable on Ω, such that

$$
\left.
\begin{aligned}
\mathbf{w} + \operatorname{grad} p &= \mathbf{F} \\
\operatorname{div} \mathbf{w} &\geqslant 0 \\
p &\geqslant 0 \\
p \operatorname{div} \mathbf{w} &= 0
\end{aligned}
\right\} \quad \text{on } \Omega
$$

$$\text{(6.9)}$$
$$\text{(6.10)}$$
$$\text{(6.11)}$$
$$\text{(6.12)}$$

with the boundary conditions

$$ p = P \qquad \text{on } L \tag{6.13} $$

$$
\left.
\begin{aligned}
\mathbf{w} \cdot \mathbf{n} &\leqslant A \\
p(\mathbf{w} \cdot \mathbf{n} - A) &= 0
\end{aligned}
\right\} \quad \text{on } S
$$

$$\text{(6.14)}$$
$$\text{(6.15)}$$

We shall interpret this problem as a decomposition problem with respect to a pair of superdual functions on the Hilbert space $H = L^2(\Omega, \mathbf{E}_n)$. Let $C \subset H$ be the totality of the vector fields w which are continuous on $\bar{\Omega}$, continuously differentiable on Ω, and satisfy the conditions (6.10) and (6.14). Let $D \subset H$ be the totality of the vector fields s which are continuous on $\bar{\Omega}$ and have the form $s = \operatorname{grad} p$, where p is a numerical function continuous on $\bar{\Omega}$ satisfying the conditions (6.11) and (6.13).

Define on H two numerical functions a and b by

$$a(w) = \begin{cases} +\infty & \text{if } w \notin C, \\ \displaystyle\int_L P\mathbf{w}\cdot\mathbf{n}\,d\sigma & \text{if } w \in C, \end{cases}$$

$$b(s) = \begin{cases} +\infty & \text{if } s \notin D, \\ \displaystyle\int_S p\,A\,d\sigma & \text{if } s = \operatorname{grad} p \in D. \end{cases}$$

To prove that these two functions are superdual, one remarks that, for arbitrary w and s, the expression

$$a(w) + b(s) - (w|s)$$

has the value $+\infty$ unless $w \in C$ and $s \in D$; in that case the expression is written

$$\int_L P\mathbf{w}\cdot\mathbf{n}\,d\sigma + \int_S pA\,d\sigma - \int_\Omega \mathbf{w}\cdot\operatorname{grad} p\,d\xi$$

$$= \int_L P\mathbf{w}\cdot\mathbf{n}\,d\xi + \int_S pA\,d\sigma + \int_\Omega p\operatorname{div}\mathbf{w}\,d\xi - \int_{S\cup L} p\mathbf{w}\cdot\mathbf{n}\,d\sigma$$

$$= \int_S p(A - \mathbf{w}\cdot\mathbf{n})\,d\sigma + \int_\Omega p\operatorname{div}\mathbf{w}\,d\xi.$$

This expression is nonnegative by virtue of the definition of the sets C and D; clearly its value is zero if and only if the vector fields w and $s = \operatorname{grad} p$ satisfy the conditions (6.10) to (6.15). Thus the problem turns out to be equivalent to the following one: *to find w and s in H such that*

$$w + s = F,$$

$$a(w) + b(s) = (w|s).$$

This is a strong problem according to the scheme presented in Section V.B. By the statements of this section the (unique) solution, say w_1 and $s_1 = \operatorname{grad} p_1$, *if it exists*, possesses the following variational properties:

(1) w_1 is, in H, the minimizing point of the function

$$w \to \tfrac{1}{2}\|F - w\|^2 + a(w),$$

or, equivalently, discarding the term $\frac{1}{2}\|F\|^2$, which does not depend on w, the solution w_1 is, in the set C, the minimizing point of the function $\mathscr{A}(w)$ defined in (6.7).

(2) $s_1 = \operatorname{grad} p_1$ is in H the minimizing point of the function

$$s \rightarrow \tfrac{1}{2}\|F-s\|^2 + b(s),$$

or, again discarding the term $\frac{1}{2}\|F\|^2$, the solution $s_1 = \operatorname{grad} p_1$ is, in the set D, the minimizing point of the function $\mathscr{B}(p)$ defined in (6.8).

These extremal characterizations might alternatively be derived in the same way as in Section V.B; conversely, the linear problem in that section might be interpreted in terms of a strong decomposition problem with respect to a suitable pair of superdual functions.

In general, the superdual functions a and b possess an infinity of dual minorants, so that the present problem admits an infinity of weakened problems.

On the other hand, the existential study of strong solution is to develop according to the ideas presented, for a special case, in Section I.E: *constructing a "hull."*

D. Conclusions

As was noted before, the preceding problem takes its origin in the dynamics of fluids with unilateral incompressibility (cavitation). Problems of statics concerning elastic media with unilateral boundary constraints or with unilateral internal reactions arise under a quite similar mathematical aspect [see Fichera (*1*) and Prager (*1*)]. It would be interesting to handle these problems by the same scheme, especially when boundary conditions are expressed as nonhomogeneous inequalities.

References

J. C. Aggeri and C. Lescarret,

1. Fonctions convexes duales associées à un couple d'ensembles mutuellement polaires, *Compt. Rend.* **260**(1), 6011–6014 (1965).
2. Sur une application de la théorie de sous-differentiabilité à des fonctions convexes duales associées à un couple d'ensembles mutuellement polaires, Faculté des Sciences de Montpellier, Séminaires de Mathématiques, 1965.

R. Bellman and W. Karush,
1. On a New Functional Transform in Analysis: The Maximum Transform, *Bull. Am. Math. Soc.* **67**, 501–503 (1961).
2. On the Maximum Transform and Semi-Groups of Transformations, *Bull. Am. Math. Soc.* **68**, 516–518 (1962).

A. Beurling and A. E. Livingston,
1. A Theorem on Duality Mappings in Banach Space, *Arkiv Mat.* **4**, 405–411 (1960–1963).

Z. Birnbaum and W. Orlicz,
1. Über die Verallgemeinerung des Begriffes der zueinander konjugierten Potenzen, *Studia Mat.* **3**, 1–67 (1931).

A. Broendsted,
1. Conjugate convex function in topological vector spaces, *Mat. Fys. Medd. Dansk. Vid. Selsk.* **34** (2) (1964).

A. Broendsted and R. T. Rockafellar,
1. On the Subdifferentiability of Convex Functions, *Proc. Am. Math. Soc.* **16**, 605–611 (1965).

F. E. Browder,
1. On a Theorem of Beurling and Livingston, *Can. J. Math.* **17**, 367–372 (1965).
2. Multivalued Monotone Nonlinear Mappings and Duality Mapping in Banach Spaces, *Trans. Am. Math. Soc.* **118**, 338–351 (1965).

R. Courant and D. Hilbert,
1. "Methods of Mathematical Physics," Vol. 1, Wiley (Interscience), New York, 1953, Chap. IV, Par. 11.

J. B. Diaz,
1. Upper and Lower Bounds for Quadratic Integrals and at a Point for Solution of Linear Boundary Value Problems, in "Boundary Problems in Differential Equations" [Proc. of a symposium conducted by the Mathematics Research Center (1959), Madison], Univ. Wisconsin Press, Madison, Wisconsin, 1960, pp. 47–83.

W. Fenchel,
1. On Conjugate Convex Functions, *Can. J. Math.* **1**, 73–77 (1949).
2. Convex Cones, Sets, and Functions, lecture notes, Princeton Univ., Princeton, New Jersey, 1953.

G. Fichera,
1. Un Teorema generale di semicontinuità per gli integrali multipli e sue applicazioni alla fisica matematica, *Atti del Conv. Lagrangiano* (Torino, 1963), Accademia delle Scienze, Torino, 1964.

W. L. Jones,
1. On Conjugate Functionals, Doctoral dissertation, Columbia Univ., New York, 1960.

S. Karlin,
1. "Mathematical Methods and Theory in Games, Programming, and Economics," Vol. 1. Pergamon Press, New York, 1959.

S. Mandelbrojt,
1. Sur les fonctions convexes, *Compt. Rend.* **209**, 977–978 (1939).
G. J. Minty,
1. Monotone (Nonlinear) Operators in Hilbert Space, *Duke Math. J.* **29**, 241–340 (1962).
2. On the Monotonicity of the Gradient of a Convex Function, *Pacific J. Math.* **14**, 243–247 (1964).
J. J. Moreau,
1. Decomposition orthogonale d'un espace hilbertien selon deux cônes mutuellement polaires, *Compt. Rend.* **255**, 238–240 (1962).
2. Fonctions convexes en dualité, Faculté des Sciences de Montpellier, Séminaires de Mathématiques, 1962.
3. Fonctions convexes duales et points proximaux dans un espace hilbertien, *Compt. Rend.* **255**, 2897–2899 (1962).
4. Applications "prox," Faculté des Sciences de Montpellier, Séminaires de Mathématiques, 1963.
5. Les liaisons unilatérales et le principe de Gauss, *Compt. Rend.* **256**, 871–874 (1963).
6. Propriétés des applications "prox," *Compt. Rend.* **256**, 1069–1071 (1963).
7. Inf-convolution, Faculté des Sciences de Montpellier, Séminaires de Mathématiques, 1963.
8. Inf-convolution des fonctions numériques sur un espace vectoriel, *Compt. Rend.* **256**, 5047–5049 (1963).
9. Fonctions à valeurs dans $[-\infty, +\infty]$; notions algébriques, Faculté des Sciences de Montpellier, Séminaires de Mathématiques, 1963.
10. Remarques sur les fonctions à valeurs dans $[-\infty, +\infty]$ définies sur un demi-groupe, *Compt. Rend.* **257**, 3107–3109 (1963).
11. Etude locale d'une fonctionnelle convexe, Faculté des Sciences de Montpellier, Séminaires de Mathématiques, 1963.
12. Fonctionnelles sous-differentiable, *Compt. Rend.* **257**, 4117–4119 (1963).
13. Sur la fonction polaire d'une fonction semi-continue supérieurement, *Compt. Rend.* **258**, 1128–1131 (1964).
14. Théorèmes "inf-sup," *Compt. Rend.* **258**(1), 2720–2722 (1964).
15. Sur la naissance de la cavitation dans une conduite, *Compt. Rend.* **259** (2), 3948–3951 (1964).
16. Semi-continuité du sous-gradient d'une fonctionnelle, *Compt. Rend.* **260**(1), 1067–1070 (1965).
17. Proximité et dualité dans un espace hilbertien, *Bull. Soc. Math. France* **93**, 273–299 (1965).
18. One-Sided Constraints in Hydrodynamics, to appear in "Non Linear Programming: a Course" (J. Abadie, ed.). North-Holland Publ., Amsterdam.
19. Quadratic Programming in Mechanics: Dynamics of One-Sided Constraints, *J. SIAM Control* **A4**(1) (Proc. 1st Intern. Conf. Programming Control) 153–158 (1966).

W. Prager,
1. Unilateral Constraints in Mechanics of Continua, *Atti del Conv. Lagrangiano* (Torino, 1963). Torino, Accademia delle Scienze, 1964.

W. Prager and J. C. Synge,
1. Approximations in Elasticity Based on the Concept of Function Space, *Quart. Appl. Math.* **5**, 241–269 (1947).

R. T. Rockafellar,
1. Convex Functions and Dual Extremum Problems, Doctoral dissertation, Harvard Univ., Cambridge, Massachusetts, 1963.
2. Level Sets and Continuity of Conjugate Convex Functions, to appear in *Trans. Am. Math. Soc.*
3. Extensions of Fenchel's Duality Theorem for Convex Functions, *Duke J. Math.* **33**, 81–90 (1966).
4. Characterization of the Subdifferentials of Convex Functions, *Pacific J. Math.* **17**, 497–510 (1966).

J. C. Synge,
1. The Hypercircle in Mathematical Physics, Cambridge Univ. Press, London and New York, 1957.

The First Nondistributive Algebra, with Relations to Optimization and Control Theory

C. MUSES

Centre de Recherches en Mathématiques et Morphologie
Pully-Lausanne, Switzerland

I. Introduction

Within the limitations of time and of space that circumstances have made unavoidable, only a brief outline of this ramified subject can be made here. The reader interested in further details is referred to a forthcoming monograph, "Theory of Nondistributive Multiplication and Algebraic Structures" (Muses).

Matrices are isomorphic with hypercomplex numbers; and projective geometry, affine geometry, the theory of vector spaces (hence that of function spaces), and linear algebra are all isomorphic, forming one of the most significant and profound convergences of meaning in all mathematics.

This convergence, in one or more of its aspects, is treated, for example, in the following works: H. Weyl, "Mathematische Analyse des Raumproblems" (1923); B. Segré, "Lezioni di geometria moderna" (Vol. I, 1948); G. Birkhoff and S. MacLane, "A Survey of Modern Algebra" (1948); C. C. MacDuffee, "Vectors and Matrices" (1943); O. Schreier and E. Sperner, "Introduction to Modern Algebra and Matrix Theory" (first English edition, 1951); and H. Schwerdtfeger, "Introduction to Linear Algebra and Matrix Theory" (1951). A. A. Albert's "Modern Higher Algebra" (1937) and "Structures of Algebras" (1939) are highly recommended as well.

Full awareness of the fact and significance of the above-mentioned convergence has not yet been realized, however; nor has the fact that hypercomplex numbers and their related rings and fields are the most

171

economical way to represent it. Group theory is related to the same fundamental idea, its algebra stemming from that of matrices, and hence from linear algebras, i.e., the algebra of hypercomplex numbers.

In his modern classic, "Algebraic Theory of Numbers" (1940), Hermann Weyl observed on p. 222: "... enormous progress has been made in the theory of class fields ... but in spite of all efforts I have the feeling that the theory has not yet assumed its final form."

The reason for Weyl's penetrating appraisal is found, for instance, in the predicament of G. Voronoi, who in his theory of cubic number fields was forced to speak of ideals that were "existent" and of those that "have no real existence", by which it turns out that he means representable (or not) in terms of roots of complex numbers. The entire theory of ideals, and hence of class fields, suffers from the same defect: the limitations of complex numbers.

It is as if we said that 3 was an absolute prime because it has no explicit factors, complex or real. But it is less well known that $3 = (1+i+j) \cdot (1-i-j)$ than that the number 5 factors into $(2+i)$ and $(2-i)$. For 7 we need complete quaternion factors, i.e., $7 = (2+i+j+k) \cdot (2-i-j-k)$. No more than quaternion factors are required for any real integral prime, and thus H-algebra is sufficient to "dissolve" all such real primes. However, if we stop there, we need to hypostatize "ideals" (together with their modern and rather artificial extensions, "ideles" and "adeles") to eliminate apparent paradoxes arising from the investigation of complex and hypercomplex primes. But we need not stop there; and since $\sqrt{-1}$ is the point at which all number systems remain open, we are indeed forced to go on to nonassociative and then to nondistributive algebra.

Just as real algebra is not closed, but open at the operation "square root of minus unity," so are Gaussian and quaternion algebra similarly open, for $\sqrt{-1}$ is *multivalued*, i.e., j, k, etc., also satisfy it, leading us from real (R) to Gaussian (G) to quaternion or Hamiltonian (H) to Cayley (C) algebra, and beyond.

Thus hypercomplex algebra contains complex or Gaussian algebra, and the latter contains real algebra; or $R \subset G \subset H \subset C \subset N$. The last term in this sequence is new, and previous attempts to extend Cayley algebra have failed because of not realizing the theorems that: (1) any extension of R must have nonamalgamative addition; (2) any extension of G must have noncommutative multiplication; (3) any extension of H must have non-associative multiplication; and (4) any extension of C must have non-distributive multiplication. Thus all linear algebras with less than 5 and more than 2 i-elements are contained in H; all with more than 3 and less than 8, in C; all with more than 7 and less than 16, in N. It is in this sense that R, G, H, C, and N are the only complete linear algebras with less than 17 elements in all, for all linear algebras contain the real element $i_{\pm 0} = 1^{\pm 1} = 1$, as well as the self-orthogonal elements $i_{\pm \infty} = 0^{\pm 1} = 0$, ∞i_n.

In general, $i_{\pm n} = i_n^{\pm 1} = \pm i_n$; and $i_n^2 = -1$ $(0 > n < \infty)$, where $i \equiv i_1$ $j \equiv i_2$, $k \equiv i_3$. The above nonarbitrary notation and its properties are indispensable in handling hypercomplex numbers efficiently and usefully. A table of all the complete linear algebras with finite factor multiplication follows, zero being regarded not as a finite, but as an infinitesimal number.

A complete algebra has 2^n distinct elements, none of which represents merely the same nonreal element extended along a different real dimension. Clifford algebras, since they apply i_1 to successively higher real dimensions in order to form their 2^n elements, are not complete algebras. Thus the only complete algebra requiring a representation space of four dimensions is quaternion algebra (H): the only complete algebra similarly requiring eight dimensions is octave algebra (C); and the only complete algebra similarly requiring sixteen dimensions is N-algebra. A characteristic of complete algebras is successively to require a more precise formulation of what is meant by addition or multiplication, and that each embeds in itself all the complete algebras below it, thus preserving the self-consistency of mathematics. The rules of arithmetic really do not "break down"; they merely become more sensitive, taking more distinctions into account in higher algebras. A *complete algebra* is also one whose elements form a kind of multiplication loop, regenerating each other, except for zero formation when the number of elements exceeds 8. Finite factor (ff) multiplication is that which does not entail the equation $a \cdot 0 = b$, where a, $b \neq 0$, ∞, although it may involve $a \cdot b = 0$, $a \neq b$, as in N-algebra.

Thus non-ff multiplication entrains what may be termed *zero revival*, whereas the nondistributive multiplication of N-algebra involves mutual annihilation or zero creation. To perform ff multiplication, the precise kind of zero product must be specified, the rules for such specification (deducible from the wave-operator interactions) being necessary in the process of zero revival, i.e., the operation $a \cdot 0 = b$; a, $b \neq 0$, ∞. All non-ff multiplication is nondistributive. The converse is not true, however, since there are four forms (R, G, H, and C) of ff multiplication that are distributive.

TABLE I

FIVE COMPLETE LINEAR ALGEBRAS, INVOLVING THREE KINDS OF HYPERCOMPLEX NUMBERS

Algebra		No. of elements	No. of units	Characterization	
				Addition	Multiplication
Real		R 1, 0	$T_1 = 2$	am	co, as, di
Gaussian	(di)	G 1, 1	$(2/3)^a T_2 = 4$	$-am$	co, as, di
Hamiltonian		H 1, 3	$T_4 = 24$	$-am$	$-co$, as, di
Cayleyan		C 1, 7	$T_8 = 240$	$-am$	$-co$, $-as$, di
Nondistributive		N 1, 15	$T_{16} = 4320^b$	$-am$	$-co$, $-as$, $-di$

[right brace spanning Hamiltonian, Cayleyan, Nondistributive rows] $(-am)$

[a] This fraction is not *ad hoc* but involves the Eisenstein integers based on the cube roots of minus and plus unity, and involving the imaginary angles $\pm (2/3) \pi i$.

[b] This is the probable figure based on the densest packing yet achieved [see Leech (*14*)] for D_{16}. However, this figure does not stand on the same footing as the prior four, since the polytope of centers is no longer convex, and there is no longer distributive multiplication, which in geometric terms means that in the D_{16} lattice pack, every sphere of T_{15} no longer touches the D_{16} portions of T_{16}. This phenomenon appears from D_9 onward, since D_8 is the last dimension to have a convex *polytope of centers*, which is the D_n figure with its vertices at the centers of the hyperspheres in the T_n shell, which centers in turn may be regarded as an infinitesimal portion of a $_K D_{n-1}$ space where $K = 1$ if $2 \leqslant n \leqslant 8$, and $K < 0$ if $\infty > n > 9$. The T_n refer to maximal-contact tangent sphere shells in D_n.

Thus R, G, H, C, and N may be considered to have Euclidean dimensionalities of 1, 2, 4, 8, and 16, respectively, T_n being the maximal number of equal tangent hyperspheres that can be fit about another such sphere of the same radius in D_n, a parabolic space of n dimensions. In the same terminology $_{\pm K} D_n$ is an elliptic $(+)$ or hyperbolic $(-)$, i.e., a convex or concave space of curvature K and n dimensions. Since $_{\pm K} D_{n-1}$ is always embedded in $_0 D_n \equiv D_n$, the parabolic, flat, or Euclidean spaces are of prime importance, and hence the linear algebras.

There is a close connection between the groups of tangent hyperspheres mentioned in the last paragraph and error-correcting computer codes, which in itself suggests the importance of the present theme for optimization and control theory. (See also pages 200ff.)

We now have the complete algebras R, G, H, C, N, each of whose multiplications is embedded toward the right; i.e., N-algebra contains R, G, H, and C. N is the first algebra with nondistributive $(-di)$ as well as nonassociative $(-as)$ and noncommutative $(-co)$ multiplication; $(-)am$ denotes (non)amalgamative addition, only R being am, co, as, and di, just as N only in this fundamental table of the real multiplication linear algebras is characterized completely negatively as $-am$, $-co$, $-as$, and $-di$.

Before commenting further on these characterizations and on the meaning of the T_n and their relation to optimization and control, we shall append the other tables necessary to complete the multiplication table for N-algebra.

II. The A_N Multiplication Table (Unlisted triplets are $-as$)

(a) *The Linear Triplet* (as, co): $n \cdot n = -0$

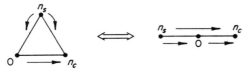

FIG. 1. Thus $n_s \cdot 0 = n_c$; $0 \cdot n_c = n_s$; $n_s \cdot n_c = -0$; i.e., $i_n \cdot i_n = -i_0 = -1$.

This linear triplet, as our diagram shows, involves by the theory of its multiplication the distinction of a separating center or source (n_s) and a combining center or sink (n_c). Thus in $i \cdot i = -1$, the two (i)'s are not identical. This subtle distinction does not affect ordinary hypercomplex algebra.

Subscript rules:

(1) $\quad -i_n = i_{-n} = i_n^{-1}, \qquad 0 < |n| < \infty.$

(2) $\quad \pm i_0 = \pm i_{-0} = \pm 1^{\pm 1} = \pm 1.$

(3) $\quad \pm i_\infty = \pm 0 i_n = 0; \qquad \pm i_{-\infty} = \pm (0 i_n)^{-1} = \pm \infty i_n$

$\left. \vphantom{\begin{matrix}1\\2\\3\end{matrix}} \right\} i_{\pm n} = i_n^{\pm 1}$

Thus $i_{-\infty}$ is doubly indeterminate, and here $0 \leqslant n < \infty$.

(b) *The* H-*type Triplets* $(as, -co)$, *Each with 6 Variants*

[1]1.	$3 \cdot 2 = -1$	19.	$3 \cdot 13 = 14$
[1a]2.	$4 \cdot 1 = -5$	20.	$12 \cdot 8 = 4$
[1a]3.	$7 \cdot 6 = -1$	21.	$13 \cdot 9 = -4$
4.	$9 \cdot 1 = 8$	22.	$10 \cdot 14 = -4$
5.	$10 \cdot 1 = -11$	23.	$15 \cdot 4 = 11$
6.	$13 \cdot 12 = -1$	24.	$8 \cdot 13 = 5$
7.	$14 \cdot 1 = -15$	25.	$12 \cdot 9 = -5$
[1a]8.	$6 \cdot 4 = 2$	26.	$10 \cdot 5 = -15$
[1a]9.	$7 \cdot 2 = 5$	27.	$5 \cdot 11 = 14$
10.	$8 \cdot 10 = -2$	28.	$14 \cdot 8 = 6$
11.	$11 \cdot 2 = 9$	29.	$15 \cdot 6 = 9$
12.	$12 \cdot 14 = -2$	30.	$10 \cdot 6 = 12$
13.	$13 \cdot 15 = 2$	31.	$6 \cdot 11 = 13$
[1a]14.	$4 \cdot 7 = 3$	32.	$15 \cdot 7 = 8$
[1a]15.	$5 \cdot 6 = 3$	33.	$7 \cdot 9 = 14$
16.	$11 \cdot 3 = 8$	34.	$7 \cdot 10 = 13$
17.	$10 \cdot 3 = 9$	35.	$7 \cdot 11 = 12$
18.	$15 \cdot 12 = -3$		

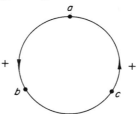

FIG. 2. The H-type or cyclic triplet, $ab = c$, etc., $ba = -c$, etc. Counterclockwise is taken as the positive sense.

Each of the above equations represents a set of six (see Fig. 2), obtainable by cyclic permuting. Since each such triplet is isomorphic to an H-algebra, which in turn is isomorphic to a D_3 sphere with a D_4 axis of rotation, such triplets may be also termed H-spheres.

[1] Pertains to H as well. The equations are indicial throughout.
[1a] Pertain to C. All others pertain to N only.

(c) *The Partially Cyclic Triplets* $(as, -co)$

FIG. 3.

1. 2 6 8̲	9. 3 10 13	17. 6 13 3̲	25. 10 14 8
2. 2 7 9	10. 3 11 14	18. 6 14 4̲	26. 10 15 9
3. 2 10 12	11. 4 6 1̲0̲	19. 6 15 5̲	27. 11 1̲3̲ 8
4. 2 1̲1̲ 13	12. 4̲ 14 2	20. 6 7̲ 13	28. 11 1̲4̲ 9
5. 3 5̲ 8	13. 5 6 1̲1̲	21. 7̲ 11 2	29. 1̲2̲ 14 10
6. 3 6̲ 9	14. 5 7 1̲2̲	22. 7 13 4	30. 1̲3̲ 14 1̲1̲
7. 3 7 1̲0̲	15. 5 14 3̲	23. 7 1̲4̲ 5	
8. 3 9 1̲2̲	16. 6 · 12 2̲	24. 9̲ 11 4	

For example $(2 \cdot 6)8 = 2(6 \cdot 8)$, each triplet specifying four such equations. Underscores indicate apex members. See Fig. 3.

Triplets excluded by the scheme are $(-as)$, *e.g.,* $(6 \cdot 8)2 = -6(8 \cdot 2)$.

III. The (-di) Mutual Annihilators

Just as commutators are definable as

$$co \equiv (a, b) = ab - ba$$

and associators as

$$as \equiv (a, b, c) = (ab)c - a(bc),$$

we may also define a "distributor" as

$$di \equiv (a; b, c) = a(b+c) - (ab+ac).$$

In commutative, associative, and distributive algebra it is respectively true that $co = 0$, $as = 0$, and $di = 0$. But in nondistributive algebra the distributor is no longer equal to zero, since now ab or ac or both may be zero even though neither b, a, nor c is zero. This behavior of our distributor is analogous to that of commutators and associators, which are also not zero in $(-co)$ and $(-as)$ algebras.

Thus we have in N-algebra the possibility of two operators "zeroing out" or forming a mutually annihilating pair, agreeing with our basic $(-di)$ condition: $a \cdot b = 0$; $a, b \neq 0$. Such behavior should not be regarded as abnormal; on the contrary it is natural, and preserves the continuity of algebraic structure even after the breakdown of the norm-product rule, which extends only through Cayley algebra. The fact that the norm of a product should equal the product of the norms of the factors is intimately bound up with the representability of the product of two sums of n squares as the sum of n squares. This representability is in turn directly related to the possibility of continuing pure hypertetrahedral symmetry in higher spatial dimensions. Such symmetry extends only through eight dimensions, the representation space of C-algebra. With nondistribution we are entering spaces of nine or more dimensions, and in such spaces there is in general no longer a homogeneous or single-valued contact number (the number of spheres touching a given sphere) in lattices formed of equal tangent hyperspheres in such spaces. Also, in such spaces the hyperspheres of a D_{n-k} lattice section may not touch all those of the D_{n-k+1} section.

Mutual annihilation, which may be conceived of as the interference of two waves of π phase difference, finds its algebraic expression through disagreeing patterns of parity, each operator being characterized by such a pattern (see Section IV). In addition to the patterns of operators i_8 through i_{15}, given in the next section, patterns are also assignable to i_1 through i_7. Thus we have, where the numbers to the left signify the index,

1	0	4	$++$
2	$+$	5	$--$
3	$-$	6	$+-$
		7	$-+$

All nonfitting patterns "zero out" if in any binary factor pair there are three or more parity tracks in any one operator; $i_1 \equiv i$ fits with all patterns. Thus $i_3(-) \cdot i_4(++) = i_7(-+)$, but $i_3(-) \cdot i_8(+++) = 0$; whereas $i_3(-) \cdot i_{11}(-++) = i_{14}(+-+)$, for here there is no track annulling, since the minus in track 1 (the only track that i_3 possesses) agrees with the minus in track 1 of i_{11}. Thus also $i_7(-+) \cdot i_{15}(-+-) = -i_8(+++)$; but $i_7(-+) \cdot i_{14}(+-+) = 0$, and also $i_8 \cdot i_9 = 0 = i_8 \cdot i_{10}$, etc. Hence there are in

N-algebra $28+4(8)=60$ binary combinations of operators that produce zero, making 120 possibilities when anticommutation is considered.

There are structural rules governing the parity-pattern changes and assignments. But the basic table of Section II, showing multiplicative-operator subscript changes, together with the parity patterns given for each operator in this and the following sections, plus the basic rules for mutual annihilation already given, will enable the reader to work out any result without the extra labor of employing the parity-pattern structure rules.

Without entering into further detail here, one may summarize the interaction structure by the statement that a minus on any track of a factor reverses the parity of the same track of the following factor with more tracks, leaving all other tracks unchanged, whereas a plus sign on any such track preserves the parity of the corresponding track but changes the following tracks. Thus $(-)\cdot(-+)=(++)$; $(+)\cdot(-+)=(--)$; and $(++)\cdot(---)=(--+)$; and there are similar variations of the basic interaction rules for other parity patterns.

The operator $i \equiv i_1 \equiv i_1(0)$ has the effect of a parity reversor; for example,

$$i_1(0)\cdot i_{10}(+--) = i_{11}(-++);$$

$$i_1(0)\cdot i_2(+) = i_3(-);$$

$$i_1(0)\cdot i_5(--) = -i_4(++),$$

etc.

If both operator and operand have the same number of tracks (with different patterns) then each track acts only on its correspondent; opposite parities yield (0), but like parities in the first track yield $(+)$, whereas in the second track $(-)\cdot(-)=(+)$ and $(+)\cdot(+)=(-)$. Thus

$$(++)\cdot(--)=(00)=(0)\equiv i_1; \quad (+-)\cdot(++)=(+0)=(+);$$

$$(--)\cdot(+-)=(0-)=(-); \quad (--)\cdot(-+)=(+0)=(+);$$

$$(-+)\cdot(++)=(0-)=(-),$$

this last parity equation referring to the operator equation in Cayley algebra, $i_7\cdot i_4 = -i_3$ or $i_4\cdot i_7 = i_3$. When simply the index of the resultant operator is considered, without reference to sign, then parity pattern multiplication can be regarded as commutative.

Similarly, the principal rule for the assignment of parity patterns is that in the case of an operator of even index the parity pattern is the compound one formed by adding together the patterns of the two factors of the index, the first being 2; and the parity pattern of the operator of next higher (i.e., odd) index is the polar or annihilating pattern for the preceding operator. Thus i_{14} is assigned $(+ - +)$ since $14 = 2 \cdot 7$, the patterns of the two factors being $(+)$ and $(- +)$, which combine to give $(+ - +)$. Then by the second rule the pattern for i_{15} is polar to the preceding, i.e., $(- + -)$. The ultimate validation for all these rules is that they optimally achieve a consistent algebra that embeds Cayley algebra and differs from it by the minimal number of structural and operational changes necessary to conform with the minimal type of nondistribution demanded by the breakdown of the modulus-product relationship in nine or more dimensions.

With algebras beyond N, which have operators of four and more tracks, there is a new possibility: $a \cdot 0 = b$; a, $b \neq 0$, ∞. This may be called *zero revival* and leads to the fact that $i_n \cdot i_m^{-1}$ may be equal to zero as well for $n, m \geqslant 16$. It is also true that our investigations show that viable (i.e., unique product) linear algebras are no longer possible in more than 128 dimensions. It is this phenomenon (which geometrically shows up as two or more sphere lattices with the same maximum contact number) which forces the appearance of *quadratic algebra* in a compound space of minimally 256 dimensions. At this stage a new type of number appears, characterized by $p^2 = 0$, $p \neq 0$. The writer discovered that for D_n, $n \geqslant 128$, these numbers must appear; and only later learned that Eduard Study had also deduced (from projective kinematics) the existence of such a number, although Study had no idea of the algebraic application or significance of his so-called "duale Nummer." From his method he could not know that the algebra demanding such numbers as $p^2 = 0$, $p \neq 0$, has a representation space of 128 dimensions and ends the viable linear algebras.

More will be said about quadratic algebra later, but this paper is concerned primarily with N-algebra, which has a quasi-isotropic representation space of 16-D rather than higher anisotropic algebraic spaces. Details of the still higher algebras we have found must await later occasions. N_C is the highest viable (nonschizoid) algebra permitting a finite number (128) of elements and the existence of a Laplacian operator, which, along with positive entropy, disappears in "cubic" algebra where a third kind of number, q, appears, with the characterizing equation $q^{\pm 4n} = \text{RIP}(q_n) = 0$, where "RIP" means "real, imaginary, and dual (p) parts." In the multiplication of two powers of p (and *a fortiori* of q), the addition of exponents is not in general commutative. Both $p^0 = q^0 = 0$.

IV. The (-*di*) Elements of N-Algebra

1. $i_8(+ + +)$ 5. $i_{12}(+ + -)$
2. $i_9(- - -)$ 6. $i_{13}(- - +)$
3. $i_{10}(+ - -)$ 7. $i_{14}(+ - +)$
4. $i_{11}(- + +)$ 8. $i_{15}(- + -)$

V. Beyond N-Algebra

A summary: $N_G \to N_H \to N_C \to N_N \equiv N^2$, i.e., quadratic algebra, after an isomeric transformation which involves the introduction of a new kind of concept: the *quadratic* operator implied by q. This algebra has an infinity of elements and a morphology possessing relations with the elliptic modular function. These will not be discussed now. (There is also an absolute idempotent algebra to which one is naturally led by considerations stemming from the infinite-elements algebra above mentioned.) The two algebras beyond p involve q- and w-numbers (see pages 209 ff.).

VI. Commentary

This section, as explained in the Introduction, will be brief, and not exhaustive, dealing only with clarifications of certain salient points through the addition of further details.

The first such point concerns an apparently prevalent misconception pertaining to the nature of division algebras or those possessing unique factorization, that is, $(a \cdot b = 0) \Leftrightarrow (a \vee b = 0)$. C. S. Peirce corrected and simplified his father's unwieldy and arbitrary classification of algebras and first defined the concept of a division algebra. Charles Peirce also first concluded that R, G, and H were the only associative division algebras. Leonard Dickson in his otherwise very valuable work on algebra does not adequately refer to Peirce, and indeed commits the lapse in his "Algebras and Their Arithmetics" of saying that H is the last division algebra. The useful and valuable Condon and Odishaw's "Handbook of Physics" has in the last two editions repeated Dickson's lapse[2] but now as an apparent misconception—that quaternions "are the only hypercomplex system, apart from the reals and the complex numbers, which has no divisors of zero." This would mean that all division algebras are associative, which is not the case. Thus in Cayley or octave algebra if $\sum_{k=0}^{7} a_k i_k \cdot \sum_{k=0}^{7} b_k i_k = 0$, then $a_k = 0$ or $b_k = 0$; that is, there are unique divisors. W. W. Sawyer in his "Prelude to Mathematics" further repeats this repetition of Dickson's oversight, showing the present need for clarification of this point. That need is shown also by another omission in the handbook article: the absence there in the definition of Cayley algebra of the nonassociative multiplication and its rules, which form the distinctive and essential portion of the definition of that algebra.

The correct statement is that, although H is the highest associative division algebra, C is the last division algebra, as well as the last distributive algebra. After seven nonreal elements, the product of the norms no longer equals the norm of the product of two factors. The norm of such a product is then less, thus giving rise to nondistributive multiplication. Thus if N_1 and N_2 are two numbers in $A_N \equiv N$ (the first complete algebra after C-algebra), then if $N_1 \cdot N_2 = N_{12}$, $|N_1| \cdot |N_2| > |N_{12}|$. The dot in the equation refers to the (required) nondistributive multiplication of N-algebra, as defined in the foregoing tables, whereas the dot of the inequality refers to the ordinary multiplication of R-algebra.

Table I has shown how algebras are specifiable by their type of multiplication. In the two cases, R and G, indistinguishable by this criterion, the

[2] Dickson knew better, as his original discussion of quasi-quaternion treatment of C algebra in his "Linear Algebras" shows. A similar confusion arises in a 1963 paper (L. Inglestam, Hilbert Algebras with Identity, *Bull. Am. Math. Soc.* **69**, p. 794)—that a division algebra must mean R, G, or H. However, division algebras include the nonassociative C-algebra. The same error of omitting C (all stemming from Dickson's ellipsis in "Algebras and their Arithmetics,") is made in a 1965 paper quoting Inglestam (M. F. Smiley, Real Hilbert Algebras with Identity, *Proc. Am. Math. Soc.* (p. 440)), the error in both cases escaping the referees and the editors of the Society. This is not a reflection implying incompetence, but a simple demonstration of how rushed information-processing has become, with inevitable losses in our societal memory.

additional and important distinction between amalgamative and non-amalgamative addition must also be taken into consideration. This distinction is defined by the fact that in R the sum of any two summands is expressible as a single (amalgamated) symbol, whereas in G this is not necessarily so, e.g., $(1+i)$ is not so expressible. The reason for nonamalgamation is meta-dimensional (see pages 209 ff.).

It is worth noting in passing that only the minimal changes of operational meaning are demanded by the successive algebras. Thus the noncommutation of H is simply anticommutation $(ab = -ba)$, which is the very least change that could be made to render the multiplication noncommutative. Similarly, the $(-as)$ multiplication of C is not even mandatory except in certain specified triplets (i.e., those which are not $1 \cdot 2 = 3$, $1 \cdot 4 = 5$, $1 \cdot 6 = 7$, $2 \cdot 4 = -6$, $2 \cdot 5 = 7$, $3 \cdot 4 = 7$, $3 \cdot 5 = 6$, or any cyclic permutation thereof);[2a] and moreover, the nonassociative multiplication then resulting is again only minimally changed; i.e., it is merely antiassociative, that is, $a(bc) = -(ab)c$. If we consider a doublet as d and a singlet as s, $(-as)$ multiplication may be regarded as a meta form of $(-co)$, since $s \cdot d = -d \cdot s$.

The negative sign of any result in $(-co)$ may be interpreted as traversing the H-triplet in the opposite sense [see the diagram in Section II(b)]. Similarly, it may be shown that given the system of fixed singlet and doublet channels shown in Fig. 4, if we want to shift from flow pattern 1, $a(bc)$ to flow pattern 2, $(ab)c$, we must introduce a, b, and c into the channels formerly employed for c, b, and a, respectively.

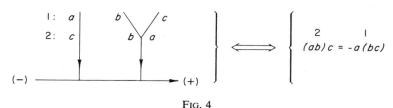

FIG. 4

[2a] Modulo-7 arithmetic (together with the rule that two even members in ascending order of value on the left-hand side will yield a negative result) directly generates the associative subscript equations of Cayley algebra. Similarly modulo-15 arithmetic generates the associative or H-triplets of N-algebra, in which, however, the additional complication of partially associative triplets exists, there being 35 H-triplets and 30 partially associative triplets (see the tables).

We have spoken of cyclic or H-triplets, which could also be called H-spheres. Each of these consists of three independent nonreal elements, thus forming an H-type of algebra. Now $i_{1,2,3} \equiv i, j, k$ may be considered as generating mutually perpendicular circuits (each containing the two real points ± 1) of unit radius such that the subscript equation $1 \cdot 2 = 3$ and its cyclic permutations governs the sense of all three rotations. (We noted this in a 1962 lecture at Naples, and it is discoverable in Hamilton actually— before Du Val's interesting book on quaternions and 3-space rotations appeared in 1964.) If we wish to remain entirely in D_3, it has not been generally noted, however, that the k-circuit must change size, since the i_3 or k-circuit must contain the points $+1 = k^0 = k^{4m}$ and $-1 = k^2 = k^{4m+2}$, where m is any integer. Thus the k-circuit expands, like a cone, with a base radius of zero (at k^0) to one of unity (at $k^1 = k$), then shrinks again to zero at $k^2 = -1$, the base plane of the cone moving so that its center traverses the real axis from $+1$ to -1 as $k^0 \to k^1 \to k^2$, the radius of k^1 being unity as already stated, and the slant height of the cone remaining unity, with vertex at the origin. At $k^{\pm 1}$ the altitude is zero, and the cone, a circle.

However, springing from the multivalued nature of $\sqrt{-1}$, H-algebra actually demands that $i_{1,2,3}$ be all on the same footing, which means a fixed size and position for all three circuits. If this requirement is thoroughly imposed, 3-space is no longer adequate, and we minimally need three fixed, mutually perpendicular unit circuits all intersecting in the points ± 1, which means a 4-space arrangement, such that only two i-circuits plus the real axis, i_0 (i.e., $i_{0,1,2}$, $i_{0,1,3}$, or $i_{0,2,3}$) could be represented in D_3 at any one moment. Thus quaternions do not exactly map 3-space rotations.

Since i_1 and i_2 imply $i_1 \cdot i_2 \neq i_1$ or i_2, we have, in our subscript notation, $(1,2) \to 3$. Similarly, $(1,2,3,4) \to (5,6,7)$ and $(i_k; k = 1, 2, \ldots, 8) \to i_{9,10,\ldots,15}$. Thus the (2^n)th i-element generates the algebra $A(2^{n+1})$ from $A(2)^n$. Thus $(i_0, i_1) \to G$; $(G, i_4) \to C$; and $(C, i_8) \to N$, n being $2^{0,1,2,3,4}$, respectively, for R, G, H, C, and N, the number of i-elements in $A(2^n)$ being $2^n - 1$. This phenomenon is the basis of the notion of a complete algebra, which has been previously defined.

Since a D_4-sphere can have three mutually perpendicular great circles all intersecting a given pair of poles, any fully or cyclic (as) triplet may be called an H-triplet or H-sphere, each such H-sphere containing a quaternion algebra. N-algebra contains 35 H-algebras, just as C contains 7. The structure of N-algebra is extraordinarily richer and more complex than that of C, and far supersedes the richness of C with respect to H. There is a tremendous gap between the distributive and the nondistributive algebras.

It has not hitherto been realized that the norm-of-product/product-of-norms inequality characterizes $(-di)$ multiplication, nor that this in turn implies a volume-shrinkage relation among hyperspheres. Thus $\left(\sum_{k=0}^{m} a_k^2 \right)^{1/2}$, where the a_k are all integers, is the modulus (positive square root of norm) of a number in $A(m)$, i.e., a linear algebra of m-elements. But it is also the radius of a D_m-sphere, as the D_m distance element proves.

Thus the relation $\prod$ (norms) = norm($\prod$) that characterizes all distributive algebras means that $r_1^2 \cdot r_2^2 = r_{12}^2$ or $r_1 \cdot r_2 = r_{12}$, where r_1, r_2, and r_{12} are the radii of three D_m-spheres corresponding respectively to the two numbers and their product. Hence H-multiplication involves four-dimensional spheres, and C-multiplication involves spheres of eight dimensions.

From Table I and its footnotes, it is clear that the maximal number T_n of equal tangent hyperspheres that can fit about another central sphere of the same radius has an intimate connection with the number of units in a given linear algebra. It is hence of some interest to make brief mention of these tangent-sphere groups.

The writer has been interested in this problem since 1948, and approached it from the point of view of the convex polytope, which he called the *polytope of centers*, that might be formed by joining the centers of the shell spheres of a tangent sphere group. This led him to the discovery that contrary to the usual statement that the 24-celled regular polytope of D_4 has no ancestors and no descendants, it actually has both; for it is one of an infinite sequence of convex polytopes which the writer termed the hyper-cuboctahedra, since, like the cuboctahedron (the D_3 member of the family), all the other members also have a circumradius equal to any edge. This family is formed by the hypertruncation of the $(n-2)$th element of the hypercube. By this process the cuboctahedron, the 24-cell (the last regular, finite member of the family), and a 42-celled D_5 figure all arise as the representatives of this polytope sequence in three, four, and five dimensions, respectively. The family arises also from truncating hyperoctahedra.

What makes these three members most interesting is that they are also the packing polytopes ($\mathbf{P}_{3,4,5}$) or polytopes of centers for $D_{3,4,5}$. The author later found that the family of hypercuboctahedra could also be regarded as the ordinary linear truncations of the hyperoctahedra. The author then went on to define the more general family, $\mathbf{P}_n$, by the condition that (1) $_0r = e$; i.e., circumradius = edge, and (2) N_0 = max, i.e., the number of vertices to be a maximum, subject to the first condition. This is a much more fundamental sequence of polytopes than the hypercuboctahedra; and the writer learned that they had all been specified through $n = 8$, although never realized to be members of one family. Indeed, although they had all been separately discovered by 1912, even in 1930 their connection with dense sphere packs was not realized, nor has the family been hitherto defined.

In a letter (May 1965), Professor H. S. M. Coxeter kindly noted that the packing polytopes' existence was implied by his 1951 paper in the *Canadian Journal of Mathematics*, p. 414, although not realized as such or defined by a family. In Coxeter's valuable graphic notation the members from $n = 1$ through $n = 8$ can be written

$\mathbb{P}_1$ •   ; $\mathbb{P}_2$ ••   ; $\mathbb{P}_3$ •••   ; $\mathbb{P}_4$ •⊥••   ;

$\mathbb{P}_5$ •⊥•• ; $\mathbb{P}_6$ ••⊥•• ; $\mathbb{P}_7$ •••⊥•• ; $\mathbb{P}_8$ ••••⊥•• ,

a notation which can be regarded as mapping whole dimensions into points, as does (in a different manner and independently arrived at) the writer's archemorphic notation for classifying differential equations (*17*, p. 256). That $N_0(\mathbf{P}_8) = 240$ was first discovered by the genius of Thorold Gossett in 1897, although the connection of the number 240 with the eight-dimensional tangent sphere group (T_8) was not realized until H. F. Blichfeldt's brilliant work on minimal quadratic forms in 1935; and even thereafter the geometric connection with Gossett's work was slow in coming, Coxeter being the first to realize it in an insightful paper (1946) which linked that number also to C-algebra.

In 1963 the writer found the following results, the summary formula of which is quoted in (*8*, p. 66).

Define T_n as the maximal number of equal tangent hyperspheres that can all touch another sphere of the same radius in n-dimensional parabolic space, D_n. Then for $1 \leqslant n \leqslant 8$,

$$T_n = n\left(\left\{\frac{2^{n-2}}{3}\right\} + n\right),$$

where $\{m\}$ is the least integer containing m.

Coxeter ("Regular Polytopes," 2nd ed., 1965, p. 234) requires five (the last three being quite complicated) separately derived equations and expressions to gain h, the period of the product (order of multiplication irrelevant) of the finite symmetry group generated by reflections of a hypertetrahedral fundamental region. These groups are extremely important, are all irreducible, and can extend only up to eight dimensions, inclusively. After $n = 8$, the fundamental region is reducible or factorable, and there are no more such groups. The graph is then disconnected.

The expression (in the above formula) multiplying n is h for these groups, thus furnishing the periods of the products of their generators in remarkably uniform, concise, and simple form using one equation only. The geometric basis of our expression for T_n extends very deeply into the fundamental nature of irreducible groups generated by reflections. The expression in brackets contains the heart of the matter, and represents the maximal number plus one[3] of hypertetrahedral vertices (i.e., the kind with three cells, all also of hypertetrahedral shape, about a vertex) that can be formed given 2^{n-2} hypertetrahedral cells. That number of cells in turn is the number of cells bounding the hyperoctahedron in $(n-2)$ dimensions.[4] Thus the

[3] The extra "1" refers to the $n(n+1)$ vertices always formable in n dimensions by translating the $(n+1)$ cells of an n-dimensional hypertetrahedron outwardly along their respective altitudes (drawn from the center of the figure to the centers of each cell).

[4] The regular D_n octahedron has the symmetry of a hypersphere in D_n with all its $(n-2)$ mutually perpendicular axes of rotation drawn with respect to a given equatorial plane. The $(2n-4)$ poles of such a sphere have the symmetry of the $2(n-2)$ vertices of an $(n-2)$-dimensional octahedron, since the n diagonals of a regular D_n octahedron are all mutually perpendicular. In the prior equation, $\frac{1}{2}T_n$—the number of diameters in T_n—is the number of hyperplanes of symmetry in the irreducible group of period $h = T_n/n$ generated by reflections. The fundamental region for such a group is always a hypertetrahedron in elliptic or parabolic space, and such groups extend only through $n = 8$, as mentioned above.

previous equation by no means simply epitomizes existing information on these groups but provides a new and fundamental insight into the nature of finite groups generated by reflections, as well as a demonstration of the unity of the first eight dimensions in concise, elegant fashion.

From our formula, $N_0(\mathbf{P}_n) = 2, 6, 12, 24, 40, 72, 126, 240$ for $1 \leqslant n \leqslant 8$, which are also key numbers in the theory of quadratic forms, sphere packs, and tetrahedral symmetry groups. It is a consequence of their definition that in all these convex polytopes the number of edges meeting at each vertex is the same in each such polytope; i.e., $2N_1/N_0 = N_{1/0}$. Also all the dihedral angles of such a polytope are equal, the dihedral being defined as the angle between two D_{n-1} elements. These facts in turn imply that each vertex can be surrounded by not more than two kinds of surface cells c_1 and c_2, so arranged that in the hypersurface pattern all c_1's are adjoined at all D_{n-2} elements by c_2's, and vice versa. For $n = 2$ or 4, $c_1 = c_2$, and we have all α_1's and all β_3's, respectively, as surface cells, that is, a regular figure; in a more trivial sense, $n = 1$ also produces a regular figure. After $n = 4$ this phenomenon can never occur again in any finite positive dimension, and in all other cases $\mathbf{P}_n$ must be a special type of Archimedean figure such that if ϕ be the angle at the center between any two vertices, $\phi = \pi/3$ radians.

After $n = 8$ tremendous changes occur, in line with the vast shift from distributive to nondistributive algebras. Put in terms of the theory of sphere packs, the polytope of centers is no longer convex.[5] The writer's findings (17, pp. 230 and 262) for tangent sphere groups with $n \geqslant 9$ refer to the maximal numbers of equal tangent spheres surrounding another of greater radius such that the difference between the two radii is minimal, since the two radii can no longer be equal and the polytope remain convex. The writer's previous work was done under the assumption of a convex

---

[5] Note that the edges of a "polytope of centers," and hence of a "packing polytope" ($\mathbf{P}_n$), are all lines of centers between pairs of *tangent* (hyper)spheres in the T_n (hyper)shell. A packing polytope, as will appear from the exposition, is simply a maximal-vertex (N_0 max) polytope of centers for a monoradial (hyper)sphere pack in a given D_n, "monoradial" referring to the fact that both the shell (hyper)spheres and the central one all have the same radius. When the radius of the central member is different from that of the shell members, all of which are alike, we have a biradial pack, also considered in pages 192 ff. The packing polytopes summarize in their structure the sphere-packing or lattice possibilities of their dimensions.

polytope of centers as his theorem that for $n > 8$, the polytope of centers is no longer convex, was only recently found. The proof of this theorem in quickest form may be made to devolve upon the equation

$$4 \csc^{-1} \sqrt{n} - \sec^{-1} n = 0,$$

which has as its only real solution $n = 8$.

This equation represents the last finite member of our *alphabet honeycombs*, a remarkable series of hyperspace lattices, all the cells of which consist only of alphas and betas, i.e., of regular hypertetrahedra and hyperoctahedra; hence our designation "alphabet." Where the following coefficients represent numbers of dihedral angles of the indicated polytopes, we have for the six finite members of the series (all the several expressions in parentheses being equal to 2π radians), in D_2, D_3, D_4, and D_8:

$$(6\alpha_2) = (3\alpha_2 + 2\beta_2) = (4\beta_2) = (2\alpha_3 + 2\beta_3) = (3\beta_4) = (1\alpha_8 + 2\beta_8).$$

There is also a seventh member belonging to D_∞ $(2\alpha_\infty + 1\beta_\infty = 2\pi)$, since the dihedrals are now, respectively, $\pi/2$ and π.

The reason for the great symmetry and density of the packing structures in D_4 and D_8 is intimately connected with the following facts, the significance of which has not been noted: the circumradius of the D_4 cube (γ_4) is equal to its edge, and in γ_8 it is equal to the face diagonal. Thus the basic symmetry possibilities of the cube are fully exploited at $n = 8$ in so far as single straight lines can be related. There is one simple symmetry possibility, but even this involves two perpendicular straight lines related to a third line; the circumradius of γ_{16} is equal to the sum of the two sides of the isosceles right triangle whose hypotenuse is the face diagonal. This D_{16} relationship breaks the simplicity of the single linear pattern, of which D_8 is the last representative; however, D_{16} is still simple enough to be the highest dimension in which a simple $(-di)$ algebra may exist, i.e., a nondistributive algebra without the complication of zero revival, that is, without $a \cdot 0 = b$, where $a \cdot b \neq 0$, ∞, but with $a \cdot b = 0$.

There is not space here to enter into the indicated processes, which rest upon derivable rules of zero formation. Suffice it to say that six levels of zero arise through the interaction of nondistributive operators in N through N_N algebra, these six falling into a hierarchy of three parity pairs. Hence six kinds of zeros result, which are indicated by the following table, showing alternative symbols. These have relevance in quadratic algebra.

TABLE II

THE SIX ZEROS OF ($-di$) MULTIPLICATION (cf. Sections III and IV)

Thus $(+ - -)(- + +) \to (0\bar{0}0)$; $(0\bar{0}0)(\bar{0}0\bar{0}) \to (\circ \bar{\circ} \circ)$; $(\bar{\circ} \circ \bar{\circ})(\circ \bar{\circ} \circ) \to (\bar{\oplus}\oplus\bar{\oplus})$, etc. It should be noted that $\oplus$ and $\bar{\oplus}$ do not interact, each containing a self-polar system of rotations as the fourth symbols of rows 5 and 6 show. In N_C-algebra is thus attained the highest level zero of the hierarchy, i.e., $\oplus$ or $\bar{\oplus}$ on each of six "tracks" or channels (a "6-track zero"), the $(-di)$ operators in that algebra being able to have as many as six channels or guides for their parity waves; whereas N, N_G, and N_H may have only 3, 4, and 5 parity wave channels respectively. Six channels is a limit that may be compared to a coaxial cable formed by six helical strands around a core of equal diameter. There is not space for further development here, but class numbers of higher cyclotomic number fields are relevant.

Although nondistributive multiplication and its possible algebras have not hitherto been considered, they constitute as fundamental and basic an extension of mathematical thinking as the extension from positive to negative, and then to complex and hypercomplex numbers. What has delayed such specification was the unreasonable fear of a non-division algebra, that fear being no more tenable than it was in number theory, where Kummer freed us from confinement to algebraic number fields with unique factorization in terms of real or complex numbers.

The same problem arose in vector algebra. Thus if v and v' are two perpendicular vectors, and v_1 is another vector not perpendicular to either, we have for the scalar product $v \cdot v_1 = v_2$, but $v(v' + v_1) = v_2$, since the scalar product of two perpendicular vectors vanishes. Thus nondistribution may arise in vector algebra, rendering vector quotients nonunique, since any other vector v_p, perpendicular to v, would yield $v \cdot v_p = 0$.

On another occasion (*17*, p. 216) we have also shown that $(-di)$ multiplication enters into the theory of nonlinear operators, with the consequence in electronics that undistorted modulation is not possible with a nonlinear operator, and neither are superposition or classical harmonic analysis; and we add *en passant* that distorted modulation is deeply connected with any theory of mathematical esthetics, a field that has interested mathematicians from ancient times, notably G. Birkhoff in our times, although Birkhoff did not reach the connection between nonlinearity and esthetics. In this connection the volumes brilliantly edited by G. Kepes of the Massachusetts Institute of Technology (published by Brazilier, New York) on structure and the visual arts should also be noted, even though not quite relevant to the present technical bibliography. They reached the writer's attention after this paper was in press and hence could receive only brief mention. [See also (*17*, p. 227 ff.) and pages 200 ff. of this paper for relations to biological patterns and coding structures.]

Professors Antoniewicz, Conti, and Moreau have, each in their own way, stressed the relation of convexity to control. We are suggesting that this relation can be made more precise, analytic, and applicable by the following *Theorem*: The *unit packing structure* of a parabolic dimension n governs the controllability problem in such a space. *Lemma*: That packing structure is in turn specified by the maximum number T_n of equal tangent hyperspheres in D_n that fit about another of equal radius; then $T_n = N_0(\mathbf{P}_n)$, defining the *polytope of centers* by its number of vertices; that all its edges are equal follows also.

There is a natural hyperplane separation of these sphere groups (cf. Conti's "ball of controllability") which we characterize thus: two "polar caps," each of $\frac{1}{2}(T_n - T_{n-1})$ spheres, are separated by an $(n-1)$-hyperplane of "equator" T_{n-1} sphere units.

Concluding our previous remarks on sphere packs, we note that it is therefore now possible by means of the concept of the *polytope of centers* to unify the geometry of all sphere-inscribable polytopes of equal edge in terms of rigid groups of tangent spheres (radius r) about a central one of radius R. If $_0R$ is the circumradius of such a polytope, whose edge is e, then $[2(_0R)/e] - 1 = R/r$. Thus R/r determines the polytope. If $R < r$, we have all the regular figures (except γ_4 for which $R = r$); and for $n < 8$, the Gossett polytopes. If $R = r$ we have all the packing polytopes $\mathbf{P}_n$, all the truncated cross polytopes (it is interesting to note that $t\beta_n = \mathbf{P}_n$ for $n = 3, 4, 5$), and all the expanded simplexes. For other ratios of R and r we have the truncated expanded simplexes, and the hemifigures of these truncations, all those ratios being of the form R/r, as are all γ_n for $n > 4$. The hemigammas for $n > 8$ have $R > r$; for the hemigamma $n = 8$, $R = r$; and for $n < 8$, $R < r$. The 240 vertices of $\mathbf{P}_8$ are thus obtainable by compounding a $h\gamma_8$ and a truncated β_8 ($128 + 112 = 240$); this is believed to be a new construction.

Thus all the Archimedean figures are subsumed under the theory of rigid configurations of equal spheres on a central sphere of usually larger radius.

The ratio $R/r = \sqrt{5}$ is particularly interesting. In D_2 it yields the decagon, in D_3 the icosidodecahedron, and in D_4 the 120 cell as well as a figure of 96 vertices (see below). It appears to be the only finite ratio other than unity which generates polytopes that, like the packing polytopes, possess analogous sections in lower dimensions which are all maximal-contact packs for that ratio. Thus with $R/r = \sqrt{5}$, no more than 10 spheres fit about 1 in D_2; no more than 30 in three dimensions; and no more than 120 in D_4. In five or more dimensions, the ratio no longer yields a rigid pack.

In four dimensions, rigid packs (for $R \geqslant r$) can be formed from 16, 20, 24, 32, 96, 600, or 720 equal spheres. It is interesting to note that the group of 96 has also the ratio $R/r = \sqrt{5}$. Similar theorems may be enunciated for the higher dimensions with this theory. In all dimensions ($n > 2$) the number of rigid packs is *finite*, as is the number of viable ratios R/r.

Thus the subject of generalized sphere packs, as here outlined, has an intimate connection with the theory of polytopes. The group 360-about-1 in D_9 is the "first" convex figure in that it is the first convex pack in D_9 with the number of contacts to the central sphere exceeding 272 and with $(R/r) - 1$ a minimum. This group forms a polytope of centers that could be called a "$hte\alpha_9$", i.e., a hemitruncated, expanded D_9 simplex, using the notation introduced by Coxeter in his 1930 paper.

One can go further and treat the theory of all equal-edged convex polytopes, whether sphere-inscribable or not, in terms of maximally dense packs of equal spheres, using the notion of a polytope of centers. Similarly, equal-edged nonconvex polytopes may also be treated and generated, but there is no room here for the interesting details. We shall heneforth adopt the names *alpha, beta, gamma* as more convenient than the relatively awkward "simplex" or (hyper)tetrahedron, "crosspolytope" or (hyper)-octahedron, and "measure polytope" or (hyper)cube, respectively. Indeed, "simplex" is somewhat of a misnomer. For the (hyper)tetrahedrons are one of the subtlest and most elegant of all polytopes, ensuring as we have seen they do that the eighth dimension is the principal key to the theory of structure.

Related to this fact is the writer's expression $(\Delta_g)^{1/2}/g$ ($g = 9 - n$, n referring to D_n, and Δ_n being the nth triangular number, where $\Delta_1 = 1$, $\Delta_2 = 3$, $\Delta_3 = 6$, etc.) for the governing structural ratio of circumradius to edge in the dimensionally successive vertex-truncation figures of $\mathbf{P}_n$ ($n = 9$ yields a lattice or infinite polytope). This series of polytopes was first discovered by the geometrical genius of Thorold Gossett in late 19th century England, and called by him "the wedges"; although he did not recognize the series as one of successive vertex figures nor as one related to the highest possible convex polytope of monoradial centers, our $\mathbf{P}_8$.

During an interesting and stimulating conversation in London after this section had been written, but in time to include this comment, Professor C. A. Rogers kindly brought to the writer's attention his recent paper (*Mathematika*, 1963) on covering a sphere with spheres. Here Rogers, despite excellent results, reaches an impasse of sorts in considering a problem which in terms of the present theory reduces to that of a polytope of centers with $R > r = 1$.

On p. 157 Rogers states frankly that "the following results ... are not completely satisfactory." Thus when $R > n \log n$, Rogers concludes, "I do not see how to obtain a really satisfactory form of theorem 1 in this case."

The present work suggests that the initial assumption $R > r$, $r = 1$, was too restrictive, and moreover, that consideration of the ratio R/r, and not R or r considered separately, unlocks the algebraic geometric morphology of this problem and situation. The method and notion of the polytope of centers is likewise relevant, as well as the important theorem that for $n \geqslant 9$, P_n is nonconvex. There are two other important considerations in this same problem which are directly connected to the situation for large n. The first is an interesting theorem of the writer resting both on the Coxeter-Rogers-Schläfli upper bound and on the writer's formulas for sphere packs with convex polytope of centers:

$$\lim_{n \to \infty} T_{n+1}/T_n = \sqrt{2}.$$

The second consideration referred to above grows out of Rogers' fundamental result of 1958 (*Proc. London Math. Soc.*) based upon findings by the great Ludwig Schläfli. Rogers then showed that the volume ratio of the part of α_n taken up by $(n+1)$ tangent hyperspheres with their centers at the hypertetrahedron's vertices to the whole volume of α_n is, asymptotically, $\sigma_n = (n/e) 2^{-n/2}$, i.e., $\lim_{n \to \infty} \sigma_n = 0$, more simply, $\sigma_\infty = 0$, a result not explicit in Rogers' paper.

The empty portion of the simplex, i.e., the n-dimensional hole, may then be calculated to be asymptotically given by

$$H_n = \frac{(n-1)^{1/2}}{n}\left(2^{n/2} - \frac{n}{e}\right).$$

Hence

$$\frac{\text{empty portion}}{\text{filled portion}} = \frac{1}{\sigma_n} - 1 = \left(\frac{e}{n} \cdot 2^{n/2} - 1\right).$$

Thus our theorem—that for large n the empty portion increases at the expense of the filled portion in the ratio $(e/n) 2^{n/2}$, and that although the D_n content of α_n approaches zero as $n \to \infty$, the portion of α_n filled by the $(n+1)$ hyperspheres becomes progressively less with regard to the empty space, and this ratio approaches zero as $n \to \infty$.

Therefore the unusable surface of a D_n sphere, with regard to a maximal number of equal spheres tangent to its surface, increases half-exponentially with n. It is the lack of taking into account this unusable part of the hyper-surface that makes the Schläfli-Rogers-Coxeter upper bound too high. That that bound is valid as far as it goes, however, has been demonstrated by the writer from the fact that the vertex-content ratio is greater for the alpha than for any other regular or partially regular figures. This result was communicated to Professor Coxeter in October 1965, about a month after it was obtained.

Before closing this section of commentary, a few points should still be mentioned, such as that on page 176 the table of the 35 H-triplets has been deliberately "scrambled" to provide an exercise for the reader interested in gaining more familiarity with the indicial equations of N-algebra. By the use of modulo-15 arithmetic in the subscript equations, the table may be arranged in perfect sequential order. (*Hint*: Use the type of subscript equation $n \cdot m = r$ or $-r$ with $n \leqslant m$ and both n, m odd or even, respectively, where maximum r is the sum modulo 15 of n and m or a lower number determined by selection rules necessary for self-consistency.) This table involves 35 separate, but related, H-type algebras and one C-algebra. Consistency with both the C and H algebras embedded in N serves to derive the multiplication table. The eight $(-di)$ operators arise from the simplest type of parity wave oscillating about a neutral axis; namely, the eight permutations of two things ($+$ and $-$) taken three at a time, for three moments or points, are minimally required to establish oscillation or curvature. The eight forms fall into four pairs (cf. Section IV):

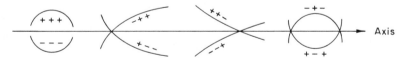

It should also be noted that the table in Section II(c) exhibits the *partially* cyclic triplets whose linearly projected flow patterns ($\triangle$ denotes vertex of triangle) are

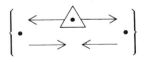

instead of

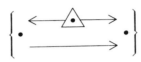

as in the (fully) cyclic or H-triplets, thus allowing two categories of non-associative multiplication by means of two triplet types that may thus be termed hyperbolic and elliptic, respectively. The *linear* "triplet" of Section II(a) can in the same spirit be termed parabolic, possessing the vertex pattern

The three patterns may be designated as hyperbolic or self-opposing; elliptic or self-affirming; and parabolic, equilibrated, or mixed, respectively.

Similarly, R-algebra, where, u being a unit, $u^2 = 1$, may be termed "elliptic"; all the complex and hypercomplex algebras, wherein $u^2 = -1$ are thus "hyperbolic"; and the quadratic algebra to which N_N leads includes $u^2 = 0$, i.e., "parabolic." There is a fourth category of unit, and hence of number, in the algebra with an infinity of elements where, although $u^4 = 0$, $|u| = 1$. This last category may be called "loxodromic." This terminology is derivable from isomorphisms to linear transformations or conformal representations, and the traces of their matrices, the matrix being loxodromic if the trace ($\equiv$ sum of elements of principal diagonal from upper left to lower right) is not real.

We have already noted that every matrix represents a hypercomplex number. In general i_n has a (2^{m-1})-element real matrix representation in all algebras $A(2^m)$, $m \geqslant n$. Thus $i_1 \equiv i$ requires a 4-element real matrix, whereas $i_3 \equiv k$ or $i_2 \equiv j$ requires a 16-element real matrix. Thus, for example,

$$\begin{pmatrix} 0 & 0 & 1 & 0 \\ 0 & 0 & 0 & 1 \\ -1 & 0 & 0 & 0 \\ 0 & -1 & 0 & 0 \end{pmatrix} \leftrightarrow i_2.$$

(Another matrix identical with i_2 is similar but smaller, containing $\pm i$ as well as ± 1 and 0.) It is not difficult to decide which notation is most elegant and least cumbersome. Thus hypercomplex numbers can be regarded as embedding in themselves entire systems of linear equations. The principal diagonal (upper left to lower right) of all real-element matrices referring to hypercomplex numbers is null.

The author found that $p^2 = 0$ was demanded when hypercomplex numbers attain a surdimensionality of 8, the mth surdimension being defined as a higher hierarchical form of a (2^m)-dimensional parabolic or Euclidean space. These surdimensions are very important in defining what we have called "complete algebras." In terms of them, real, Gaussian, quaternion, Cayleyan, and N-algebra are 0-, 1-, 2-, 3-, and 4-surdimensional, respectively. Beyond 4 surdimensions, as already indicated, there is a hierarchy of zero revival in successive complete algebras, until finally $p^2 = 0$, $p \neq 0$, is attained, in 7 surdimensions. At this point linear algebras give way to quadratic algebra and then cubic algebra (see Section IV). There is reason to regard these surdimensions as *logical closures* with respect to hierarchies of operational structures composed of independent categories (cf. (*18*), Addendum).

Beyond the first $(-di)$ algebra (i.e., N) there lie at least two higher forms of nondistribution, which may be symbolized as providing the results $a \cdot 0 = b$ and $a^2 = 0$, respectively, where neither a nor b is zero or infinity. It was with great delight that, after having confirmed the necessity for $p^2 = 0$, $p \neq 0$, in higher $(-di)$ algebra,[6] we found that Eduard Study had in 1900 arrived at the same type of number from considerations of nonreal projective geometry, arising originally out of his new approach to kinematics. These numbers, called *dual numbers*, have been regarded more or less as a mathematical curiosity, with no inkling of their transcendent importance in the theory of nondistributive algebraic structures.

The simplest kind of number characterized by the fact that the square of the unit is minus unity, is termed an imaginary number and the form of its

---

[6] Specifically in N_C, the algebra of metacomplex numbers of the p-type with 2^7 elements, i.e., the 7th surdimension or algebraic field, all fields beyond the 3rd surdimension being nondistributive.

unit power field is a unit circle on the complex plane. Similarly, the hyper-imaginary numbers $(i_n, 1 \leqslant n)$ form a series of hyperplanes, the entire series constituting what we term the hypercomplex plane. The kind of number characterized by $p^2 = 0$ where p is the unit, is related not to simple circles, but to a pair of tangent circles of unit diameters. There is a relation here to the complex function $w = z^{-n}$, which yields a family of tangent circle pairs for $n = 1$. In Cartesian coordinates one such pair, representing the unit field form of this second kind of higher number, is given by $(x^2 + y^2)^2/y^2 = 1$, the radius vector for an angle of radians from the real axis being given by $r = \sin \theta$, and hence $p^\phi = p^{2\theta/\pi} r (1 - r^2)^{1/2} + pr^2 = \sin \theta(\cos \theta + p \sin \theta)$. Thus $p^0 = 0$ and $p^2 = 0$, which distinguishes p- from i-numbers.

Just as all the i_n-operators determine the hypercomplex "plane," i.e., a hyperplane of n nonreal independent lines and one real line, so the p_n numbers determine a metacomplex "space," the rotation planes of all the p_n being perpendicular to the hypercomplex plane. The unit field form of an i_n-operator is a unit circle, and that of a p_n-operator, two tangent circles of unit diameter. In plane perspective hypercomplex space can be represented as a circle-ellipse family, metacomplex space as a double circle-double ellipse family.

These p numbers, which we arrived at through a theory of algebraic structure, and which Study arrived at through a kinematic, projective analysis inspired by some work of Laguerre, have, as J. Grünwald pointed out about 1906, an isomorphism with the quadric cone in Study's scheme, although we have found the double circle family, derivable from the complex function already given, more useful and accurate for our purpose. Actually, the two views can be reconciled when the double circle curves are regarded as the vertical sections of an infinite sequence of what we have previously termed umbilicoidal shells in a 3-space. These umbilicoids are intimately related to the even negative dimensions[7] and to our theory of

[7] A simple umbilicoid is given by $(x^2 + y^2 + z^2)^2/(x^2 + y^2) = 1$. The content of odd negadimensional umbilicoids is zero, just as that of even negadimensional spheres is zero. Conversely, umbilicoids exist in the even negadimensions, whereas spheres do not. The two are in this sense complementary forms. The (hyper)surface of an n-dimensional umbilicoid is given by

$$2(n-1) \pi^{(n+1)/2} \frac{r^{n-1}}{[(n-1)/2!]},$$

half-integer genus, with corresponding Riemann-surface representation. As the over-all horizontal diameter of these shells tends toward infinity, the finite portion in the neighborhood around the origin tends to a quadric cone, much in the same way, as we have previously pointed out (*17*, p. 258, note), as a finite portion of an infinite elliptical torus may tend toward a hyperbolic paraboloid.

It is interesting to note here that hyperspirals may be defined as projections on a D_{n-1} hyperplane of hyperconical helices in D_n. Thus the complex numbers may be ordered in terms of an Archimedean spiral of infinitesimal pitch; and it is just as incorrect to state that complex numbers cannot be ordered as that the points on such a spiral line cannot be ordered, radius vector and angle being given first and second priority, respectively, thus generating an infinity of numbers, all ordered for each member of a like infinity of radii, also all ordered.

The hypercomplex numbers can likewise be ordered by the hyperspirals we have defined above, with a hierarchy of priorities assigned to radii and angles in successive dimensions. Professor Charles Loewner, in his invited lecture before the American Mathematical Society in 1964, came close to such an ordering, but reached only the stage of hypercones, and thus

where n is the dimension (n may be negative) and r, the radius of the two generating hyperspheres. Similarly, the content of an n-dimensional umbilicoid is given by

$$\frac{2\pi^{(n+1)/2} r^n}{[(n-1)/2]!}$$

Thus, when $r = 1$, $n = 3$, we obtain a surface of $4\pi^2 r^2$ and a volume of $2\pi^2 r^3$, tallying with the equation given above. The negative dimensions are deeply related to the nature of frequency, and hence, of time, rather than space. They have not been hitherto considered. D_{-1} is by far the most important of all negative dimensions. In this connection, by use of the Riemann zeta function we have obtained the result that

$$\lim_{\epsilon \to 0} (-1 + \epsilon)! = S_\infty$$

where $\epsilon \geq 0$ and $S_\infty \equiv 1 + \frac{1}{2} + \frac{1}{3} + \frac{1}{4} + \frac{1}{5} + \cdots$, the famous harmonic series. Likewise $(-2)! = -(-1)!$ and $(-3)! = \frac{1}{2}(-1)! = \frac{1}{2} + \frac{1}{4} + \frac{1}{6} + \frac{1}{8} + \cdots$. Thus the first three negadimensions are the most important, where n is any positive integer.

$$(-n)! = (-1)^{n-1} S_\infty/(n-1)! \text{ and } (-1)!/(-n)! = (-1)^{n-1}(n-1)!$$

Thus D_{-1} enters into the nature of Euler's constant, as $n!$ and D_n are closely morphologically related. That $(-\infty)! = 0$ follows also.

attained an admitted ambiguity, which the concept of the hyperspiral eliminates. We so advised Loewner in 1964.

Finally, related to the sixth-order curve $x^4 = y^4 - y^6$ and a family based upon it through an appropriate parameter, we have the number q_n such that $|q_n| = 1, q_n^{\pm 4k} = 0$, which do not participate in any of the number spaces determined by the i- and p-numbers, but participate only in algebraic structures beyond quadratic algebra (see Section V and pages 192 ff.).

VII. Application to Error-Correcting Codes

There is a deep connection between dense-packed, error-correcting codes and maximal monoradial groupings of tangent hyperspheres about a central hypersphere. The Golay-Paige code can be derived directly from such a maximal pack in 23 dimensions, the partition of the exponent being $11 + 12$, in the sense that the 23-dimensional cube may be considered a pattern of 2^{11} vertices repeated 2^{12} times. This pattern is related directly to sphere packs in 23 and 24 dimensions, as Leech (*14*, pp. 670–671) has shown. The reader is also refered to Refs. *15* and *19*.

Higher dimensional packs suggest that still more sophisticated codes and hence computer programs would arise from packs of tangent hyperspheres with more than one lattice possible.

During a conversation at the University of London, Prof. C. A. Rogers brought to attention a very interesting paper of his (*Mathematika*, 1957), following discussions with Dr. S. K. Zaremba on the remarkable efficiency of a random redundant code in transmitting through an imperfect channel. In this paper Rogers sums up the findings, including his own and those of Professors Bambah, Davenport, Roth, and Watson, to the effect that the most economical lattice covering of a space by congruent figures whose centroids form the points of the lattice are nevertheless less economical than the most economical covering possible, which Rogers showed has an upperbound density of $n(\log n + \log \log n + 5)$ for $n \geqslant 3$, n being the dimensionality of the space.

We first venture to say that the efficiency is due to the redundancy of the code rather than its randomness, which would, however, increase Shannon information, just as a nonsense message has more unexpectedness or more such "information" than a meaningful message. This observation leads to the interesting theorem that a cipher message originally composed in some language has less Shannon information than a message of nonsense syllables; i.e., any cipher must preserve some form of the original pattern of thought, and hence less unexpectedness than complete nonsense.

The principal reason for mentioning these facts is that a random covering may be more economical than the most economical *one-rule* lattice covering. We have introduced the italicized adjective, feeling that it lies at the root of the apparent paradox, for random coverings of maximal efficiency could be defined only by *shifting* rules of formation. It is this more flexible strategy, as it were, that accounts for their possibility of being more efficient than even the most economical lattice covering, which is based on a *single* rule of formation.

VIII. Other Applications

Aside from the applications to geometry and computer coding and programming already mentioned, there are important relations both to the theory of numbers and to physics.

We shall mention the first very briefly. As long ago as 1880 Henri Poincaré had very masterfully pointed out that the ellipse and the hyperbola were the geometric keys to the structure of quadratic number fields based on $\sqrt{-K}$ and $\sqrt{K}$, respectively. It was also known by the late 19th century that the ideals of a quadratic algebraic number field (of multiple factorization) were isomorphic to lattices of constant mesh area. In the simplest cases such lattices are planar, thus suggesting at once the machinery of elliptic functions. In more complicated cases they may exist on specially defined surfaces which the writer has found are intimately related to his "curvilinear elliptic functions," which may be defined very briefly as more generalized elliptic functions based on curvilinear parallelograms. There is an extension to higher (than quadratic) number fields and their corresponding higher-space lattices, both flat and curvilinear, for which we have no space here, except to say that multiperiodic and hypercomplex functions are involved.

Such a development relates the theory of algebraic number fields to packings of hyperspheres, the centers of which would be the lattice points; just as we previously saw that such packings were intimately connected with the theory of hypercomplex numbers and hence with the structure of algebras.

The matter goes even deeper, since matrices may be treated, often with great gain in succinctness and elegance, as hypercomplex numbers. Moreover, the theory of finite groups in its most recondite aspects is related to the notions of a group of tangent hyperspheres and its polytope of centers. We have already seen the connections with error-correcting codes.

Thus groups of tangent hyperspheres, determining as they also do the packing structure of any given dimension, constitute one of the most fertile and fundamental domains of mathematics. Algebraically, hypercomplex numbers possess the same fundamentality, determining as they do even the nature of the arithmetic operations that may be performed upon them or, more accurately, in which they may be engaged. For the nature of a kind of number determines the nature of its operations. Since mathematics itself may be defined as the science of numbers[8] and their operations, it is clear that mathematics may be essentially enlarged and deepened only by enlarging and deepening our notion of number. In this sense all of mathematics after the ancient Greeks grow out of minus 1 and its square root, function theory included. Turning to physics, we now see why quaternions are becoming increasingly important despite their comparative neglect, although they were actually introduced through the back door as the basis of the vector product, the rules of which for 3-space repeat exactly the rules for quaternion multiplication of the unit vectors, except that their squares are zero instead of minus 1. This fact is the basis of Du Val's excellent observa-

---

[8] The fallacy of Bourbakian set theory is one of reductive omission: distance is ignored, although a distance function, separating the members of any set and allowing them to be distinguished, is implicit in the very notion of *set*; and distance is number, which is thus shown to be the basis of distinguishability and hence of definition. The distance may be governed by a gauge metric or even be stochastic, but it must be there for distinguishability to exist. Even so-called pure projective theorems are special cases of theorems involving angles, which in turn imply separation and distance functions. Moreover, for each so-called "pure" projective theorem there are metric theorems where a certain *non*coincidence occurs, matching a coincidence of the projective theorem, or whereby the angle implied by a given projective ratio is made explicit.

tions in his 1964 book on quaternions and rotations (Oxford University Press) and of our own observations, independently arrived at in 1962; and it is implicit in Hamilton's original work.

It is quite understandable that ordinary physics would find it inconvenient that the square of an operator should become negative. However, in quantum mechanics that is not so inconvenient, and C. W. Kilmister in 1949 was able to demonstrate that Dirac's theory could be made independent of the metric, and hence simpler, by introducing quaternions. In a London conversation with Lancelot Law Whyte, who brought to my attention for the first time his 1954 paper (among others) (27), I noted that he too had noticed this fact, and Kilmister and he have the priority for underlining it. In the history of ideas it is usually a new emphasis or implication of past knowledge rather than pure innovation that constitutes historical novelty; for quaternions-as-angles is implied in Hamilton's work.

Certain findings of quantum physics not only substantiate the conclusion of a physical (i.e., not merely pseudo-Euclidean) fourth spatial dimension, but suggest that the spatial dimensionality of our physical universe may well run as high as eight dimensions, for the almost exact rational value of the fine-structure constant 1/137 suggests strongly the existence of the unique eight-dimensional lattice composed of two kinds of cells such that every 137 of them forms an identical group whose constituents are 128 eight-dimensional tetrahedra and 9 eight-dimensional octahedra.

There is no higher finite dimension than 8 that can form a lattice composed solely of tetrahedra and/or octahedra, which are the two simplest regular forms in any dimension, since they have the fewest vertices. Therefore the eighth dimension is an upper limit for lattice regularity and simplicity. Its characteristic number, 137, interestingly points to the fine-structure constant. The exact value of that constant, 1/137.04, suggests that there is a slight curvature of the lattice in at least the ninth dimension, thus allowing slightly more cells per unit of eight-dimensional space. One cell would thus constitute approximately 1/137th of the repeating group pattern of 137 ($=9+128$) cells.

The author has also noted (17, p. 242) that the fine structure constant governs the ratio of an electron's mean radius r to the mean radius a of its orbit by the simple equation $(r/a)^{1/2} \cong 1/137$, thus suggesting that the relation of an electron to the whole configuration of its orbit about the proton is in some sense isomorphic to that of one cell of the eight-dimensional lattice considered as a unit of the entire group pattern of 137 cells. The necessity for at least a fourth physical dimension (specifically for a four-dimensional cylinder, whose cross section is a spheroid) to explain the observed phenomenon of a gravitational field (in press, National Research Council of Italy, Rome) is, however, quite independent of the existence of the spatially eight-dimensional lattice thus indicated by quantum physics.

Thus quaternions do not go far enough. I have long felt that the problems of bio-, psycho-, and sociomorphogenesis will not be solvable until placed on a firm mathematical basis, and that that basis lay in the direction of conditionally randomized hypercomplex variables and their functions, involving a hypercomplex algebra of at least 15 i-elements, which with i_0 comprise the first complete algebra where multiplication becomes non-distributive, and where pairs of annihilation operators can arise.

In a valuable technical paper[9] just called to our attention by ARTORGA's knowledgeable editor, Dr. Marcus C. Goodall of the Department of Physics, University of Boston, has already used an algebra—which he calls $Q_8(z)$—isomorphic to Cayley algebra, to resolve some basic problems of quantum field theory in both concrete and elegant fashion. Goodall is also one of the few who is aware of the pertinence of algebraic field theory to quantum mechanics. It may be noted here that this pertinence was implicit ever since the theory of Riemann surfaces was linked with that of algebraic fields by means of multiperiodic functions.

In this connection our proof of the existence of half-integer genus (presented for us at a 1965 meeting of the American Mathematical Society) is relevant, as that concept contains the key to the development of an adequate and more sophisticated theory of transformation groups and automorphisms, including anti-, enantiomorphic, or mirror transformations, and those more complicated ones which are lens-like rather than merely mirror-like. We shall end by observing that hypercomplex number theory and its related algebraic structures will be found increasingly necessary and relevant not only to quantum physics, but to biology, psy-

9 Not yet published. Based in part on a 1965 report (AFCRL-65-503), U.S. Air Force.

chology, sociology, and even to that dim vista of a scientific theory of history, i.e., *eventology*. There is much to be done and worked out, and the prospects are exciting.

IX. Relations to Function Theory

Functional analysis rests upon function theory, which in turn rests upon algebraic theory. As we have shown, an algebra is no more comprehensive than the nature of the numbers that give rise to it. Complex numbers give rise to a more comprehensive theory of functions than do real numbers, and also generate an algebra (G) which is more comprehensive than ordinary algebra (R), i.e., which embeds *R*.

Thus the theory of numbers in its deepest sense, as the theory of the kinds of possible numbers and their operations (i.e., the algebras pertaining thereto), is the basis of function theory and functional analysis. Change the kind of number and you change the algebra and hence the function theory. Such changes, moreover, are in conformity with the theory of hypercomplex numbers and their appropriate algebraic structures.

Thus number theory as here defined controls any theory of functions and functional analysis. We have already pointed out[8] that Bourbakian set theory is inadequate for functional analysis. Aside from being poorly motivated, pedantically cumbersome, inelegant, and rather artificially ugly, with far more manner than matter, it commits the reductive fallacy of attempting to deny the necessary existence of distance in any valid theory of ensembles of more than one nonnull member or element. The very fact of more than one such element presupposes distinguishability, which in turn implies, at any given moment of the existence of such an ensemble, distance or number in some context. Thus number theory as we have defined it is the *sine qua non* of the theory of ensembles. The natural extension of function theory, and hence of functional analysis, lies then in the direction of the theory of functions of one or more hypercomplex variables. Thus a C-variable is a variable all the possible values of which are Cayley numbers. There would be two kinds of right and left inverse functions of such a variable because the algebra is not simply anticommutative but also anti-associative. Similarly an H-variable would enter into quaternion or H-functions, and these would be able to have no more than one left- and right-hand inverse. Moreover, since the nonassociativity of C-algebra is not mandatory, the extra inverses of C-functions would not exist in certain cases. As an example of H-functions, let us consider the series development of one of the simplest types of right-handed analytic quaternion functions. The coefficients, it will be noted, involve $(1/2\pi^2)$ or the reciprocal unit-sphere surface in D_4, that surface thus being the measure for the integral. These coefficients in the neighborhood of the origin are given by

$$\frac{1}{2\pi^2} \int_{H_q} (q)$$

and by

$$\frac{1}{2\pi^2} \int_{H_p} (p),$$

where H_p and H_q are limiting hypersurfaces including the origin and (p) and (q) are functions involving Fueter's p- and q-functions, which may be taken as the analogues of z^n and z^{-n} in the suitably generalized Laurent expansion, respectively.

The coefficients of C-functions would, as said before, involve in general two distinct varieties of right-left parity. They would also contain as a factor the reciprocal surface of the unit hypersphere in D_8, i.e., $(3/\pi^4)$, the D_8 unit hyperspherical surface (i.e., convex D_7) being now the metric measure. Naturally, complex functions, being in G-space, have as their measure in this sense $1/2\pi$ or the reciprocal of the D_2 sphere surface, i.e., the reciprocal of a circular circumference; and this constant abundantly appears in the theory and theorems of a complex variable.

Very little is known as yet about H-functions, and C-functions have not been considered at all to the writer's knowledge. Neither of course have N-functions, since N-algebra, and hence N-numbers, have hitherto been unknown. Since the entire development of algebraic structures beyond N has been seen to rest upon the nature of zero itself, function theory in N- and higher algebras will involve precise knowledge of the laws of zero formation, of the interaction of zeros of different varieties, and of the results, in terms of the parabolic and loxodromic numbers, which lie beyond the entire hypercomplex number field, as already explained. The mathematics appropriate to biology, psychology, and even to physics in its quantum aspect will not be found distinctively to be statistical, but rather number-theoretical, the word "number" being used here in its most profound sense, which includes all the possible kinds of number (see *Addendum*).

In conclusion we must observe that aside from being rather sterile, linear black-box theory is inapplicable to either nature or manmade devices, all of which importantly and fundamentally involves hysteresis, friction, resistance, viscosity, or some other equally inescapable and pervasive form of increase of entropy; and hence involves nonlinear partial differential equations, which are the rule—any apparent exceptions being simply idealizations, that is to say fictions, and often not useful ones.

Consider now the following nonlinear partial differential system:

$$xz\frac{\partial^2 z}{\partial x^2} + x\left(\frac{\partial z}{\partial x}\right)^2 - z\frac{\partial z}{\partial x} = 0,$$

$$yz\frac{\partial^2 z}{\partial y^2} + y\left(\frac{\partial z}{\partial y}\right)^2 - z\frac{\partial z}{\partial y} = 0.$$

A solution is

$$\frac{x^2}{a^2} + \frac{y^2}{b^2} + \frac{z^2}{c^2} = 1,$$

i.e., an ellipsoid. Now if even such a comparatively simple object as an ellipsoid leads to a nonlinear partial differential equation, we can easily grasp the unreality of suggesting that far more complicated forms and phenomena could be adequately handled by linear methods.

There thus remain two open vistas for the development of the theory of functions: (1) a deepening of number theory, and hence of algebra and function theory, in the direction of more inclusive kinds of numbers; and (2) a development of a theory of nonlinear operators and nonlinear differential equations. These two paths need not be unrelated.

Closely related to the latter are the ordinary differential equations with periodic solutions, such as may arise in the solution of the wave equation by means of curvilinear coordinates. In this connection the work of Professors F. M. Arscott and Kathleen M. Erwin on ellipsoidal and paraboloidal wave functions and their differential equations deserves mention.

For some time we have felt that the theory of turbulence, and in particular of turbulent waves, might benefit if a solution of the wave equation could be found in an orthogonal system which we have termed catenoidal coordinates, formed by the two kinds (1 and 2 sheets) of catenoids of revolution plus the family of surfaces orthogonal to both. Such a system would not simply be based on a quadric equation, but upon one of infinite degree which would, we have reason to believe, have direct relevance to a system of turbulent waves. We have not had time to work out the separation of the wave equation by this means, but enough has been said for any with the necessary interest to do so.

The end of our journey is thus a panorama of open vistas, which is not only appropriate to the hypercomplexly multivalued nature of $\sqrt{-1}$ with which we began, but to mathematics itself, which is in so many ways the least dogmatic and most unexpected of all sciences.

In connection with the hypercomplex, multiple values of $\sqrt{-1}$, a defect of the present theory of ideals should be noted, to which earlier passing reference was made. Ideal numbers have been considered to be either roots of complex numbers or inexpressible, which would be inconsistent. To remedy this defect, ideal numbers must be considered as roots of hypercomplex numbers.

Although all ideals of quadratic fields can be expressed as roots of complex numbers, those of cubic and higher fields cannot in general be so expressed unless "complex" be extended to "hypercomplex." The lack of this theorem, that all ideal numbers are expressible as roots of complex or hypercomplex numbers, is the principal source of obstacles in G. Voronoi's otherwise satisfying exposition of cubic number fields, and in modern works on number fields.

Thus we return, in a new and higher sense, to the conception that ideals are lattices, a conception implicit in Kummer and explicit in Poincaré and other contemporaries. It can further be shown that the mesh area of such lattices is constant. Higher ideals would then become higher-dimensional lattices, and we are again at the fundamental conception of a tangent hyper-sphere group and the loops of units and theory of multiplication of higher algebras, which has already been commented upon.

X. Addendum on Group Theory

The valuable result of Hall (*10*), termed "exciting" by Coxeter, that there exist ternary and not only binary operation groups, is, however, but the beginning of an infinite sequence. The operation that is the basis of Hall's ternary groups is $ax + b$, i.e., an operation combining multiplication and addition, either of which alone is but a binary operation. But a quaternary group is formable on the operational basis of $ax^2 + bx + c$, and an n-ary group, on the basis

$$\sum_{k=0}^{n} a_k x^k.$$

Hence the theory of n-ary groups becomes a mathematico-linguistic transformation of the existing theory of polynomials, and thus is full of interesting isomorphisms, relevant also to function theory.

XI. Addendum on Higher Kinds of Number

The Greeks considered suspect and abnormal any number x such that $k \cdot x < 0$ where k was any positive number. Renaissance man, though he had long accepted negative numbers as just as natural as positive numbers, still balked at x where $x^2 = -1$, although he used such numbers to solve some quadratic equations.

It took until the 19th century until man's mind could regard these numbers too as nonpathological, although the designation "imaginary" still clings to them.

In the 20th century, Eduard Study first considered a number x not equal to zero and such that $x^2 = 0$; although Study still had no realization that this implies also $x^0 = 0$, and an advanced form of nondistributive multiplication. The present survey has revealed the evolutionary ancestors of p namely, numbers such as a and b, neither zero nor infinite nor equal, and such that $a \cdot b = 0$; the next higher nondistributive number being given by $a \cdot 0 = b$.

The foregoing paper has also developed numbers beyond p, namely, a nonzero q, such that $|q| = 1$; $q^4 = 0$; $q \neq q^2 \neq q^3 \neq 0$; and, unlike all the preceding numbers, with q^2 and q^3 irreducible to any real number or any lower power of q.

It is also noteworthy that $1/u \neq u^{-1}$ is true for $u = q$; and that $1/u^2 \neq u^{-2}$

and $1/u^3 \neq u^{-3}$ are true also for $u = q$. The nonrepresentability of reciprocals in terms of powers of their denominators is deeply related to the enantio-morphic phenomena that begin to be noticeable in what may be called the third metadimension, that of the p-numbers, the realm of the q-numbers constituting the fourth metadimension, whereas that of (hyper)imaginary or i-numbers constitutes the second, while the real axis represents the first metadimension, since it may represent any dimension of real space; all these being copies of each other. But the dimensions of the higher metadimensions are not copies of each other. For even the two first dimensions, i_1 and i_2, of the second metadimension cannot be exact copies, since it is no longer true that $i_1 \cdot i_2$ and $i_2 \cdot i_1$ are equal.

The metadimensions are isomorphic to the kinds of number, which in turn are characterized by their unit power fields, i.e., the function their unit traces out in a suitably defined representation plane, when it is reiteratedly multiplied by itself. Thus the unit field form shows the self-reflexive operation of the given unit or kind of number.

The forms for the five kinds of number with unit power fields of real, finite degree are shown in Table III. In another context, in 1962, we defined the first six metadimensions: those with real field forms.

TABLE III

Meta-dimen-sion	Kind of number	Character-istic unit operation	Unit field form	Degree
1	Real	$u^2 = 1$	$x^2 = 1$ or $x = \pm 1$	Bilinear
2	Imaginary and hyperimaginary	$u^2 = -1$	$x^2 + y^2 = 1$	Quadratic
3	p-Numbers ⎫ meta-	$u^2 = 0$	$(x^2 + y^2)^2/y^2 = 1$	Quartic
4	q-Numbers ⎬ imag-	$u^4 = 0$	$y^2 = x^4 - x^6$	Sextic
5	w-Numbers ⎭ inary	$1/u^8 = 0$	$y = x^4 \pm (x+2)(x^2-1)^{1/2}$	Octic

It will be observed that the q-numbers are the last with a finite, symmetric unit field form. The w-numbers have no longer either a finite or symmetric field form, and hence develop another (asymmetric enantiomorph) type of field form when the factor $(x+2)$ is replaced by $(x-2)$. The *orders* of w-

numbers (analogous to $i_1 \equiv i$, $i_2 \equiv j$, $i_3 \equiv k$, etc.) may be represented by

$$y = x^4 \pm (x+1+n)(x^2-1)^{1/2}, \quad |n| = 1, 2, 3. \dots$$

The negative orders from (-2) asymmetrically mirror the nonnegative orders from the zeroth onward. But the (-1)st order yields the equation $y^2 = x^4 \pm x(x^2-1)^{1/2}$ which interestingly yields, on the substitution $x \rightarrow ix$ the cognate form $x^4 \pm x(x^2+1)^{1/2}$.

Beyond the w-numbers, more vast changes occur. The unit field form of the sixth metadimension is no longer representable by an equation of finite degree; and the seventh metadimension requires a unit field equation which is a function of a nonreal variable.

Finally, it can be shown that the eighth metadimension is necessarily non-representable in any representation space, and that it contains all meta-dimensions beyond itself by an inherent, self-induced continuation.

It thus turns out that there are eight possible basic kinds of number (each with their own infinities), plus zero.

The higher kinds of number for the first time yield concrete hope of placing the profound and subtle characteristics of bio-, psycho-, and socio-transformations and processes on an adequate mathematical basis. Such kinds of number would thus introduce the humanities to their appropriate mathematics, which will not do them the grave and unscientific injustice of forcing them to fit some Procrustean bed of inadequate hypothesis or reductive definition. Man and man's sciences are now ready to go beyond the square root of minus one. With each new and higher kind of number a new and deeper algebra and arithmetic become possible, and hence a new and deeper functional analysis.

REFERENCES

1. R. Baer, "Linear Algebra and Projective Geometry." Academic Press, New York, 1952.
2. W. Blaschke, Anwendung dualer Quaternionen auf Kinematik, *Suomalaisen Tiedeakat. Toimituksia* (1958).
3. R. Brown and N. McCoy, Prime Ideals in Non-Associative Rings, *Trans. Am. Math. Soc.* **89**, 245 (1958).
4. R. H. Bruck and E. Kleinfeld, The Structure of Alternative Division Rings, *Proc. Am. Math. Soc.* **2**, 878 (1951).

5. H. S. M. Coxeter, Integral Cayley Numbers, *Duke Math. J.* **13**, 561 (1946).
6. H. S. M. Coxeter, Extreme Forms, *Can. J. Math.* **3**, 391 (1951).
7. H. S. M. Coxeter, An Upper Bound for the Number of Equal Nonoverlapping Spheres That Can Touch Another of the Same Size, *in* "Convexity" [*Proc. Symp. Pure Math.* **7**, 53 (1963)].
8. H. S. M. Coxeter, *in* "Lectures in Modern Mathematics," Vol. III (T. L. Saaty, ed.), Chap. 2, pp. 63–71. Wiley, New York, 1965.
9. P. Du Val, "Homographies, Quaternions, and Rotations," Oxford Univ. Press, London and New York, 1964.
10. M. Hall, "The Theory of Groups," Macmillan, New York, 1959.
11. W. R. Hamilton, "Elements of Quaternions," Dublin, 1866. (The second, posthumous edition was revised by C. J. Joly.)
12. W. R. Hamilton, Collection of Letters, Trinity Coll. Library (Division of Manuscripts), Dublin.
13. A. Hurwitz, Mathematische Werke, *in* "Algebra, Zahlentheorie, Geometrie," Vol. II. Birkhäuser, Basel, 1933.
14. J. Leech, Some Sphere Packings in Higher Space, *Can. J. Math.* **16**, 657 (1964).
15. M. H. McAndrew, On Error-Correcting Codes, *Math. Computation* **19**, 68 (1965).
16. C. Muses, Systematic Stability and Cybernetic Control, in "The Cybernetics of Neural Processes" (E. R. Caianiello, ed.), Fig. 6, pp. 174–177, Quaderno 31, National Research Council of Italy, Rome, 1965.
17. C. Muses, Some Crucial Problems in Biological and Medical Cybernetics, *in* "Progress in Cybernetics" (J. Schadé, ed.), Vol. 2, pp. 216, 230, 261–262. Elsevier, Amsterdam, 1965. [The formulas on pp. 230 and 262 refer to *convex* polytopes of centers and hence to biradial packs for $n > 8$. Printers' errors: exponent of first equation p. 240 should read 1/3 and line 4 of note p. 261 should read $(n-2) \geqslant 8$.]
18. C. Muses, An Introduction to Higher Kinds of Number, Annals, *N.Y. Acad. Sci.* (1966); in "Interdisciplinary Perspectives on Time."
19. W. W. Peterson, "Error-Correcting Codes," M.I.T. Press, Cambridge, Massachusetts, 1961.
20. C. A. Rogers, "Packing and Covering." Cambridge Univ. Press, London and New York, 1964. (Includes bibliography of Rogers' papers.)
21. R. D. Schafer, Structure and Representation of Nonassociative Algebras, *Bull. Am. Math. Soc.* **61**, 469–484 (1955); see also B. Brown and N. H. McCoy, Prime Ideals in Non-Associative Rings, *Trans. Am. Math. Soc.* **89**, 685–707 (1958).
22. L. Schläfli, "*Gesammelte Mathematischen Abhandlungen*," Birkhäuser, Basel, 1950.
23. S. L. Sobolev, On the Theory of Nonlinear Hyperbolic Equations (in Russian). *Mat. Sb.* (1939).
24. E. Study, "Geometrie der Dynamen." Leipzig, 1901–1903, 2 vols.
25. O. Teichmuller, Der Elementarteilersatz fur nichtkommutative Ringe, *Sitzber. Preuss. Akad. Wiss., Phys.-Math. Kl.* **14** (1937).
26. H. Whitney, Tensor Products of Abelian Groups, *Duke Math. J.* **4**, 495 (1938).
27. L. L. Whyte, A Dimensionless Physics? *Brit. J. Phil. Sci.* **5**(17), 1 (1954).

Suboptimal Supervisory Control

A. STRASZAK

*Polish Academy of Sciences
Institute for Automation
Warsaw, Poland*

I. Introduction

Most papers on optimal-control theory have been directed toward the development of methods which give optimum control as a function of time (*1, 3, 4*). Much less has been done on the optimal regulator problem. The synthesis problem was solved only for very special low-dimension optimal control problems [see, for example, (*1*)]. Most current research on optimal control theory is directed toward the development of methods which will give optimum control for the infinite-dimensional problem.

Sometimes, we hear that the finite-dimensional optimal-control problem is a classical one. It is probably true, from the control theory viewpoint, but only if the dimension of optimal control problems is extremely low ($n = 1$, 2, or maybe 3). However, many optimal control problems have now appeared whose dimensions are 100 or even 1000 or more. This is due to the widespread use of on-line computers in control systems, as well as to the application of control theory in economic, management, and biological research.

An increase in dimensions in optimal control systems introduces new problems to control theory and new difficulties to control engineering. One of these is connected with computing the optimal control law, another one with realizing the optimal controller.

The purpose of this article is to present a method which simplifies high-dimension optimal control problems by introducing two-level (supervisory) control. The original optimal control problem is divided into two types: low-dimension, first-level optimal control problems, and optimal supervisory control problems. In general, such control is not optimal; therefore, we call it suboptimal control.

II. Statement of the Problem

Let us consider a set of optimal control systems S_1, S_2, ..., S_k. By the optimal-control system S_i we mean a dynamic process P_i governed by the vector equation

$$\frac{dx_i}{dt} = F_i x_i + G_i u_i, \tag{1}$$

where x_i is an n_i-vector, the state of the system P_i; u_i is an m_i-vector, the control of system P_i; and F_i, G_i are $(n \times n)$ and $(n \times m)$ matrices of real constants and optimal controller C_i, which is described by the vector equation

$$u_i = C_i^0(x_i). \tag{2}$$

The equation of the optimal controller C_i^0 is the "feedback" form of the solution of the following optimal-control problem.

Minimize the functional (performance criterion)

$$I_i = \int_{t_1}^{t_2} g_i(x_i, u_i) \, dt, \tag{3}$$

where x_i and u_i are connected by (1) and are or are not subject to the constraints

$$M_i(u_i) \leqslant U_{i0}. \tag{4}$$

It is assumed that such a solution exists. For example (2) if

$$I_i = \int_0^\infty [(x_i^T Q_i x_i) + (u_i^T R_i u_i)] \, dt, \tag{5}$$

then if the optimal solution exists, the optimal feedback control is given by

$$u_i = C_i x_i, \tag{6}$$

where C_i is an $(m_i \times n_i)$ matrix of real constant.

Let us now introduce the global optimal control problem by introducing the global functional

$$I_g = \int_{t_1}^{t_2} g_g(x_g, u_g)\,dt, \tag{7}$$

where $x_g \in X = X_1 \times X_2 \times \cdots \times X_m$ is the $\sum\limits_{j=1}^{k} n_{ij}$-vector, the state of the global system, and $u_g \in U = U_1 \times U_2 \times \cdots \times U_m$ is the $\sum\limits_{j=1}^{k} m_{ij}$-vector, the control of the global system. The global dynamic process is governed by the vector equation

$$dx/dt = Fx + Gu, \tag{8}$$

where F, G, $\left(\sum\limits_{j=1}^{k} n_{ij} \times \sum\limits_{j=1}^{k} n_{ij} \right)$ and $\left(\sum\limits_{j=1}^{k} n_{ij} \times \sum\limits_{j=1}^{k} m_{ij} \right)$ are matrices of real constants.

The global constraint is a function of the local constraints

$$M_g = M_g[M_i(u_i)]. \tag{9}$$

For example, if

$$I_g = \int_{0}^{\infty} [(x^T Q x) + (u^T R u)]\,dt, \tag{10}$$

then the global optimal-feedback control is given by

$$u = C_g x, \tag{11}$$

where C_g is the $\left(\sum\limits_{j=1}^{k} m_{ij} \times \sum\limits_{j=1}^{k} n_{ij} \right)$ matrix of real constant. The property that the general pattern of feedback of the optimal solution does not depend upon dimensionality of the optimal control problem is also true for many nonlinear optimal controllers (1). It is well known that dimensionality presents difficulties in numerical analysis (3). Therefore, it is a proper question to ask if dimensionality difficulties exist in the realization of the optimal control system.

To study this question it was useful to introduce the function which would give the complexity (costs, reliability, etc.) of the optimal controller.

It was established (7) that such a function exists, and that for the linear optimal controller is given by

$$K_{\mathrm{L}} = n^2 k_1 + nk_2,$$ (12)

where $k_1 > 0$, $k_2 > 0$ are constants, and $n = \dim x = \dim u$, and respectively. For the nonlinear optimal controller

$$K_{\mathrm{NL}} = K(n^3, n^2, n).$$ (13)

It is not difficult to find such $\dim x = n$ that K will overcome the admissible value. In this case the optimal controller is not applicable. To overcome these difficulties, wholly or in part, we must lose the global optimality.

III. Controlled Optimal Control Systems

The optimal-control system S_i minimizes the functional I_i subject to (1) and (4) or only subject to (1); therefore, any change of the minimal (optimal) value of this functional is possible only by change of (1) and/or (4). This problem was studied recently for the minimum-time optimal-control system (5) and may be extended without special difficulties for more general cases.

Let us consider for example, the minimum-time optimal control for a second-order linear plant,

$$\dot{x}_i = \begin{bmatrix} 0 & 0 \\ 1 & 0 \end{bmatrix} x_i + \begin{bmatrix} 1 \\ 0 \end{bmatrix} u_i$$

with constraint

$$\sup |u_i| < U_i.$$

Let us suppose, additionally, that

$$x_{i1}(t_1) = 0, \qquad x_{i2}(t_1) = 0, \qquad x_{i1}(t_2) = 0, \qquad x_{i2}(t_2) = x_{i20}.$$

Then $I_i = T_i$ can be expressed in the very simple form

$$T_i = 4(x_{i20}/\mathrm{const.}\, U_i)^{1/2}.$$

This form is shown in Fig. 1 as a function of x_{i20} and U_i. In general, the minimal (optimal) value of the functional as a function of the constraint U_i,

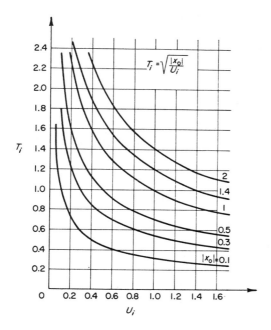

FIG. 1

$$I_i^0 = I_i(U_i),$$

is a monotonic decreasing function (4). Therefore, if the constraint U_i is subject to change, we can control the performance of optimal control systems.

IV. Supervisory Control

Following the same approach as in Section III, we introduce the set of local functionals $I_1(U_1, x_{10})$, $I_2(U_2, x_{20})$, ..., $I_k(U_k, x_{k0})$. Let us now introduce a new global functional

$$I_g^* = \sum_{j=1}^{k} \min_{u_j} I_j(U_j, x_{j0}). \tag{14}$$

In place of the problem of minimizing (7),

$$I_g = \int_{t_1}^{t_2} g_g(x_g, u_g) \, dt$$

subject to the global constraint (9),

$$M_g = M_g[M_i(U_i)]$$

for the global dynamical process (8)

$$dx/dt = Fx + Gu,$$

we consider, first, the problem of minimizing the modified functional

$$I_g{}^* = \sum_{j=1}^{k} \min_{u_j} I_j(U_j, x_{j0})$$

subject to the constraint

$$M_g = M_g[M_i(u_i)] \leqslant U_g,$$

Second, we consider a set of problems of minimizing

$$I_i = \int_{t_1}^{t_i} g_i(x_i, u_i)\, dt,$$

where x_i and u_i are connected by the equation

$$dx_i/dt = F_i x_i + G_i u_i$$

subject to the constraints

$$M_i(u_i) \leqslant U_{i0},$$

where U_{i0} is for the moment a fixed parameter. The optimal allocation of the resources U_{i0} is obtained from the solution of the first minimizing problem.

Once the original global optimal control problem has been replaced by the optimal supervisory control problem we must show that

$$I_{g1} \leqslant I_{g2} \leqslant I_{g3}, \tag{15}$$

where I_{g1} is the minimal (optimal) value of the global functional for the global optimal control system, I_{g2} is the minimal (optimal) value of the global functional for the supervisory optimal control system, and I_{g3} is the minimal (optimal) value of the global functional for a set of local optimal control systems. It follows from definition of the global optimal control problem that

$$I_{g1} \leqslant I_{g2} \quad \text{and} \quad I_{g1} \leqslant I_{g3}.$$

From the definition of the optimal allocation of the resources it follows that

$$I_{g2} \leqslant I_{g3};$$

therefore, inequalities (15) are fulfilled. The optimal supervisory control problem can also be solved by using mathematical programming machinery (6).

V. Example

Let us consider a very simple example. Assume that we have two dynamic processes P_1 and P_2, which are governed by the equations

$$\dot{x}_1 = u_1 \qquad \text{and} \qquad \dot{x}_2 = u_2,$$

respectively. Local optimal control problems are formulated as follows: Minimize

$$I_1 = \int_0^{t_{21}} dt \qquad \text{and} \qquad I_2 = \int_0^{t_{22}} dt$$

subject to the constraints

$$\sup |u_1| \leqslant U_1 \qquad \text{and} \qquad \sup |u_2| \leqslant U_2.$$

Let us introduce a global optimal control problem: Minimize

$$I_g = \int_0^{t_{2g}} dt, \qquad \text{where} \quad t_{2g} = \max_i t_j \quad (i = 1, 2)$$

subject to the constraint

$$\sup ||u_1| + |u_2|| \leqslant 1 = U_g = U_1 + U_2.$$

Following the same approach as in Section IV, we introduce

$$I_g{}^* = \min_{u_1} \int_0^{t_{21}} dt + \min_{u_2} \int_0^{t_{22}} dt.$$

From (4) we know that

$$\min_{u_1} \int_0^{t_{21}} dt = T_1 = x_{01} U/_1,$$

$$\min_{u_2} \int_0^{t_{22}} dt = T_2 = x_{02}/U_2.$$

Therefore,

$$I_g^* = \frac{x_{01}}{U_1} + \frac{x_{02}}{U_2}.$$

Minimizing I_g^* subject to

$$\sup ||u_1| + |u_2|| \leqslant 1,$$

we solve the supervisory control problem. The optimal solution is

$$U_{1_{\text{opt}}} = \left(\frac{\alpha - 1}{\alpha - 1}\right)^{1/2}, \qquad U_{2_{\text{opt}}} = 1 - U_{1_{\text{opt}}},$$

where $\alpha = x_{02}/x_{01}$.

REFERENCES

1. L. S. Pontriagin, V. G. Boltyanskii, R. V. Gamkrelidze, and E. F. Mishchenko, "Mathematical Theory of the Optimal Processes." Fizmatgiz, Moscow, 1961.
2. R. Kalman, Contributions to the Theory of Optimal Control, *Bol. Soc. Mat. Mex.* **5**, 102–119 (1960).
3. R. E. Bellman and S. E. Dreyfus, "Applied Dynamic Programming." Princeton Univ. Press, Princeton, New Jersey, 1962.
4. R. Kulikowski, Optimal Control Systems, *Arch. Automat. i Telemech.*, No. 2–3, 1961.
5. R. Kulikowski, Optimal Control as a Function of Plant Parameters, *Arch. Automat. i Telemech*, No. 2, 1964.
6. S. Karlin, Mathematical Methods and Theory in Games, Programming and Economics." Pergamon Press, New York, 1959.
7. A. Straszak, On the Partitioning Problem in Large-Scale Multivariable Control Systems, *Arch. Automat. i. Telemech.*, No. 2, 1965.

Author Index

Numbers in parentheses are reference numbers and indicate that an author's work is referred to although his name is not cited in the text. Numbers in italic show the page on which the complete reference is listed.

A

Aggeri, J. C., 156, *166*
Antosiewicz, H. A., 1(1), 2(1), 3(1), 4(1), 4, *54*
Artola, M., 130, *130*
Aubin, J. P., 9(1), 13(1), *14*, 120, 130(2), *130*

B

Babunashuili, T. G., 4(2), *4*
Baer, R., *211*
Balakrisanan, A. U., 4(3), *5*, 15(2, 3, 5, 6), 16(2), 17(2, 3), 22(2), 23(2), 24(2, 3), 33(2), *35*, 115(3, 4), *130*, *131*, 143
Baltyanskii, U. G., 69(17), *84*
Barbashin, E. A., *54*
Bellman, R., *83*, 154, *167*, 213(3), 215(3), *220*
Beurling, A., 156, *167*
Birnbaum, Z., 154, *167*
Blagoveščenskiĭ, Yu. N., 68(2), *83*
Blaschke, W., *211*
Boltyanskii, U. G., *5*, *54*, 55(1), 59(1), 61(1), *63*
Boltyanskii, V. G., *5*, *54*, *220*
Broendsted, A., 154, *167*
Browder, F. E., 156, *167*
Brown, R., *211*
Bruck, R. H., *211*

C

Caianiello, E. R., 37(1), *46*
Caligiuri, G. P., 62(13), *63*
Cesari, L., *131*

Chang, S. S. L., *63*
Conti, R., 1(4), 2(5, 6), 3(6), 4(6), 4(4), 5, *54*
Courant, R., 147, *167*
Coxeter, H. S. M., 186(8), *212*
Crocchiolo, C., *46*

D

De Backer, W., 55(11, 12), 59(8, 12), 62(8–10), *63*
de Luca, A., *46*
Desoer, C. A., 15(1), 16(1), *35*
Diaz, J. B., 147, *167*
Dixmier, J., *131*
Doob, J. L., 70(3), *83*
Drago, A., *46*
Dreyfus, S. E., 213(3), 215(3), *220*
Du Val, P., *212*
Dynkin, E. B., 67(5), 70(4), 71(4), *83*

E

Egorov, Yu. V., *54*, 115(6), *131*

F

Fattorini, H. O., *54*
Fattorini, H. P., 115(7), *131*
Fenchel, W., 154, *167*
Fichera, G., 166, *167*
Fleming, W. H., 74(7), 76(7), 78(7), *83*
Freĭdlin, M. I., 68(2, 9), 70(9), 76, *83*
Friedman, A., 71(10), 72(10), *83*

G

Gabasov, R., 4(7), *5*, *54*

221

Subject Index

A

Adiabatic learning hypothesis, 37
Adjoint variables
  jump conditions for, 59–60
  normalized, 56–57
Affine minorants, 150
Algebra, nondistributive, 171–211

B

Banach spaces, bang-bang principle and, 47–49
Bang-bang principle, Banach spaces and, 47–49
Bilateral problem, 161–164
Bipolar function, 150

C

Closure theorem, 118–119
Controllability, 51–54
  and observability, 133–143
  linear control systems, 1–4
Convex cones, 156–157
Convexity
  duality and, 145–166
  nonlinear control theory, 90–92

D

Decision equations, 37
  nonlinear problems posed by, 38–46
  reverberations and, 38–39
Degenerate parabolic equations, generalized solutions of, 77–80
Deterministic control problems, 68–70
Diffusion processes, optimal control of, 67–83
Dual functions, 152–156
Duality, 145 ff.
Duality mapping, 155–156

E

Effective excitation, 41
Error-correcting codes, nondistributive algebra and, 200–201
Existence theorem, 80–83

F

Function theory, nondistributive algebra and, 205–208

G

Γ-convolution, 157

H

Hamilton-Jacobi equation, 69–70
Hilbert space, duality and, 159–161
H-type triplets, 176

I

Inf-convolution, 157–159

J

Jump conditions, for adjoint variables, 59–60

L

Linear autonomous control processes, 133–137
  controllability and observability, 138–142
Linear controllability, 1–4, 51–54
Linear parabolic equations, some optimization problems for, 115–130
Linear problem, 161–164
Linear system, 17
Linear time-invariant system, space-state theory, 18–24

224